The Assassination of King Shaka

The Assassination of King Shaka

John Laband

Jonathan Ball Publishers
JOHANNESBURG AND CAPE TOWN

All rights reserved.
No part of this publication may be reproduced or transmitted,
in any form or by any means, without prior permission
from the publisher or copyright holder.

© Text John Laband, 2017
© Published edition, Jonathan Ball Publishers, 2017

First published in South Africa in 2017 by
JONATHAN BALL PUBLISHERS
A division of Media24 (Pty) Ltd
PO Box 33977
Jeppestown
2043

ISBN 978-1-86842-807-6
EBOOK ISBN 978-1-86842-808-3

Every effort has been made to trace the copyright holders and to obtain their permission for the use of copyright material. The publishers apologise for any errors or omissions and would be grateful to be notified of any corrections that should be incorporated in future editions of this book.

Twitter: www.twitter.com/JonathanBallPub
Facebook: www.facebook.com/JonathanBallPublishers
Blog: http://jonathanball.bookslive.co.za/

Cover by MR Design
Design and typesetting by Triple M Design
Printed and bound by CTP Printers, Cape Town
Set in 11.5/15pt Van Dijck MT Std

Contents

PREFACE ix

Introduction They Are Still Fighting, Even Now 1

Part I Three Spears
1 Stabbed While Dancing 13
2 A Royal Spear? 20
3 An Ndwandwe Spear? 30
4 A Qwabe Spear? 43

Part II Always Talking of War
5 He Who Beats But Is Not Beaten 55
6 People of Our House 65
7 Fighting Stick of Thunder 73
8 The Elephant Took What Belonged to It 80

Part III A Wolf Without a Place to Hide His Head
9 What Has Killed My Mother? 89
10 I Am Lamenting Because of My Mother's Death 95
11 Splasher of Water with an Oxtail 102

12 Buffalo That Stood Glaring with a Spear 107
13 This Is King Chaka's Name 112

Part IV Are You Stabbing Me, the King of the Earth?
14 They Hate Him 119
15 Are You Not Going to Stab Him? 128
16 What Is the Matter My Father's Children? 136
17 You Were Warned 141

Part V The Wild Beasts of Jama Have Killed One Another
18 The One With the Red Assegai Shall Not Rule 147
19 Wizard Whose Liver Is Black 152
20 Did You Not Bring Harm to Yourself? 159

GLOSSARY OF ZULU WORDS 169
TIMELINE 172
CHARACTERS 181
KINGDOMS, PARAMOUNTCIES AND CHIEFDOMS 185
NOTES 189
READING LIST 209
ACKNOWLEDGEMENTS 218
INDEX 219

Maps

1 The Zulu region at the outset of Shaka's reign 12

2 Migrations during the consolidation of the Zulu kingdom 32

Preface

It is not only in fantasy sagas like George RR Martin's *Game of Thrones* that kings fall to the assassin's blade or poisoned cup. Rulers, no less now than in the past, know that the assassin's shadow menaces their every step. An attempt on a ruler's life might fail thanks to lucky chance, or it might succeed despite every precaution taken. The would-be killer might be motivated by private grievance or paranoia, or by religious or ideological conviction.

Especially in a monarchy, the assassin might be driven by personal ambition to usurp the throne. In a traditional society, this was an act not to be undertaken lightly where there was something particularly awful in killing a king whose right to rule was enforced by divine sanction. And what made the deed the more reprehensible was that the assassin would usually possess a plausible hereditary claim to the crown, and this meant that the victim must be of close kin. This in turn required the usurper, once he had seized power, to purge all rival claimants who shared his royal blood lest they challenge him for the crown then or in the future.

The record of Africa, no less than that of Europe, Asia and the Americas, is replete with royal assassinations and their blood-filled aftermaths. There is one instance, though, that eclipses all others in Africa because of the legendary eminence of the victim: Shaka Zulu, whose name so luridly conjures up all the brutal, warlike glamour of the precolonial continent.

In writing this book, my objective is not to undertake another scholarly investigation into the formation of the Zulu kingdom in the reign of King Shaka. Several excellent historians – notably John Wright, Carolyn Hamilton and Elizabeth Eldredge – have already expertly mastered this field. Nor do I wish to attempt a fresh biography of Shaka himself. In several recent books, Dan Wylie has the jump on me there.

Rather, what I am attempting is a focused inquiry into a single, pivotal event in Shaka's life: his assassination. By teasing out the circumstances surrounding the plot to slay him, by investigating the individuals involved and their possible motives, and by considering the implications and consequences of the violent deed, I hope to throw some strong light on the functioning of the early Zulu kingdom and on the elusive character of Shaka himself.

The reader is invited to follow along with me as I try to make sense of the case. Since writing history is not simply selecting, organising and presenting facts in an objective fashion, but also a literary act in which the author inevitably possesses a personal point of view, I shall be open with the reader. In pursuing my investigation, I shall pose a series of questions seeking answers from the available evidence, and it is up to the reader to decide whether these queries are sufficient, on target or misdirected. Likewise, I shall explain my reasons when I find the answers I come up with to be convincing, or at least plausible, and when I can find no satisfactory answer at all. Once again, it is for the alert reader to better me at my own game.

Of course, to approach the controversial subject of Shaka is to venture into a tangled and dangerous forest with mantraps set across the twisting paths. 'History perhaps does not furnish an instance of a more despotic and cruel monster than Chaka,' declared Lieutenant Francis George Farewell, RN, one of the first hunter-traders established at Port Natal in 1824, who witnessed Shaka at the height of his power.[1] Through their writings, he and his fellow pioneers, Henry Francis Fynn and Nathaniel Isaacs, disseminated their vision of Shaka as a forbidding savage ruling over a nation in arms, imbued with a fierce military ethos. Indeed, Isaacs went so far as to declare: 'I am not aware that history ... can produce so horrible and detestable a savage. He has deluged his country in innocent blood.'[2] Future white settlers, missionaries, officials and soldiers all elaborated on this ferocious image until it became fixed in the Western imagination.

Indeed, as the founder of the Zulu warrior kingdom, Shaka has understandably been the subject of biographers, artists and filmmakers. Henry Cele's compelling portrayal of Shaka in the lavish ten-part SABC mini-series *Shaka Zulu*, first screened in 1986, indelibly imbedded screenwriter Joshua Sinclair's and director William Faure's larger-than-life vision of Shaka the ruthless warrior-king in viewers' minds. Viewers were duly intrigued, even if many critics attacked *Shaka Zulu* for historical inaccuracy and inherent racism.[3] Several popular authors, notably EA Ritter and Donald Morris, have also employed considerable licence to sensationalise and romanticise Shaka's career. More recently, academic critics such as Carolyn Hamilton and Dan Wylie have leapt into the fray and, employing the intricate tools of literary deconstruction, have exposed the historical invention and literary mythology that have 'created' the Shaka of popular imagination.

Despite such critiques, which cut vigorously away at the legends that shroud the historical figure, we should not ascribe the strong survival of the Shaka warrior stereotype only to Western sources. The Zulu people have always celebrated him as a great conqueror. As his praises, or *izibongo*, expressed it:

> The nations he hath all destroyed
> Whither shall he now attack?
> He! Whither shall he now attack?
> He defeats kings
> Whither shall he now attack?
> The nations he hath all destroyed
> Whither shall he now attack?
> He! He! He! Whither shall he now attack?[4]

In recent decades, many Zulu intellectuals and politicians have exploited the Zulu past, with its military traditions, and have invoked the towering personality of Shaka to promote and legitimate Zulu nationalism – none perhaps with greater élan than the late Mazisi Kunene in his epic of 1979, *Emperor Shaka the Great*. Their message has resonated with ordinary Zulu people who continue to believe in their ethnic characteristics as a warrior nation. As a male Zulu migrant labourer vigorously put it: 'The Zulu Nation is born out of Shaka's spear. When you say "Go and fight," it just happens.'⁵

'Chaka King of the Zoolus' by J Saunders King
(NATHANIEL ISAACS, *TRAVELS AND ADVENTURES IN EASTERN AFRICA*, 1836)

Indeed, outside the Legislative Assembly Building in Ulundi – opened in 1984 when the Zulu nationalist Inkatha Freedom Party ruled the self-governing KwaZulu 'homeland' between 1977 and 1994 – is a highly idealised bronze statue of Shaka holding his great war-shield and brandishing his spear. Yet, when in 2010 a statue of the king accompanied by Nguni cattle was erected at the new King Shaka International Airport, it caused an immediate outcry because Shaka was not depicted carrying weapons. With accusations by the Zulu royal house that this rendering of Shaka made him look more like a herd boy than a warrior, the statue was removed for reconsideration. It has not yet been replaced because no one can agree exactly how to depict Shaka's features, the problem being that nobody knows for sure what the king looked like.

And this points to another significant problem in approaching the subject of Shaka. The decidedly problematic sources are limited, complex and contradictory. They consist of the dubious, highly coloured and self-serving accounts of white trader-hunters who actually encountered Shaka, mostly penned or reworked later after a long lapse of time; of remembered and recurrently embellished *izibongo* handed down over generations; of popular and oft-repeated Zulu traditions; and of the oral testimony of witnesses. This testimony was not systematically recorded until the very late nineteenth and early twentieth centuries, when the interviewees had distant childhood memories of the Shakan period, or could only relate what the previous generation had to say of Shaka, in itself a subjective response. The archives hold an assortment of official British documents – the staple of conventional historians – which convey little but a gullible and misinformed grasp of Shaka and his kingdom. And, finally, there is the archaeological evidence, patchy at best and useful only in helping us envisage Shaka's material environment. It is no wonder, perhaps, that Dan Wylie has concluded that 'we know almost nothing for certain about Shaka', and that what has come down to us 'is an extraordinary palimpsest of half-understood rumours, speculations and plain old lies'.[6]

Still, this is no reason to despair. When one thinks about it, the sources for the history of Ancient Rome (for example) are hardly any more soundly based: partially surviving histories written decades – if not centuries – after the events described or the tantalising summaries made of them;

a scattering of copied and re-copied letters, speeches, poems and other pieces of literature; inscriptions, coins, dubious portrait busts and the rest of a fragmented archaeological record. Nevertheless, these considerable shortcomings and difficulties with the evidence have not put off classical historians, who continue to write about the Ancient World with unabated enthusiasm. So why would historians of the early Zulu kingdom shrink from a similar challenge?

Yet this in turn presents a problem for this book. An academic monograph would lay out the full panoply of evidence in exhaustive footnotes and references. However, the nature of this book is such that I do not believe I should allow it to become tiresomely overburdened with the scholarly apparatus. I have therefore adopted the practice of confining my notes to direct quotations and to every piece of evidence specifically deployed to buttress my investigation into the case of Shaka's assassination. Otherwise, for the sources for my supporting and contextualising account of the history of the early Zulu kingdom and its political, military, social, religious and economic milieu, the reader is referred to the Reading List at the end of the book.

Zulu words are explained when they are first encountered in the book, but the Glossary provides the singular and plural forms, as well as the meaning, of those used more than once. Modern Zulu spelling is employed in the text, but the obsolete form is retained in direct quotations.

INTRODUCTION

They Are Still Fighting, Even Now

Had it not been for the sudden appearance one morning in the late 1860s of two enormous snakes with black and green markings,[1] it would have been a day as any other at kwaNodwengu, King Mpande kaSenzangakhona's principal royal military homestead, or *ikhanda*. The mammoth assemblage of a thousand or more domed grass huts lay in the very heart of the Zulu kingdom, in the Mahlabathini plain ('the place of sands') enclosed by a sweep of hills just north of the White Mfolozi River. It is not easy nowadays, from the poor archaeological remains of hut floors and postholes, to picture the massy scale of an *ikhanda* such as this, nor its hulking impact on the open grassy landscape, with its patches of acacia bush where aloes and euphorbias stood sentinel.

The layout of kwaNodwengu followed that of the *amakhanda* of Mpande's two royal predecessors and half-brothers, Shaka and Dingane. As with all the other *amakhanda* situated at strategic points across Zululand, it functioned as a hub of royal authority. All mirrored in colossal form the tens of thousands of humble circular clusters of thatched beehive huts dotting the undulating countryside. Each was a self-sufficient family homestead, or *umuzi*, the half-dozen or so huts arranged around a circular cattle byre, or *isibaya*, protected by a wooden palisade.

The wealth of the Zulu kingdom: Nguni cattle in the cattle byre of an *umuzi*
(GEORGE FRENCH ANGUS, *THE KAFFIRS ILLUSTRATED IN A SERIES OF DRAWINGS*, 1849)

It was only appropriate that the *isibaya* should form the core of every *umuzi* or *ikhanda* because the Zulu were above all a pastoralist people. Cattle were central to their culture and religious ritual, and were the prime indicator of wealth in a society that had little other means of accumulating it. Iron Age Bantu-speakers migrating southwards through Africa had introduced domestic cattle into southern Africa about two thousand years before. Nguni cattle, with their spreading horns, multicoloured skins and black-tipped noses, were the favoured indigenous strain in the Zulu country. The Zulu language contains hundreds of terms by which to identify the distinctive shapes of horns, the presence or absence of a hump, and the numerous different colours and patterns. Favourite cattle had praise-names and were trained to respond to whistled commands.

At kwaNodwengu the huts within the stout outer palisade enclosed an elliptical, open parade ground too extensive for a man to be heard if he tried to shout across it. A number of cattle enclosures were built against the inner palisade of reeds and grasses. At the top end of the parade ground, opposite the main gate to the *ikhanda*, was the great cattle *isibaya*, sacred

King Cetshwayo's chief *ikhanda*, oNdini. The general aspect of his father Mpande's kwaNodwengu *ikhanda* would have been identical.

(*GRAPHIC*, 22 FEBRUARY 1879)

to the king. There Mpande and the members of his inner royal council (*umkhandlu*) would discuss matters of state and he would pass judgment on the wrongdoers grovelling before him. It was also the place where he would perform the religious rituals required of the monarch and would officiate over the great national ceremonies.

Directly behind the *isibaya* was the royal enclosure, or *isigodlo*, sacred to the king and divided into two sections of about fifty huts in all. In the central, 'black' section dwelt the female members of the royal house, or *amakhosikazi*, comprising Mpande's wives, the widows of his predecessors, sisters, aunts and other relations. As married or senior women they were crowned with complexly worked topknots of hair, in Shaka's time 'greased and clotted with red ochre clay',[2] and wore leather skirts reaching to the knees. They decorated themselves with beads around the forehead, ankles and arms. Like all Zulu people, women as well as men, they wore ear plugs of carved, polished wood, about two to five millimetres in diameter. Just before puberty their earlobes had been pierced as the first of the rituals marking the transition from childhood to adulthood.

Alongside the *amakhosikazi* lived the king's favoured maids-of-honour, the *umndlunkulu*, women who had been given to him as tribute and who served as his concubines. Unmarried girls across the kingdom had a front covering of beadwork or leaves to shield their nakedness, or perhaps a fringed waistband of skin, but these *umndlunkulu* were reputed to wear nothing other than strings of beads. If they were favoured, they sported

Zulu women in their *umuzi* brewing beer (*utshwala*) from ground sorghum, millet or maize and water. The low-alcohol drink was essential on social and ceremonial occasions.
(GEORGE FRENCH ANGUS, THE KAFFIRS ILLUSTRATED IN A SERIES OF DRAWINGS, 1849)

brass coils around their arms as well as four brass collars that were so tight it was almost impossible to turn the head. It was death to look upon these maids-of-honour when they left the *isigodlo* under armed escort to bathe or to relieve themselves at a distance. The only male who could freely enter the *isigodlo* was the king himself, and the life of any other man who did so without being summoned was forfeit. The king's great hut, larger by far than any other in the *ikhanda*, was in the black *isigodlo*, and there he might hold audience. At night the gates to the *isigodlo* were barred and the king was the only man to sleep there.

His *umndlunkulu*, secluded and unoccupied except for entertaining the king with song and dance, grew corpulent on the staple diet of the *isigodlo*, blood clots and fat cooked into a rich soup and washed down with whey. This fare was in stark contrast to that of ordinary people, who ate meat only when they had sacrificed a beast and subsisted on sour clotted milk, beer made from sorghum, pounded grain boiled as porridge, and fresh vegetables.

In the 'white' *isigodlo* lived the younger *umndlunkulu* who had not attracted the king's eye, the royal children – who, as elsewhere in Zululand, had shaven heads and were nude except for a string of beads around the waist and (if a boy) a penis sheath of woven grass – and the *izigqila*. These last were women who had been captured in war or were the wives or daughters of men the king had executed. Their status was slave-like, for they could never be ransomed or freed. Not only were they obliged to be at the sexual disposal of men of the royal house but they also performed all the menial domestic chores in the *isigodlo*. Their days were filled cultivating the gardens, fetching water, gathering firewood, cooking food and waiting on the women of high status whose clay chamberpots they emptied.³

Daily, the king would enter the *isibaya* to inspect his cattle – every Zulu man's greatest source of pride – and regularly review the warriors barracked in the two great wings of huts standing in rows six or eight deep that enfolded the parade ground. Then he would position himself on an anthill or large rock and peer over the palisade of the *isibaya*, encouraging his warriors and his great nobles, or *izikhulu*, as they sang his *izibongo* (praises), leapt high into the air and rhythmically stamped their feet, showing off their highly disciplined and intricate dancing skills.

Before one is swept up by the undoubted pageantry and excitement of life in an *ikhanda*, the harsher realities of life there should be considered. On the memorable day of the two battling snakes, the young unmarried men of the uKhandempemvu *ibutho*, or age-grade regiment, were taking their turn to serve their king at kwaNodwengu. Life there was Spartan despite generous servings of beef, otherwise reserved for the conspicuous consumption of the rich and powerful. It was easy to become lost in the confusing maze of almost identical beehive huts, and when a man wandered into a section occupied by another unit, he risked being beaten up and chased away. Because different *amabutho* were always being rotated in and out, huts would periodically be left empty. Then they would be filled with wood ash and excrement by those living in neighbouring huts and required much cleaning to be made habitable again. Lunguza – born in about 1820 and one of the nearly two hundred informants whose invaluable testimony was meticulously recorded by the colonial magistrate, James Stuart – recalled that for lack of supervision the warriors regularly relieved themselves very close by the outer palisade. Consequently, in the *ikhanda* 'the stench was very bad'. Indeed, men even 'voided' in the streams where others drew their water.[4]

The young warriors' day of labour began at dawn when they set about their regular tasks of gathering wood and grass to repair the huts and palisades, tending the king's fields of crops and guarding his extensive herds of grazing cattle. Through the custom of *ukusisa*, royal cattle such as these were entrusted to the care of all the *amakhanda* (and often to *imizi* as well). They remained the property of the king, but their carers had the right to make use of them for milk or dung and to keep their offspring.

Herdsmen such as those at kwaNodwengu were armed. The other warriors going about their chores had stowed away their great, man-height, cowhide war-shields in huts raised on wooden stilts to preserve these valuable items (only two could be cut from the hide of a cow) from the rats; while their menacing stabbing-spears, or *amaklwa*, were piled out of sight in their huts. Likewise laid aside on this routine working day was the panoply of precious furs and feathers that made up the warriors' superb and intricate ceremonial dress. Instead, in a society where there was no shame in nakedness, they wore no more than a cowhide penis sheath for modesty beneath a thick bunch of animal skins twisted to resemble tails. These tails might be continued all around the waist like a kilt, or be replaced over the buttocks by an oblong cowskin flap, often supplemented by further tails. Woven blankets, which were to become an increasingly favoured item of outer wear in cool weather, were only introduced in 1824 with the arrival of the first white traders at Port Natal and were initially luxury garments confined to the elite. The unmarried men of the uKhandempemvu *ibutho* would have worn their hair long and intricately worked into fantastical shapes.

Unconscious of the supernatural drama about to be played out before him, Masiphula kaMamba, the hereditary chief, or *inkosi*, of the emGazini people, was stationed as usual in front of his hut halfway down and at the forefront of the left of the two great wings of barrack huts at kwaNodwengu. As Mpande's chief appointed officer of state, or *induna*, he was the most powerful man in the kingdom after the king. Like all men of high status, he grew his fingernails long and wore an *ingxotha*, the heavy and excessively uncomfortable brass armlet that reached from wrist to elbow and was conferred as a royal mark of distinction. He was notorious for his cruelty, likened in his violent rages to a wild animal,[5] and his subordinates grouped around him that morning maintained a wary and respectful distance as he kept his ferocious eye on the warriors going about their tasks in the great enclosure.

The day grew pleasantly warm, for it was that mild season of early summer when women across the kingdom, sometimes joined by their husbands and children, were weeding the shooting sorghum and millet in the small, irregular fields that adjoined their *imizi*. Masiphula and his companions were suddenly startled to see two great snakes chase each other up and down the reed screen that shielded the low doorway to his hut. They twined furiously around each other until they tumbled to the ground, where they continued to writhe in the dust, now one on top, and then the other, their thrashing coils dripping with blood from the savage bites they inflicted on each other. Drawn by the commotion, a crowd of warriors formed to watch in awed dread. Those witnessing the extraordinary spectacle – including Mtshapi (born in about 1846) and Ndukwana (born in about 1824), whose testimony Stuart recorded towards the end of their lives – were in no doubt as to what was happening.

In Zulu religious belief, the living and the dead were bound together as a single community in which the shades of the ancestors, or *amadlozi*, were the senior members. The shades brooded and watched over the living, who in turn consulted them in everything they did, propitiating them with offerings when they sensed their disfavour, and making contact with them through blood sacrifice in the *isibaya*. When an *idlozi*, who normally lived below the ground, wished to revisit the world of the living it did so manifested in the form of a snake. As King Cetshwayo clarified, when asked how you could tell when an ordinary snake was an *idlozi*, it was uncharacteristically untimid, and you could recognise one 'even as you recognise a human acquaintance'.[6] Because the *amadlozi* retained their mortal personality and characteristics, and maintained the same status in the other world they had experienced while alive, a commoner would materialise into a small, sluggish, harmless brown snake.

THE ASSASSINATION OF KING SHAKA

'Umpanda [Mpande], the King of the AmaZulu'
(GEORGE FRENCH ANGUS, *THE KAFFIRS ILLUSTRATED IN A SERIES OF DRAWINGS*, 1849)

Large green or mottled black snakes (*izimamba*), on the other hand, such as those tussling at kwaNodwengu, were known to manifest as the *amadlozi* of great chiefs.[7] And, to clinch their identification that day, it was crucial that, out of a thousand huts at kwaNodwengu, the two *amadlozi* had specifically chosen to enact their eternal quarrel in the spirit world in front of that of Masiphula, the king's chief *induna*, and no other.

Consequently, when a number of *izikhulu* hurried up to the scene of combat and tried to intervene, they cried out: 'Our pardon, kings! What is happening?'[8] They addressed the snakes as 'kings' because it was perfectly obvious to them that they were beholding the implacable, never-ending struggle between the *amadlozi* of King Shaka, the founder of the Zulu kingdom, and of King Dingane, who had assassinated him in 1828 some forty years before – Dingane, who had gone on to seize the throne and ruthlessly hunt down all his perceived rivals in the royal house.

While the mounting throng looked on, the larger and greener of the two snakes overcame the other, which broke away and fled. Masiphula knew that the appearance of the *amadlozi* of kings in the form of snakes must always be reported to the monarch so that, should the *amadlozi* be offended in some way, he could propitiate them through the ritual sacrifice of cattle and by praising them. Accordingly, Masiphula dispatched a messenger at the run who approached Mpande as protocol demanded, singing his *izibongo* as loud as he could and stooping down as a sign of respect. The king, as was usual at that time of day, was in the *isibaya* holding a confidential meeting with his councillors, who were ranged deferentially in front of him. They were dressed like every other Zulu man, but with more beads and ornaments.

Mpande was only too aware that the Zulu royal succession had always been decided by force, and that in 1840 he himself had overthrown his half-brother Dingane at the battle of the Maqongqo hills. It was later recounted that when, in 1856, his own two sons, Cetshwayo and Mbuyazi, were about to go to war over the right to the succession, Mpande had declared: 'Our house did not gain the kingship by being appointed to sit on a mat. [In Zululand when a father appointed one of his sons his heir he would sit on a mat on account of his rank.] Our house gained the kingship by stabbing with the assegai.'[9]

When Mpande's *izinduna* all exclaimed in awe of the snakes, 'Hau! They are still fighting, Nkosi, even now',[10] Mpande could not ignore the fact that the *amadlozi* of two kings were brawling in his own *ikhanda*. He immediately consulted the diviners, or *izangoma*, attached to his court. *Izangoma*, who could be either men or women, were easily differentiated from ordinary people on account of their bizarre apparel, weird hairstyles and body paint. They were chosen and possessed by the *amadlozi*, and so were able to translate the shades' supernatural messages to the living and to prescribe the correct ritual responses to avert calamity or illness, or to counter witchcraft.

Assured by his *izangoma* that the snakes were indeed the *amadlozi* of Shaka and Dingane, and that he must come to the defence of the former, the founder of the Zulu nation, Mpande peremptorily commanded his councillors: 'Drive off that evil-doer of Mgungungdhlovu [Dingane].'[11] 'So,' he continued with angry indignation, 'he is fighting with Tshaka when it was he who finished off the sons of Senzangakona? He used to say he had killed Tshaka for troubling the people; in fact it was he who finished off the Zulu house.'[12]

PART I

Three Spears

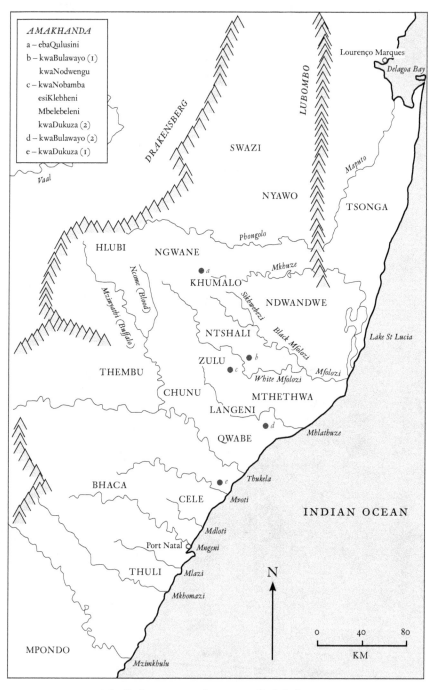

The Zulu region at the outset of Shaka's reign

CHAPTER I

Stabbed While Dancing

In 1824, four years before Shaka fell bleeding under the remorseless spear thrusts of his assassins, there was an earlier attempt on his life. His subjects, believing he would die, gave way to wild and extravagant mourning. Depending on just how they regarded their king, their lamentations were genuine or feigned, but were stringently enforced regardless.

The attack took place at Shaka's esiKlebheni *ikhanda*, south across the White Mfolozi River from kwaBulawayo in the Mahlabathini plain, his principal *ikhanda* at the time. EsiKlebheni had been established by his father, Senzangakhona, who, when he reached manhood, had moved out of kwaNobamba, the modest *umuzi* of his father and grandfather, who had been only very minor *amakhosi*.[1]

EsiKlebheni was situated in the emaKhosini valley, the 'Valley of the Kings', the most sacred locality in Zululand. It was so named because Shaka's royal predecessors were reputedly all buried there. Who they were is a matter of dispute. Even King Cetshwayo, who recounted the story of his people while held captive in the Castle in Cape Town after his defeat in the Anglo-Zulu War of 1879, had to admit that 'very little is known of them and their doings'.[2] The missionary and pioneer anthropologist, the Rev AT Bryant, collected no fewer than 11 versions of the genealogy of early Zulu *amakhosi*, and came to the conclusion that the most likely line

13

of descent was Malandela, Zulu, Phunga, Mageba, Ndaba, Jama and finally Shaka's father, Senzangakhona.[3] Be that as it may, Shaka and his successors as king always visited the presumed sites of these graves when there was a national crisis. They consulted the royal *amadlozi*, sacrificed cattle to them, recited their praises and sang 'the great and ancient anthems' (*amahubo*) honouring the mighty deeds of the ancestors and famous warriors of the past.[4]

The attempted assassination occurred during the annual *umkhosi*, or first-fruits ceremony, which, following his father's practice, Shaka celebrated at esiKlebheni.[5] This was the most significant event in the Zulu ritual year. As king, Shaka was the great rainmaker, and the fruitfulness of the crops depended on him. At several crucial moments in the agricultural cycle he was strengthened with ritual medicines to ensure a good harvest, but the *umkhosi* festival capped all others.

In preparation, all the *amabutho* made their way from their homes or distant *amakhanda* to assemble in the cluster of *amakhanda* in the vicinity of esiKlebheni. From there they proceeded to esiKlebheni itself for the three days of intense *umkhosi* ceremonies. Then the king, his *amabutho* and all his people were ritually purified, strengthened against evil influences and bound together anew. Mystical confusion was hurled out among their enemies. The ceremonies concluded with a grand review of the *amabutho* followed by the public promulgation of the laws that the king and his council of state, or *ibandla*, had decided upon for the coming year.

Something of the excitement and splendour of the *umkhosi* being celebrated in 1824 can be recaptured most vividly through the memories of the white adventurers who were seeing it through eyes quite unaccustomed to the sight. The ten-year-old Charles Rawden Maclean, known as 'John Ross', was shipwrecked at the rudimentary settlement of Port Natal in October 1825. As he wrote, nearly fifty years later, 'three years were, with little interruption, passed at King Shaka's residence. He kept me with him, first as a sort of rare pet animal ... and latterly as a confidential companion, as far as companionship could be held with such a mighty potentate, who could only be approached on all fours.'[6]

Maclean attended an *umkhosi* festival and remembered the 'immense gathering' of people in the *ikhanda* itself and encamped all around it.

'Utimuni, nephew of Chaka'
(GEORGE FRENCH ANGUS, *THE KAFFIRS ILLUSTRATED IN A SERIES OF DRAWINGS*, 1849)

The great majority were warriors and only 'a small portion of women and children were to be seen'. Maclean was in the *isibaya* with Shaka, who was discussing the coming grand review with his councillors while seated before them 'perfectly naked' and 'anointing his body with grease, preparatory to investing himself with the royal war dress'. A 'large body of warriors, in full war costume ... carrying white shields spotted black' then advanced from the bottom end of the parade ground and 'drew up in front of the King, in the form of a crescent, three deep, with Dingane, the King's brother, at their head. Having saluted the King with a simultaneous blow on their shields with the handle of the Umkhonto (a short-handled assegai or spear) and a general exclamation of, "Great master, Great King, you great as the world," the whole squatted on the ground ... their shields laid transversely on their breasts.'[7]

The festival attire of these warriors was indeed magnificent, and differentiated one *ibutho* from another, as did the distinctive colours and patterns of their war-shields. (Maclean noted separate *amabutho* carrying shields that were uniformly entirely black, white with black spots, white with brown spots, brown or pure white.)[8] The warriors' dress consisted of at least twenty skins of various varieties, but only especially favoured *amabutho*, *izikhulu* and members of the royal house were permitted to wear leopard skin. All wore the basic kilt of tails; white ox and cow tails were fastened around the neck like a cape to hang down the back as far as the knees, and down to the waist in front. More of these tails were tied above the elbows and below the knees to cover the shins. No footwear was worn. Bracelets of beads and bangles ornamented the arms. The headdress, individual to each *ibutho*, was held together by a thick, padded animal skin headband. More skins hung down from this headband as flaps or tassels either side of the face or down the back of the neck. Combinations of feathers arranged in bunches or in single plumes, worn upright or slanting backwards, completed the headgear. Maclean thought the ensemble gave the warriors 'a very warlike and commanding appearance'.[9]

The king and the great men of the kingdom wore the same style of ceremonial dress as the warriors, but their higher status was indicated by the costliness and rarity of their furs and feathers and by a greater display of ornaments. When paying Shaka a visit in 1825, two hunter-traders, James King and Henry Francis Fynn, admired Shaka's ceremonial headdress. A band of stuffed otter skin surrounded his head, adorned with 12 bunches of gorgeous red lourie (turaco) feathers and, in front, a single blue crane plume, 60 centimetres in height.[10] On a similar occasion, Maclean noted that Dingane, although garbed equally royally as Shaka, simply could not boast so large a display of beads as the king, who had 'a long band of these thrown over his shoulder in the manner of a soldier's belt [bandolier]'.[11]

Dancing was an integral part of the ceremonies. Warriors brought special dancing shields to the occasion, and Shaka's was pure white with a single, large black spot in about the middle.[12] Nathaniel Isaacs, a trader who, like Maclean, was shipwrecked at Port Natal in 1825, published a journal in 1836 in which he purported to have recorded his experiences in Zululand. On 16 April 1826, he saw warriors dance with Shaka, having first (as they did for certain dances) set aside their shields:

> They formed a half circle ... The king placed himself in the middle of the space within the circle, and ... [*umndlunkulu*] girls stood opposite to the men three deep, in a straight line, and with great regularity. His majesty then commenced dancing, the warriors followed, and the girls kept time by singing, clapping their hands, and raising their bodies on their toes ... The king was remarkable for his unequalled activity, and the surprising muscular powers he exhibited. He was dressed with a profusion of green and yellow glass beads ... This ceremony was performed with considerable regularity, from the king giving, as it were, the time for every motion. Wherever he cast his eye, there was the greatest effort made.[13]

Even in normal circumstances, Ndukwana (one of Stuart's informants) recalled, the *umkhosi* 'was invariably characterised by quarrelling and fighting among the different regiments, when indunas [officers] used to interfere and strike out among them with sticks right and left'.[14] EsiKlebheni in 1824 would have been no different: a seething gathering of thousands of overexcited people, their bodies jammed together, incessant noise, clouds of dust raised by the dance, and the king right in the midst of it all. His *izimbongi* (praise singers) added to the general furore. One of them, with bushbuck horns attached to his forehead, his hair dressed in female style and wearing a woman's leather skirt, went among the press of spectators, praising the king and pretending 'to butt or stick them as a beast would do'. The people played along, scrambling away as if afraid of being hurt, and 'the noise would resound'.[15] What better opportunity ever presented itself to a would-be assassin, especially one who calculated his realistic chances for escape in the dense, panicking crowd on the great parade ground and in the confusing network of closely packed huts surrounding it?

The hunter-trader Fynn, who had set up at the tiny settlement of Port Natal in May 1824, was present at esiKlebheni when the assassination attempt was made.[16] There is no doubt that he was an eyewitness to events in Zululand in the 1820s, but his heavily edited 'diary', produced between 1832 and 1861, is a very problematic source. That said, his is the fullest account we have of the circumstances.

Dancing similar to that described by Isaacs had been going on all day. It did not abate even when dusk fell, and Shaka ordered 'lighted bundles of dried reeds' to be held up to illuminate the pulsating scene. Fynn decided to watch, and had just entered esiKlebheni when he 'heard a great shriek and the lights were immediately extinguished. Then followed a general bustle and crying.' Shaka, 'while dancing, had been stabbed'. It was said that the would-be assassin was trembling as he tried to push his spear home.[17] Shaka, recounted Jantshi (who had been born in about 1848 and had gleaned his information from Nongila, who had served as an official spy for Shaka), 'drew the assegai out himself and ran into a hut'.[18]

Fynn shoved his way with considerable difficulty through the uproar to the *isigodlo*, where the screaming women were 'in a state of madness'. He tried to enter Shaka's great hut, where he supposed the king must be. However, he was pulled away by one of the king's confidential household attendants and advisors, or *izinceku*, one of the trusted men who undertook delicate missions on Shaka's behalf. This *inceku* led Fynn out of the *isigodlo* to a small *umuzi* some distance from esiKlebheni where Shaka's attendants had hustled the stricken king for his greater security.

Zulu testimony is consistent in stating that Shaka was stabbed through the left upper arm and that the blade barely penetrated his left breast.[19] Fynn, while agreeing about the direction of the thrust, insisted that the blade passed 'through the ribs' and that Shaka spat blood. Doubtless to enhance his own role in ministering to the wounded king with imported British ointments, mild purgatives and fresh dressings, Fynn seems greatly to have exaggerated the gravity of the wound. With distinct relish, he even asserted that 'Shaka cried nearly the whole night' anticipating imminent death.

Yet the king's own *izinyanga*, or traditional healers, who were accustomed to handling stab wounds, clearly had the case well in hand themselves. They would have applied herbal poultices to the open wound to prevent inflammation and encourage healing, and then have tied it up with grass. Their greatest concern appears to have been that the blade had been poisoned. It had not, and within five days Shaka was on the mend, his recovery celebrated with the plentiful sacrifice of cattle in thanksgiving to the royal *amadlozi*.

Meanwhile, Fynn had witnessed disquieting scenes of hysteria as Shaka lay wounded. Increasing crowds thronged around the *umuzi* where the king had been taken, shouting and screaming and throwing themselves about. The *umndlunkulu* were in particular distress since they dared not eat while their lord apparently hovered between life and death. The whole great, exhausted assemblage went through the incessant motions of intense mourning, since not to weep – or to be caught feigning to do so – or to sit down, or to wear ornaments or even to wash meant (Fynn dramatically assures us) being put to death.

The most urgent question in the minds of Shaka, his *izikhulu* and the general throng throughout all this mourning uproar must have been: who was behind the assassination attempt? Three possibilities occurred to them, any one of which represented a dire threat to Shaka's regime, which, despite its triumphalist façade, rested on shallow and untested foundations.

CHAPTER 2

A Royal Spear?

Makewu, *inkosi* of the Dube people, declared in 1899 that, when Shaka drew out the spear that had wounded him, he recognised it as being of the variety he had distributed to two of his brothers, Dingane and Mhlangana, who lived at the isiPhezi *ikhanda* on the banks of the Mphembeni River a few kilometres to the west of the emaKhosini valley.[1] As princes of the royal house, or *abantwana*, they possessed a status that was a reflection of Shaka's own, and he had no choice but to delegate to them considerable authority in his kingdom.

These two *abantwana* would indeed succeed in killing Shaka, in 1828, and there was clearly some conflation in Zulu memory of the first and subsequent attempts on his life.[2] Yet it was not inherently unlikely that they could have been plotting against Shaka in 1824 too. In Zulu society succession was governed by complex procedures made necessary by the large number of wives and children in the household of a man of high status. The automatic succession of the eldest son was considered too dangerous for an ageing sire, so the naming of his heir was delayed until the last moment to reduce the possibility of violent usurpation.

Shaka avoided any threat from an impatient heir by acknowledging no son of his own. As Baleka (who was born in 1856) remarked to Stuart: 'A person like Tshaka is like a wild beast, a creature that does not live with its own young, its male offspring.'³ However, Shaka was himself one of 18 brothers born of Senzangakhona's 15 wives. We do not know the date of his birth. It is most often said to have been 1787, although Dan Wylie has persuasively argued for about five years earlier.⁴ The only concern the more ambitious of his surviving brothers had in the unsettled principle of royal succession was that the royal mat should fall to one of them. (In those days there were no European-style chairs, and for a throne Zulu rulers sat on a rolled-up mat, or *umqulu*.)⁵ Tellingly, King Cetshwayo, Shaka's nephew, reputedly had a dream in which he was visited by the *amadlozi* of Ndaba and Dingane. They said to him, 'we shall give you only one son, for you of the Zulu are always killing one another in disputing the kingship if there are many of you'.⁶

Shaka may have been the glorious founder of the powerful Zulu kingdom, but to the royal family – especially those with their eye on the royal *umqulu* – his claim to the kingship was compromised. Not only was he a usurper and regicide who had overthrown the rightful *inkosi* of the Zulu people, but his very legitimacy was also open to question.

Was Shaka indeed illegitimate? The most authoritative word on that score must surely come from his nephew, King Cetshwayo, who voiced the tradition current in the royal house. When Senzangakhona began his reign, declared Cetshwayo, 'he was unmarried; but had a natural son, only a year or two old, by [Nandi], daughter of [Mbhengi kaMhlongo], chief of the [Langeni] tribe, named Chaka, or the "bastard"'. In Zulu society, marriage was only legalised – and its issue legitimised – through the *ilobolo* system, that is, with the handing over of cattle by the man's family to the father or guardian of the bride in exchange for the loss of the valued domestic labour of the young woman. 'Soon after he became king,' continued Cetshwayo, Senzangakhona 'married Chaka's mother', but they had no other son.

Senzangakhona apparently came to believe that the illegitimate Shaka 'would become troublesome when he grew up', recounted Cetshwayo, and when he was about fifteen (closer to twenty if Wylie is correct) his father decided to kill him. However, Shaka received warning and in about 1802 fled to Jobe kaKhayi, the powerful *inkosi* of the Mthethwa people in southeastern Zululand between the White Mfolozi and Mhlathuze rivers, where he would greatly prosper as a war leader. Nandi, meanwhile (according to

Cetshwayo) remained Senzangakhona's favourite wife, even if most other traditions (as we shall see) took a very contrary view. But Cetshwayo was insistent that Senzangakhona, whether to please or placate Nandi, eventually gave Shaka to her 'for a son', or, in other words, legitimised him.[7]

Ndhlovu (born in about 1858), who was descended of the Zulu royal house and whose grandfather had been prominent in Senzangakhona's day, has left us the fullest recorded oral version of Shaka's youth.[8] He confirmed Cetshwayo's account of Shaka's eventual legitimisation, as did others.[9] Nevertheless, the strong belief persisted in some Zulu and colonial circles that Shaka remained illegitimate.[10] What gave credence to this position was the tradition that Nandi could not abide seeing Shaka grow up in Senzangakhona's household while she shamefully remained with her father as an unmarried woman. So, the story goes, she eventually left to marry Ngendeyana, a man of substance among the Qwabe people – or perhaps just to enter his *isigodlo* as a concubine until Senzangakhona claimed her.

What does seem well accredited is that she had a son, Ngwadi, by Ngendeyana, although the paternity of her daughter, Noncoba, is disputed.[11] To complicate matters, a tradition did persist that Ngwadi was really Senzangakhona's son. This serves to explain why Shaka grew very close to him, which he would not have done if they had not shared the same sire. According to Mayinga, born about 1839 and another of Stuart's informants, it was a deliberate insult on Dingane's part to suggest Ngendeyana was Ngwadi's father, and was typical of the slanders that succession disputes engendered.[12]

Even if we accept the certainty of the Zulu royal house that Shaka was eventually legitimised, the fact that he was Senzangakhona's eldest son still did not automatically make him his heir, or *inkosana*. That person, according to custom, would be the son of the woman Senzangakhona decided to declare his 'great wife', and she was not Nandi. Rather, she was Bhibhi, his eighth wife and Senzangakhona's undisputed favourite. In the early twentieth century, the Zulu still had a popular proverb: 'You are beautiful like Bibi ka Nkobe, who, whenever the king appeared, was also to be seen.'[13] Bhibhi's son by Senzangakhona was Sigujana (otherwise known as Nomkwayimba or Mfokozana), who was of much the same age as Shaka. There seems general agreement that Senzangakhona recognised him as his *inkosana*.¹⁴ Did that make Shaka a usurper? There can be no doubt that it did.

Shaka seized the Zulu chieftainship with the energetic support of his patron, Dingiswayo, the Mthethwa *inkosi*. As we have seen, he had entered the service of Jobe kaKhayi, Dingiswayo's father, in about 1802. When Jobe died, in around 1807, Dingiswayo killed his *inkosana*, his own brother Mawewe, and usurped the throne. Such fratricidal violence was anything but unusual in Shaka's world of iron, an environment far removed from the bucolic, peaceful, pre-Shakan Eden of later legend. Rather, this disgruntled but ambitious outcast reached maturity in a setting that encouraged him to hone his ruthless political flair from example, and to whet his remarkable military talent with frequent practice.

Hunting and warfare had long been the honourable occupations of men in Shaka's sphere, and in the youthful Shaka's day warfare was intensifying between the numerous chiefdoms in the lands between Delagoa Bay to the north and the Thukela River to the south. In the sixteenth century, the largest chiefdom in that region had probably been that of the Mbo. For reasons unknown, this chiefdom fragmented in the early eighteenth century. Several of its splinters, notably the Ndwandwe living just south of the Phongolo River, tried to rebuild their lost power. They were confronted by expanding rival paramountcies, or conglomerations of chiefdoms recognising the overarching authority of a particular ruling house. The most formidable of these was that of the Mthethwa to their south, between the White Mfolozi and Mhlathuze rivers. By the time Shaka was serving Jobe, the Ndwandwe and Mthethwa – along with other, more aggressive polities between the Black Mfolozi River in the north and the Mzinyathi and Thukela rivers in the south, such as the Hubi and Qwabe paramountcies and the Chube chiefdom – were fiercely raiding each other's cattle, struggling to control the winter and summer grazing pastures, and vying to attract new adherents at the expense of their rivals.

In their wars, all of these chiefdoms deployed their *amabutho* and Shaka would have served in their ranks. He has often been credited with inventing these large-scale military formations, or 'regiments', and with devising their fighting style. In fact, although he certainly was influential in improving their military capabilities, their organisation predated him to at least the mid-eighteenth century, while their hallmark tactic of using long throwing-spears and then finishing off their foes with short stabbing-spears went back as far as the late seventeenth century.

War served the exiled Shaka well, and he embraced military prowess as the means to personal advancement among the Mthethwa. Dingiswayo fully appreciated his martial aptitude and personal courage. As a mark of his favour, he placed him under the special care of his commander-in-chief, Ngomane kaMqomboli, who became the young warrior's father figure and mentor.

Shaka's rise to prominence among the Mthethwa came at a time when Dingiswayo found himself engaged in an increasingly deadly struggle for supremacy with the Ndwandwe, who were pushing south across the Mkhuze River under their violent and cunning ruler, Zwide kaLanga, celebrated in his *izibongo* as

> He who crouches over people that they might be killed ...
> Ford with the slippery flagstones ...[15]

Weaker neighbouring chiefdoms began to take flight west over the Drakensberg and south over the Thukela River to avoid the escalating warfare. They in turn dislodged communities in their path so that the ripples of violence spread further and further outwards. In resisting the menacing Ndwandwe, Dingiswayo relied on the smaller, tributary chiefdoms in his orbit to give him military assistance. One such was the Zulu chiefdom under Senzangakhona, which was strategically placed to secure Dingiswayo's western marches up the valley of the White Mfolozi. It was thus in Dingiswayo's interests to secure his hold on the client Zulu chiefdom, and he saw how he could do so while at the same time furthering the interests of his loyal and talented protégé, Shaka.

There is a robust tradition that it was Dingiswayo – himself a usurper – who initiated the plot for Shaka to supplant his father as the Zulu *inkosi*. The opportunity presented itself when Senzangakhona paid his overlord a visit in search of a new wife. Perhaps he was also impelled by curiosity to see his long-estranged but increasingly famous son.

It seems that Shaka felt no qualms at falling in with Dingiswayo's plan to deploy occult powers against Senzangakhona. The Zulu believed that since an overlap existed between this world and the world of the *amadlozi* there was dangerous scope for a mystical force, *umnyama* – which was darkness, evil influence and misfortune – to seep out among the living. To set this malevolent, supernatural force in motion, harness it and direct it against a specific individual, it was necessary to resort to witches, or *abathakathi*. Their most potent magic potions, or *imithi*, always included snippets of the human body and its waste products, such as nail clippings or urine. (The Zulu were always careful to prevent their *insila*, or body dirt, from coming into the hands of those who wished them harm.) Correctly prepared, these wicked potions could do incalculable harm, calling down disease or death.

Shaka, it is said, played his full and willing part in the actual bewitching of his father. One version has Shaka climbing on top of the hut where Senzangakhona was sleeping. He then washed himself with the malevolent *imithi* prepared for him by the *abathakathi* so that the potions dripped through the thatch onto the Zulu *inkosi*. Another version has Senzangakhona bewitched when his mat and spears were smeared with these magical brews to ensure that Shaka gained occult ascendancy when his shadow fell across his father, or (in another account) suddenly leapt over him. Whatever the occult means used, Senzangakhona began to feel mortally ill, and returned home from Dingiswayo to kwaNobamba, where he fell into a rapid decline and died.[16]

King Cetshwayo blandly declared that, on Senzangakhona's death (which Fynn understood to have occurred in 1816),[17] 'the Zulu tribe sent to him [Shaka] and begged him to be their king: he consented ... and he was made king with great rejoicing. His brothers acquiesced.'[18] This sanitised version flies in the face of all other surviving accounts, which are unanimous that Shaka usurped the Zulu throne by eliminating Senzangakhona's favourite son and designated *inkosana*, Sigujana.[19]

It seems that, on hearing of Senzangakhona's death, Dingiswayo – no stranger to regicide and fratricide – promised to support Shaka's claim should Sigujana be put out of the way. Shaka turned to his half-brother Ngwadi, Nandi's son supposedly by Ngendeyana, with whom he had developed a close rapport. The story goes that Ngwadi, who was also in Sigujana's fatally misplaced confidence, accompanied the new *inkosi* alone to the river to bathe. But Ngwadi had accomplices stationed in the long grass by the river bank. As the unsuspecting Sigujana stooped and washed alongside Ngwadi, these assassins ran the young man through from behind with two spears. Ngwadi sent immediate word to Shaka that he had eliminated Sigujana. In commemoration of his treacherous deed he would come to be known appropriately as 'the stick of one who cuts down trees'.[20] He would remain a close favourite of Shaka's, who 'gave him authority over a large number of people'.[21] Ngwadi would suffer the dire consequences of this partiality when Dingane came to power.

Dingiswayo, as he had promised he would, lent Shaka his full backing in his bid for the now-unoccupied royal *umqulu*. He dispatched Shaka to the Zulu chiefdom with a daunting military escort under the command of the Mthethwa commander-in-chief and Shaka's old mentor, Ngomane, who would in due course become his chief councillor. Once arrived, Shaka seized power with exemplary ruthlessness, executing the prominent men associated with Senzangakhona's regime – including a number of uncles – as well as others whom he suspected of opposing his claim to rule. Only then did all of Shaka's surviving brothers, thoroughly cowed, give up any immediate ambitions they might have harboured to succeed Sigujana, and tender him their allegiance.[22] But, as we have seen, *abantwana* were raised with ingrained notions of the very likely possibilities of violent usurpation. So, if the spear that wounded Shaka at esiKlebheni in 1824 was not one of theirs – and it does indeed seem it was not – there was scant reason why in future another spear should not be.

Even so, it is unlikely that any of the *abantwana*, no matter how disgruntled or ambitious, would ever contemplate a deadly move against Shaka without the prior knowledge and approval of the most influential person in the royal house, the individual Cetshwayo believed had 'carried on all the negotiations' for Shaka's return:[23] their formidable aunt, Mnkabayi kaJama, Senzangakhona's older sister.

Mnkabayi clearly possessed a ruthless taste for power. As Ngidi (one of Stuart's informants, born in about 1818) later put it, the Zulu kings were 'placed' by her.[24] She first came to prominence on the death of her father, Jama, when she ruled as co-regent with Mudli kaNkwelo kaNdaba of the Zulu royal house until Senzangakhona came of age.[25] Zulu society may have been overtly patriarchal, but royal women in the *isigodlo*, especially *amakhosikazi*, were positioned to manipulate the outcome of succession disputes. Their hands were strengthened if they had no sons of their own to enter the ring – and it seems Mnkabayi and her younger twin sister, Mmama, remained unmarried.[26]

There is a sturdy tradition that Mnkabayi, while she was regent, saved the infant Shaka's life. When Senzangakhona learned that he had an illegitimate child by Nandi, so this particular story goes, he was enraged and sent armed men to kill the infant. But Mnkabayi hastily concealed Shaka and convinced her brother that she had poisoned him. Senzangakhona was satisfied and commended his sister's action. Once his back was turned, though, she urged Nandi to flee with her baby to the safety of her father's *umuzi*, where Shaka grew up.[27]

Whether this was really so or not, the tale served to connect Mnkabayi closely with her promising young nephew, and it does seem she kept a proprietary eye on his career. She and Mmama encouraged Shaka's ambitions while in exile, and were reputed to have been deeply instrumental in encompassing Sigujana's assassination and persuading other members of the royal house to go along with them.[28] With Sigujana out of the way, Mnkabayi assumed temporary power as regent (as she had once before after the demise of her father, Jama), and kept Shaka's royal *umqulu* warm for him until he arrived from the Mthethwa country.[29] Yet again, Shaka was deeply beholden to his aunt, while she, for her part, had consolidated her considerable political clout in the kingdom she had secured for him.

For Mnkabayi, the practical exercise of power lay in Shaka's need for dependable representatives to govern his most significant *amakhanda* as extensions of the royal household. The *amakhosikazi* from his *isigodlo* were ideal for this role. One such was Bhibhi, Senzangakhona's widow and the mother of Sigujana. Her fate, though, was to be as tragic as her son's. She retained her high status and usefulness to the monarch during the reigns of both Shaka and Dingane. But, when Mpande defeated Dingane at the battle of the Maqongqo hills in 1840, the usurper's victorious forces hunted down the members of Dingane's household as they tried to take refuge in the bush, and Bhibhi was among those butchered. Mpande was aghast, for Bhibhi was one of those experienced *amakhosikazi* upon whom he was intending to build his administration, and before the battle he had specifically ordered: 'Let her not be killed. I shall need her to rule.'[30]

Besides Bhibhi, other *amakhosikazi* who were prominent under Shaka as the administrators of his *amakhanda* were Langazana, Senzangakhona's fourth wife; Songiya, his half-brother Mpande's mother; Noncoba, his half-sister (who was remembered as good-tempered, light-skinned, very fat and with a short, wide nose said to be like Shaka's);[31] and Mmama, his aunt. However, the most important *amakhanda* were reserved for Mnkabayi to preside over.

Mnkabayi ruled over not only the sacred kwaNobamba homestead itself, where Senzangakhona was buried, but also the strategic ebaQulusini *ikhanda* that dominated northwestern Zululand and guarded that vulnerable frontier.[32] She was also in charge of esiKlebheni and entrusted with the sacred *inkatha* kept there. The *inkatha* possessed the mystical power of binding together, rejuvenating and protecting the king and the nation. It was a circular grass coil about a metre in diameter, and the thickness of a man's calf, wrapped in a python skin and bound with grass rope by the leading men of the nation. Among other ingredients it contained the *insila* of the king, his ancestors and relations, shreds of *izinkatha* captured from vanquished *amakhosi* and pieces of flesh cut from their bodies, vomit from the *amabutho* when they were being ritually purified, and *imithi*. It was handed down from king to king, growing in size as it was added to, until the British destroyed it in the Anglo-Zulu War.[33] Besides these *amakhanda*, eMahlabeni was also Mnkabayi's. This prestigious *ikhanda* was known as the seat of war. It was where the army used to *ukuthetha*, or go through the ceremonies of giving praise to the ancestors under her command, and where, from the reign of Shaka to that of Cetshwayo, the marching orders for a major campaign were issued.[34]

Indeed, such was her power and prestige that after the death in 1827 of Shaka's mother, Nandi, Mnkabayi effectively replaced her as the Queen Mother and was known as the Great She-Elephant, or *iNdlovukazi*. Her imposing physical presence matched her sobriquet. Taller and lighter in colour than her twin, Mmama (who was dark brown), she had a large stomach and was described as an *isitubesikazi*, or a person whose prime-conditioned body was sleek and softly fat.[35] In her *izibongo* – where she is sometimes addressed as a male on account of her power (thus opening up a gender duality) – she was celebrated for her honest, incorruptible ability to resolve her adherents' problems and for her success in confronting any evil forces that might threaten Zulu power:

> Father [sic] of guile!
> … Who devours a person tempting him with a story …
> The opener of gates so that all people may enter …
> Sipper for others of the venom of cobras.[36]

When she died during King Mpande's reign, her grave near the kwa-Gqikazi *ikhanda* in the Mahlabathini plain became a place of secure refuge for fugitives, and her name long continued to be invoked when people took a sacred oath.[37]

This, then, was the highly respected, if domineering, personality who had assured Shaka's succession, and who served with great effectiveness as a mainstay of his rule. However, should she come to disapprove of his policies, and suspect that they were undermining the kingdom he had built, she was unlikely to scruple at conspiring to bring down her protégé. She, who had saved Shaka's life as a child and had presented him with his throne, could equally well command the spears to deprive him of both.

CHAPTER 3

An Ndwandwe Spear?

If the spear that had wounded Shaka did not belong to his royal brothers, whose, then, was it? Fynn recorded in his diary that six men besides Shaka had been stabbed in the affray, and that 'from the road they took' the assassins must have been sent by Zwide kaLanga, the *inkosi* of the Ndwandwe.[1] Dr Andrew Smith, naturalist, explorer and government agent, who visited King Dingane on a diplomatic mission from the Cape in 1832, was assured then that the would-be assassins had been Ndwandwe men.[2]

The day after Shaka had been stabbed, two *amabutho* were dispatched to apprehend the would-be killers, popularly presumed to be Ndwandwe. They would have been wearing a toned-down campaign version of their precious ceremonial costume, although their officers would have retained more of their regalia to distinguish them from the rank and file. No Zulu forces would take the field until *izangoma* had ritually cleansed them beforehand of evil influences and protected them against the ritual pollution associated with the act of killing. Since this expedition was not against another army, but was more of a policing operation, scouts would have been sent out ahead to locate the supposed culprits. The main body would then have come up to surprise them where they slept or to encircle them if they attempted to flee.

On the fifth day after the assassination attempt, the *amabutho* duly returned with one or three bodies (accounts differ), which they claimed were those of the Ndwandwe responsible, and deposited them on the ground outside esiKlebheni. It is beside the point whether they really were the assassins or not, because the warriors would not have dared to report back empty-handed. In any case, the corpses satisfied the men and women still assembled in their mourning frenzy. They proceeded to beat the cadavers hysterically until they were utterly pulverised and nothing was left except an immense pile of discarded sticks and clubs.[3]

The question remains, however: why was it so readily assumed that the would-be assassins must be Ndwandwe? The answer is that Zwide was Shaka's most dangerous and persistent foe.

No sooner was Shaka sitting on the Zulu royal *umqulu* as Dingiswayo's tributary than his overlord's protracted struggle against Zwide reached its dénouement. Dingiswayo's death and the defeat of the Mthethwa was only made possible, so tradition has it, through Zwide's bewitching of Dingiswayo – a fair return, one might think, for Dingiswayo's use of *imithi* against Senzangakhona. In a feigned peace move, Zwide gave his daughter (or sister, in another version) to Dingiswayo in marriage. Zulu men, if they had sex with a woman when still unmarried or, if married, did not wish to sire offspring from a particular wife or concubine, practised external sexual intercourse (*ukuhlobonga*). Once he had ejaculated over her thighs, Dingiswayo's Ndwandwe partner gathered some of his semen into a large butterfly cocoon used as a snuffbox. She then sneaked off and brought it to Zwide. The possession of his rival's *insila* enabled Zwide to gain supernatural mastery over Dingiswayo. Under the occult power of Zwide's charm, Dingiswayo wandered into the hands of his enemies without the protection of his army, probably in 1817. Zwide, urged on by his mother, Ntombaze, put him to death, either by killing him outright or by leaping over him to consummate his spell, as Shaka is said to have done with Senzangakhona.[4]

With the Mthethwa leaderless, 'the whole country was upside down', recounted Ndhlovu, 'and it continued so until subdued by Tshaka's energetic action'.[5] Indeed, all that now stood in the path of Ndwandwe domination was Shaka's determined defiance, which brought increasing violence down on all the peoples of the region.

White traders, missionaries, settlers and officials were quick to associate Shaka and the rise of the Zulu kingdom with appalling devastation

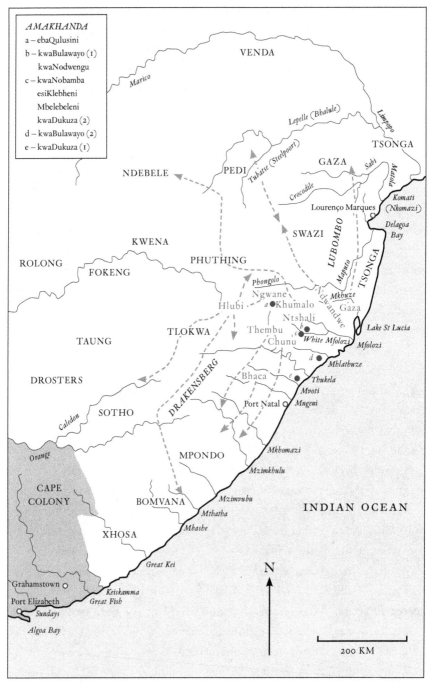

Migrations during the consolidation of the Zulu kingdom

and bloodshed, which, they claimed, decimated the local population and turned many thousands into terrified refugees or desperate cannibals. This angle conveniently allowed them to justify their commercial, proselytising and political activities as a civilising mission aimed at rescuing Africans from savage barbarism. Historians subsequently built on this approach to come up with, in the 1970s, the concept of the *mfecane* (crushing) that supposedly explained the seismic waves of unprecedented dislocation that spread across southern Africa in the early nineteenth century. The explosive rise and expansion of Shaka's militaristic Zulu kingdom, the argument went, was at the root of the mayhem.

Although this interpretation was initially widely accepted, as with all historical models it has since been modified, albeit with much more academic heat than is often the case. It is enough for us here that consensus is hardening that the Zulu kingdom, although a prominent player during the *mfecane*, was neither its sole instigator nor its only motor. Furthermore, it is accepted that the scale of dislocation, suffering and death during the *mfecane*, while not negligible, must be kept in perspective. Quite simply, the technological and physical capacity to massacre untold numbers simply did not exist, certainly not the 'two million lives' that the influential imperial historian George McCall Theal credited to Shaka's depredations on the basis of no evidence at all.[6]

Indeed, the nature of warfare the Zulu were engaged in was relatively limited, even if society in Shaka's time was increasingly militarised and 'only war was talked about'.[7] Cattle were the chief prize of combat, for they were vital to rulers – whose sole property they became – for redistribution as rewards to their successful warriors, and as a means of securing the loyalty of their nobles and of attracting new followers to their rule. Doubtless, when a community resisted the seizure of their cattle by force of arms, combat was fierce. But it would have involved only a limited number of warriors and would have been short, if sharp. We can piece together how a battle would have been fought in Shaka's time from an eyewitness account by Fynn,[8] and from later oral testimony.

Once the decision to engage was taken, the army drew up in a circle (*umkhumbi*) to be sprinkled by *izinyanga* with *intelezi*, medicinal charms to prevent *umnyama* from affecting the men with its evil influence. On one such an occasion, Fynn saw each man present his back to the *inyanga*, who flicked him with *intelezi* from an oxtail that he repeatedly dipped into the 'decoction' kept boiling in a pot.⁹ With his men now ritually assured of victory, the commander then took up position with his staff on nearby high ground. Shaka was reputed to have usually accompanied his *amabutho* on campaign,¹⁰ so we can imagine him actively directing the course of the battle, holding aloft his black war-shield with white or grey speckles only at the lower end.¹¹

When the order was given for the army to advance, it was with the tactical intention – developed from the hunt – of pinning the enemy down with a frontal attack by the centre, or 'chest', while the two flanking 'horns' rapidly encircled the foe. A reserve was kept back for support or pursuit.

Typically, when the two opposing forces were within about twenty metres of each other they halted and traded insults and battle cries peculiar to each *ibutho*. Later in the century each Zulu warrior typically carried two or three throwing-spears (*izijula*), which he normally used for hunting, and hurled them at the enemy to disrupt their ranks before charging home at a stooping run. But in Shaka's time, as Ndukwana explained and Fynn witnessed, *amabutho* were permitted to carry only one spear lest they got into the habit of throwing their spears instead of rushing in at once to close quarters.¹²

When the opposing forces clashed together, they did so with a tumultuous yell and engaged each other furiously, man to man. The weapons employed for this close fighting were the bone-crushing wooden knobbed stick (*iwisa*) commonly carried by Shaka's *amabutho*,¹³ and the obligatory short-hafted, long-bladed stabbing-spear, or *iklwa*. The warrior wielding it made an underarm stab into the enemy's abdomen, followed by a vicious rip, before withdrawing the spear. This manoeuvre, which involved hooking away an enemy's shield with one's own beforehand, required considerable skill and practice. This is where regular training under Shaka's rule was crucial; while the *iklwa* was not a new weapon, such proficiency in its use certainly was, and gave the man wielding it a considerable psychological advantage over his opponent.

This battle-winning *iklwa* was the weapon of the hero, of the man who cultivated military honour, who proved his prowess in single combat and who – as Shaka was said to have required – bore his own wounds only on his chest.¹⁴ Certainly, overt courage and insatiable ferocity were the hallmarks of the great Zulu warrior. As Shaka's *izibongo* expressed it:

> The voracious one of Senzangakhona,
> Spear that is red even on the handle ...
> The young viper grows as it sits,
> Always in a great rage,
> With a shield on its knees.¹⁵

After about three minutes of frenzied stabbing and parrying, the two sides typically fell back, temporarily sapped. They took a short pause to regroup, then re-engaged. This shattering procedure was repeated until one side finally broke. Every man's valour and daring in the deadly hand-to-hand fighting were under constant scrutiny by his peers and officers. After the battle, the king would discuss with his *izinduna* which *ibutho* had the distinction of being the first to engage the enemy at close quarters. Men who were members of that *ibutho* and who had made a kill were designated heroes. The king ordered them to wear a distinctive necklace made from small interlocking blocks of willow wood (*iziqu*), which had an occult association with the *amadlozi*. The *iziqu* were looped around the neck, or slung across the body like a bandolier, and marked out the warrior hero ever after.

By wretched contrast, those who failed to live up to the high ideals of male masculinity, and whose courage failed them in combat, were degraded and punished. The Zulu historian Magema Fuze described what happened to cowards in Shaka's time:

> Here is the war song which was sung when cowards were about to be put to death:
> Ho! Ho! Pick out the cowards!
> And all cowards were cruelly put to death when this song was chanted. The man was seized, his arm lifted, and then stabbed under the armpit like a goat, as he was told, 'Just feel the spear which you tried to avoid.'¹⁶

A young Zulu warrior in full ceremonial panoply photographed at
King Cetshwayo's coronation in 1873. Members of Shaka's unmarried *amabutho*
would have been similarly attired.

(COLLECTION OF THE LATE SB BOURQUIN)

However, if the victim managed to restrain his cries as the spear was 'turned round and round inside him', he was regarded as a hero. His wound was treated and he was given a beast, 'which was spoken of as "the tears of your mother".'[17]

In battle, once their mauled foe fell back and began to disintegrate into demoralised flight, the triumphant Zulu would closely pursue them and begin (as the saying went) 'stabbing the *ibece* melon' as they sank their *amaklwa* into their naked, unprotected backs.[18] Simultaneously, the two encircling Zulu 'horns' cut off as many of the fugitives as they could. The victorious Zulu killed all those they could lay their hands upon, for they seldom gave quarter to the defeated – although Maclean did comment that Shaka often extended amnesty to those brave survivors who would accept his rule and drafted them into his army.[19]

Having disposed of the enemy warriors, the triumphant Zulu rounded up all the captured enemy cattle for the king. Sometimes, civilians suffered directly in the fighting. This usually happened when a ruler and his adherents came under attack while they were attempting to migrate *en masse* to another region out of harm's way. The non-combatants had to stand by and watch the course of the battle in a fever of apprehension, hoping fervently that their menfolk would defend them successfully. When they lost, they faced massacre alongside them in the heat of battle. 'Let no one remain alive,' Shaka would order his *amabutho* before a battle, 'not even a dog or a child carried on its mother's back.'[20] It was believed that this style of fighting began with Shaka and was known as *umhadu*, or 'people coming to a place with violence'.[21]

There is little doubt that people in general faced privation and death from starvation in the theatres where the Zulu and other armies were operating. When the Zulu attacked a community, or simply pillaged it as they marched by, many inhabitants might take temporary refuge in the surrounding bush, in caves or on mountain tops. Once the warriors had moved on, they would re-emerge, but their situation was then dire. Their means of survival would have been destroyed or carried off: their grain pits emptied (including the essential seed for the next season's planting); their vegetable gardens stripped; their livestock rustled; and their *imizi* demolished for firewood. People would then have to move off elsewhere to find food and shelter, and there is no doubt that during the course of Shaka's wars some regions became temporarily depopulated. As Shaka's *izibongo* graphically expressed it:

> The newly planted crops they left still short,
> The seed they left amongst the maize-stalks,
> The old women were left in the abandoned sites.
> The old men were left among the tracks,
> The roots of the trees looked up at the sky.[22]

Ordinarily, though, there was no point in the Zulu annihilating the members of a defeated chiefdom since a functioning community could be usefully absorbed into the growing Zulu kingdom. The lot of those individuals captured in raids and battles could be far harder, however. Captives would be carried off to the heartland of the kingdom where they would be incorporated into Zulu households in various menial capacities.

Were these people slaves? A British naval dispatch reported that in 1823 the Portuguese export of slaves to Brazil from Mozambique between Cape Delgado to the north and Delagoa Bay to the south numbered 16 000, and that the French from Bourbon (as Mauritius was then known) were also involved in the traffic, as were Arabs from Muscat.[23] Yet it seems that Shaka's Zulu played no part in the slave export trade, unlike various chiefdoms in the Mozambique hinterland as far south as Delagoa Bay. However, domestic slave labour appears to have been long embedded in Mthethwa, Ndwandwe and Dlamini (Swazi) societies. 'Nothing in the way of slavery as ordinarily understood used to go on among the Zulu people,' Mkando told Stuart, but a form of it did persist in Shaka's time.[24]

Mention has already been made of the *izigqila* women in the king's *isigodlo*, and the servile status of captured women held in the household of an *inkosi* as concubines and domestic servants was no different. Ordinary warriors were permitted to seize two male children of the men they had killed in battle. These boys served them as their *izindibi* (baggage-carriers) on campaign. On reaching adulthood they were permitted to become members of an *ibutho* themselves, and later to marry and set up their own *umuzi*. Warriors were permitted to marry the young women they captured, and this had the advantage that no *ilobolo* had to be paid. Adult male captives could expect nothing better than to become cattle herders and labourers. In all these cases, captives were eventually integrated into Zulu society in one form or another. Even so, they had endured the trauma of being forcibly ripped away from their own kin, they had suffered many humiliations as despised aliens, and they had been kept for shorter or longer periods in menial positions.

With Dingiswayo's death in 1817, Shaka, his former tributary, was left dangerously isolated. Nevertheless, he refused to acknowledge Zwide as his new overlord. The Ndwandwe *inkosi* angrily responded by invading Zulu territory in 1818 to impose his mastery, and laid waste to the valley of the White Mfolozi. Shaka was only just able to beat the Ndwandwe off, although at one stage (according to Cetshwayo's testimony) he found himself hemmed in and in imminent danger of death or capture.[25] Badly savaged, Shaka fell back for a time on the coastal country. Yet he refused to give in. He began to regroup, carefully harboured his resources and concentrated on building up the military capabilities of his *amabutho* against future Ndwandwe attacks.

Simultaneously, Shaka deployed diplomatic skill, intimidatingly backed up by the threat – and sometimes the exercise – of his military muscle, to overawe weaker neighbouring chiefdoms into accepting him as their new overlord. They traded his stern protection from Ndwandwe ambitions against the obligation to pay him tribute in cattle and to provide manpower for his *amabutho*. In this crucial arrangement, *amakhosi* abdicated their right to raise and command their own *amabutho* and ceded this, the basis of their power, to Shaka. Thereafter the Zulu *amabutho*, raised periodically from the same age-grade in all the subordinated chiefdoms across the entire kingdom, owed their prime loyalty to Shaka, and not to their local *amakhosi*.

Shaka's preparations came none too soon, for the Ndwandwe were soon renewing their attack. The Zulu beat off a second Ndwandwe offensive thanks to a night march that caught their army unprepared. But the battle was not decisive and the Ndwandwe withdrew in good order, devastating Zulu territory as they went. In 1819, Zwide sent his army south for a third time, determined to crush the Zulu once and for all. Shaka retired before

Zwide's forces to the wooded and broken countryside of the Nkandla mountain range south of the Mhlathuze River, where the difficult terrain negated the superior Ndwandwe numbers. This time, Shaka routed and scattered the Ndwandwe in a pitched battle just where the amaZulu stream enters the Mhlathuze River from the north.

Shaka followed up this critical victory with such a rapid advance across the Black Mfolozi River into Ndwandwe territory that when his warriors approached Zwide's chief homestead, esiKwitshini, the women came out to greet them thinking it was their own victorious army returning. When they realised their mistake, Jantshi recounted, it was too late and the Zulu stabbed all the women and children as they recoiled in dismayed panic and tried to flee.[26] According to Mmemi, another of Stuart's informants and born in about 1828, Zwide himself only just had time to escape out of the back of his *isigodlo* as Shaka's men entered the parade ground.[27] Thoroughly bested, Zwide and his following withdrew northwest across the Phongolo River. Shaka's *izibongo* exalted:

> I liked him when he pursued Zwide son of Langa,
> Taking him from where the sun rises
> And sending him to where it sets;
> As for Zwide, he folded his two little shoulders together,
> It was then the elder was startled by the younger.[28]

It was very difficult for a ruler such as Zwide to hold his sprawling domain together after such an overwhelming military defeat. The membership of a chiefdom, no matter how populous and powerful, was always fluid, subject to splitting and regrouping. As would be the case with the Ndwandwe, a chiefdom might fracture when disaffected groups hived off to establish new chiefdoms of their own. What made this process so readily possible was that political power was based on control over essentially mobile resources such as cattle and the people's agricultural labour. Consequently, no chiefdom was bound inexorably to a particular territory and its members might easily migrate elsewhere in search of security, accumulating or shedding adherents as they moved on.

Inevitably, then, Zwide's humiliation at Shaka's hands brought simmering tensions within the Ndwandwe ruling house to the surface. Some sections of the Ndwandwe, such as the Gaza under Soshangane kaZikode and the Jele under Zwangendaba kaZiguda, broke away altogether and migrated north to the environs of Delagoa Bay. The Portuguese (who had in 1787 established a fort and trading post there called Lourenço Marques) first reported their presence in 1821. Soshangane and Zwangendaba settled in the vicinity for a while, extracted tribute from the weak and vulnerable Portuguese, and from the petty chiefdoms who submitted. By 1824 they had pushed further north towards the lower Limpopo River. (We shall come across Soshangane again for the part he played in Shaka's fall.)

The senior section of the Ndwandwe remained with Zwide on the northern bank of the Phongolo. He had controlled this region for some time. He now set about considerably extending his sway further to the northwest at the expense of existing states such as the Pedi Maroteng paramountcy, between the Lepelle (Olifants) and Tubatse rivers, which he shattered in about 1822. Consequently Shaka, at the time of the attempt on his life in 1824, would have been unpleasantly aware that Zwide's fortunes seemed to have revived spectacularly, and that the Ndwandwe were now undoubtedly the dominant power in all the lands between the Phongolo and the Lepelle River to its north.

Indeed, the intimidating Ndwandwe presence just over the Phongolo menaced the territory the Zulu had so recently wrested from them. What made the situation even more fraught for Shaka was that he simply did not have the resources to bring Zwide's former tributary chiefdoms between the Black Mfolozi and Phongolo rivers effectively under his direct control. A section of the Khumalo under Mzilikazi kaMashobana rejected his rule altogether and broke away, settling on the highveld to the west of Zwide's relocated kingdom. Soon known to local Sesotho-speakers as the Matabele, or Marauders, the Ndebele (as they proudly called themselves in their adaptation of this sobriquet) now lurked on the northwestern flanks of the Zulu kingdom, another latent threat.

Other chiefdoms in the former Ndwandwe territory remained potentially rebellious. For the time being, Shaka had to concede them a considerable degree of autonomy,[29] ruling through a viceroy, Maphitha kaSojiyisa, who was closely related to the Zulu royal house. Ruthless and shrewd, as his *izibongo* claim, Maphitha was a good choice and efficiently kept the newly conquered region in check:

> Jackal that escaped the trap,
> When others had been caught the previous day.
> Stabber that cannot be denied.[30]

Even so, the Ndwandwe threat to Shaka's newly founded kingdom had certainly not been dispelled, and it is understandable that the dismayed and angry crowds at esiKlebheni jumped to the obvious conclusion that Zwide must have been behind the failed attempt to assassinate their king. It is not possible, though, to prove whether he was or was not, even if it would have been most certainly to his advantage. For the moment, the production of some supposedly Ndwandwe corpses helped assuage popular Zulu fury. As for Shaka, he no more credited the Ndwandwe with the deed than he did the *abantwana*, plausible as their guilt might seem. He had his eye trained unblinkingly on another set of far more likely culprits.

CHAPTER 4

A Qwabe Spear?

When Shaka drew out the spear that had wounded him, and examined it, he found that the butt end of the wooden shaft was blunted in a manner his attendants assured him was characteristic of Qwabe workmanship. More than that, tradition asserts that the would-be assassin was called Sikwayo, identified as formerly the *induna* of the Qwabe *inkosi*, Phakathwayo kaKhondlo, whose chiefdom had been Shaka's his first major conquest.[1]

In his *izibongo* Shaka was likened to

> The threatening storm, take the children to shelter ...
> Beware, the wild beast is in the kraals.[2]

Indeed, we should never lose sight of the brutal fact that Shaka's rapidly expanding domain was a ruthless conquest state, made up of a hotchpotch of previously independent chiefdoms, 'each with its own established ruling house, its own identity, its own body of memories and traditions'.[3] Consequently, many people in freshly subjugated chiefdoms could never bring themselves to acknowledge Shaka's rule, let alone allow themselves to be more closely assimilated and take on Zulu identity. For them to do so would be a gradual process over several generations.

The reason why Shaka so readily accepted that the would-be assassin's spear must unquestionably have been wielded by a member of the Qwabe was that he was already convinced that their chiefdom harboured many malcontents. Why that should have been so is somewhat odd, though, for the Qwabe chiefdom had been incorporated on better terms than many others that had fallen to Shaka's spear.

To explain, we have to grasp on what terms Shaka cobbled his kingdom together. Zulu popular memory held that 'Tshaka did not scatter the nations; he unified … them',[4] but in the new order some were decidedly more equal than others.

The Zulu ruling house – to whose members the term 'Zulu' alone properly pertained – deliberately applied ethnic distinctions in their kingdom. On one side of the divide were the favoured 'insider' chiefdoms of the Zulu heartland, centred on the White Mfolozi. They had come under Shaka's rule early on, and their chiefly houses were absorbed into the ruling Zulu aristocracy. On the other side were the 'outsider' subject chiefdoms north of the Mkhuze and south of the Thukela. They had been subordinated later, only after Shaka had defeated Zwide, and their chiefly houses were kept at arm's length from the centre of power.

Members of the 'insider' chiefdoms came to be known as the *amantungwa*, after the *intungwa* grass that was used for thatching huts and weaving grain baskets.[5] The *amantungwa* increasingly regarded themselves of being of common Zulu descent and ethnicity. In their estimation, they were the true members of the kingdom, and it was their menfolk who filled the ranks of the *amabutho*. They looked down on the 'outsiders' whose young men Shaka did not recruit into his *amabutho* but instead deployed as lowly cattle herders and guards at outlying cattle posts. The *amantungwa* knew these 'outsiders' by a set of derogatory names, such as *iziyendane* ('those with a strange hairstyle') and *amalala*. Originally meaning 'menials', in Shaka's time *amalala* became an ethnic slur, meaning inferior people with a dialect different from that of their rulers. Madikane told Stuart that Shaka 'used to insult and frighten us by saying … we were Lala because our tongues lay flat (*lala*) in our mouths, and we could not speak in the Ntungwa fashion'.[6] Even more demeaningly, *amantungwa* said that the despised *amalala* were called that 'because they sleep (*lala*) with their fingers up their anuses',[7] and that they 'farted on the mimosa tree, and it dried up'.[8] Quite simply, they were not regarded as 'real Zulu' since they had not been 'born in the Zulu country'.[9]

According to tradition, Qwabe and Zulu were both sons of Malandela. Because they quarrelled, their father separated them, sending Zulu north and Qwabe to the coastal district south of the Mhlathuze River.[10] In other words, it was believed that the Qwabe shared a common ancestry with the Zulu, and this made them *amantungwa*, 'insiders', and Shaka regarded them as such. But they and the Zulu had a history of antagonism and of cultural differences. The Qwabe were apparently identifiable because their men always placed wood on the hearth with their right arm.[11] More obviously, it was easy to pick them out on account of their distinctive dialect, since the Qwabe characteristically used to *ukuthefula*, or to substitute a 'y' for the Zulu 'l' when speaking. Much of their mutual antipathy grew out of the original disparity in size and power between the two chiefdoms: while the Zulu initially resented Qwabe arrogance and envied their sway, the Qwabe came eventually to begrudge being overshadowed by their once weaker rival.

During the reign of Khondlo kaMncinci in the late eighteenth century, the Qwabe chiefdom was the most powerful in the coastal lands between the Thukela River and the Mhlathuze to the north, and its *inkosi* commanded his own *amabutho*. Tradition holds that, in his wandering youth as a despised exile, Shaka had been permitted for a while to live among the Qwabe because Mfunda, his grandmother on his mother Nandi's side, had been one of them.[12] It was said that Shaka and Phakathwayo, Khondlo's son who later became the *inkosi* of the Qwabe, had quarrelled as boys. Shaka never forgot nor forgave an affront, and Phakathwayo woundingly insulted both his status and masculinity by calling him 'a little Ntungwa, a little nothing in hiding, with a little penis that points upwards'.[13] Indeed, the hurtful slur about his 'stumpy little stick'[14] of a penis would long outlive Shaka to intrigue a modern age raised on popular but facile psychological theories.

Shaka entered Dingiswayo's service just when Mthethwa expansion was beginning to threaten the Qwabe. Khondlo nevertheless held fast, and consolidated his power by crushing rival neighbouring paramountcies such as the Thuli and Cele, who took flight southwards over the Thukela. However, as was so often the case in the dynastic politics of the region, a succession dispute weakened the Qwabe chiefdom. Nono had been Khondlo's choice to succeed him as *inkosi*,[15] but, soon after Shaka had himself usurped the Zulu royal *umqulu*, Nono's brother, Phakathwayo, seized power. Nono fled to Shaka for refuge along with their younger brother, Nqetho.

Harbouring these exiled Qwabe notables at his court was of the greatest political value to Shaka. As his future deeds would prove, while he habitually put defiant or recalcitrant *amakhosi* to death without a qualm – and most of their male relatives along with them – he needed to rule their conquered chiefdoms through obedient clients who would deliver up the manpower, women and cattle he required. For that to be acceptable to the freshly incorporated people of a chiefdom, smarting at their loss of independence, it was essential that Shaka's chosen puppet be of recognisable legitimacy, which meant he had to be a member of the old ruling house.

Shaka quickly identified Nqetho as his prospective choice as sub-ruler once he had brought the Qwabe to heel, and he set about winning his grateful loyalty. He treated Nqetho as a favoured companion, allowing him familiarities permitted no one else outside the Zulu royal house – even the right to spit in the king's presence[16] – and accorded him respect for his royal status enjoyed by no other. Kambi assured Stuart that '[i]f the king called anyone else but Nqeto, they would come running up, even if they were the sons of late kings. Only one would dare to respond to the summons walking; that was Nqeto.'[17]

Phakathwayo would have construed Shaka's sheltering of his exiled brothers as a hostile act. Even more provocative was Shaka's determination to build his Mbelebeleni *ikhanda* in country the Qwabe considered theirs. Both sides knew that to found an *ikhanda* was the classic ploy when staking a territorial claim.[18] Yet Phakathwayo would have seen nothing substantial to fear from the insecure and diminutive Zulu chiefdom, which was still very vulnerable to Ndwandwe attack. He is said to have contemptuously remarked of the Zulu that 'they were like a necklace which could not even go around the neck, because of their small numbers'.[19] Nor could he resist needling his bumptious rival. Jantshi recounted that Phakathwayo persisted in harping derisively on the diminutive size of his old playmate's genitalia, declaring that he wore 'as a penis cover the fruit-shell used for snuffboxes'. His jibes found their mark, and in frustrated rage 'Shaka cried until tears fell and the isigodlo also cried' in dutiful sympathy.[20]

Shaka had his revenge in full, however. Accounts differ as to how he overcame the Qwabe. The more conventional version has Shaka attacking and defeating the Qwabe at the Hlokohloko ridge, near modern-day Eshowe.[21] Phakathwayo was apparently so shocked by his unexpected reversal of fortune that he dropped dead of natural causes.[22] Jantshi filled in the details for Stuart. After easily defeating the Qwabe, Shaka's men 'found Pakatwayo seated on the ground with his head buried in his folded arms. When Tshaka came close up, Pakatwayo looked up and, as he saw Tshaka, was seized with fear ... Pakatwayo was then carried off to his kraal by the impi, which chanted war songs as it went ... [O]n the day following the battle it was found that Pakatwayo was dead, having seemingly been killed by fear alone.'[23]

Other accounts have Shaka characteristically employing treachery to overcome the Qwabe. In an apparently conciliatory move, Shaka suggested that the Zulu and the Qwabe (who, after all, shared the same lineage) should hold a friendly dancing competition (*umjadu*) at eMtandeni, Phakathwayo's principal homestead. Phakathwayo agreed, because he had no fear of Shaka, but the Zulu *inkosi* was 'stalking him'. It was agreed that no weapons would be brought to the *umjadu*, but the Zulu hid their spears in the river. They attacked and quickly overcame the Qwabe when they were dispersed after the dance, and then killed Phakathwayo in his hut.[24]

That said, we can be sure that occult means came into it, as they had when Shaka overcame his father and when Zwide destroyed Dingiswayo. The story goes, according to Mmemi (born in about 1828), that Mqayana, an *inyanga* whom Phakathwayo had unjustly exiled, took refuge with Shaka. He persuaded him of the efficacy of his supernatural powers, and undertook to 'doctor' the Qwabe *inkosi* and deliver him into Shaka's hands.

After the *umjadu* already referred to, Mqayana gathered up dirt from the ground pounded by Qwabe feet during the dance and mixed it with the excrement of hyenas and Qwabe faeces. This 'medicine' was intended to make the Qwabe shit at the mere sight of attacking Zulu warriors. To weaken them further, Mqayana lowered *intelezi* placed in grass baskets into the springs the Qwabe drank from. Toads and frogs were then put into the baskets to eat the soaked 'medicine' and then released so that they could communicate its magical influence to the Qwabe. To make quite sure, Mqayana also filled gourds containing the *intelezi* with cockroaches. Once they had eaten the medicine, the cockroaches were emptied onto and around Qwabe huts to play their part in disseminating his magic.

Certain that the Qwabe would now be unable to put up much resistance, Shaka unexpectedly raided the ekuDabukeni *umuzi* where Phakathwayo was staying. His guards, although superior in number to the Zulu, put up no resistance thanks to Mqayana's magic, for their stomachs churned and their strength failed.[25] Ngidi furnished Stuart with further graphic detail. When his guards were dispersed, Phakathwayo took refuge among palm trees near ekuDabukeni. There the Zulu discovered him, 'seated, doubled up and alone'. Shaka now came up and struck the Qwabe *inkosi*, then ritually jumped over him, 'backwards and forwards'. Shaka then ordered Phakathwayo to be dragged to ekuDabukeni where he repeated the procedure in front of his *amabutho* drawn up in a semicircle and performing a dance of triumph. Phakathwayo, not altogether surprisingly, 'now expired from a sense of abject fear and humiliation'. Shaka finally buried him with the respect due to an *inkosi* at ekuDabukeni.[26]

With the death of their *inkosi*, the Qwabe swiftly decided to submit (*ukukhonza*) to Shaka and tender their allegiance, saying, 'We are now Tshaka's people.' One tradition ascribes this politic decision to the urging of Sikwayo, Phakathwayo's *induna*, the very same man accused (unjustly, one suspects) in 1824 of trying to assassinate Shaka.[27] Rather unfairly, considering that he had employed an underhand combination of deceit and magic against them, Shaka reproved the Qwabe for not putting up more of a fight for their chief.[28] But, now that he was their ruler, he moved rapidly to draw them into his kingdom. Predictably, to bolster the authority of his own appointees over the Qwabe, he killed Phakathwayo's *inkosana*, Khathide, but to placate his new subjects he returned the cattle he had seized from them in the campaign.

Shaka's unexpected victory over the great Qwabe chiefdom had immediate repercussions. The two largest independent chiefdoms of west-central Zululand, the Chunu and Thembu, took fright, and to escape Shaka's

A QWABE SPEAR?

growing power fled south across the Thukela. Other smaller chiefdoms of the region scrambled to *khonza* to Shaka to avoid being attacked. Shaka's realm was, as a result, considerably increased.

Yet, for all that, Shaka remained insecure. Could he count on these recently subjugated chiefdoms remaining loyal? He seems to have regarded the Qwabe with especial suspicion. Their independent history had been a proud one, and they had been a major power in the region. If a revolt against his rule were to come, it would most likely originate with them.

For lack of evidence, this must remain a supposition. Regardless of who actually was behind the bid to assassinate him, it seems probable that Shaka decided to snatch the opportunity to break the Qwabe once and for all. After all, there are many stories that tell of atrocities Shaka committed against chiefdoms that had defied or betrayed him, and of the pitiless revenge he took for past humiliations or more recent insults. The Qwabe were guilty on every one of these counts in Shaka's eyes, and he did not stay his hand.

Fynn witnessed a force of 3 000 warriors being sent out to revenge the attempt on Shaka's life. He did not know or disclose their target, but he learned that their orders were 'to spare neither man, woman, child nor dog. They were to burn the huts, to break the stones on which their corn was ground, and so prove their attachment to their king.'[29] Jantshi and Baleka both told Stuart that Shaka ordered that all the Qwabe were to be 'picked out' from every part of the country and killed in reprisal.[30] Many Qwabe were quartered in the kwaBulawayo *ikhanda* close by esiKlebheni for the *umkhosi*. They were the first victims. Shaka, when asked how the Qwabe would be recognised, revealingly responded, 'by their great love of quarrelling' and 'stirring up strife'.[31] All those at kwaBulawayo identified, by whatever means, as Qwabe were driven into the great cattle enclosure and surrounded by the *amabutho*. Shaka ordered that, in vengeance, they be stabbed in the left side as he had been. After closing in and mercilessly killing the Qwabe as directed, the *amabutho* then fanned out across the Qwabe country, hunting down the Qwabe in their *imizi*.[32]

So great was the massacre that dongas were widely remembered to have been filled with corpses, and the Qwabe scattered far and wide.[33] Nandi,

Shaka's mother, was appalled, not only at the scale of Shaka's retribution but also that the Qwabe, to whom they were so closely related, should be his victims. 'Why are you taking off your covering,' she remonstrated, referring to his Qwabe kin, 'the one of your mother's people?'[34] But Shaka was not to be deterred from breaking up the Qwabe. Years later, in Dingane's reign, the Qwabe were still being excluded and discriminated against because, as Sivivi explained, they were 'perfidious' on account of having stabbed Shaka.[35]

Whether they really had tried to kill him was beside the point. Shaka's objective was the elimination of the Qwabe as a political threat to the integrity of the Zulu kingdom. Certainly, his purge succeeded in achieving that aim. But, by indiscriminately killing people accepted as *amantungwa* – Zulu 'insiders' – many of whom were his very own kin, Shaka gravely alarmed others among his recently incorporated subjects, along with members of the royal house itself. Who could be certain they would not become one of Shaka's future victims?

From Shaka's point of view, the assassination attempt of 1824 established that he stood in peril of another attempt to kill him. Within his own kingdom lurked clandestine enemies, very likely in the royal house itself and certainly among the chiefdoms he had recently conquered, especially those that did not find it easy to forget their former greatness, such as the Mthethwa and Qwabe. Foes hovering just outside his borders ached openly to bring him down, most especially the Ndwandwe, who were rapidly recovering from their defeat at his hands.

Shaka's immediate response to this bundle of threats was to shift his capital away from the valley of the White Mfolozi to within Qwabe territory. By relocating the centre of the kingdom's gravity there, Shaka was better situated to keep a close and wary eye on the Qwabe and the neighbouring Mthethwa just north across the Mhlathuze. He also put a safe distance between himself and the Ndwandwe, who were beginning to probe Zulu defences in the north and to raid their former territory south of the Phongolo. Furthermore, by moving much closer to the Thukela, Shaka was better able to consolidate his hold over the rich coastlands south of the river by quartering *amabutho* there and by establishing a string of outlying royal cattle posts.

A QWABE SPEAR?

Shaka's new capital in the Qwabe country was called kwaBulawayo. *Amakhanda* were frequently refounded in new locations, so it is often necessary to distinguish one from another as the first, second and even third of that name. The first kwaBulawayo was just north of the White Mfolozi. Shaka built the new, second kwaBulawayo just south of the Mhlathuze River at the source of the Bele stream on a ridge of hills about twenty-seven kilometres north of the present-day town of Eshowe. Symbolically, its site was close to eMtandeni, Phakathwayo's capital,[36] which it was clearly intended to overshadow, as Shaka had the Qwabe *inkosi*. According to Ngidi, kwaBulawayo means 'the "place of death", where people are killed, from the precipices near there over which people were thrown'.[37] Though, as with many other *amakhanda*, it had alternative names, and kwaBulawayo was originally known as Gibixhegu, meaning 'Defeat the Old Man'. It gained that name when Shaka defeated Zwide, because he is supposed to have said, 'I won't think of fighting with an old man (*ixegu*) who used to fight with my father.'[38]

PART II

Always Talking of War

CHAPTER 5

He Who Beats But Is Not Beaten

Shaka, having survived an assassination bid and now ruling his bellicose kingdom from his new capital, the second kwaBulawayo, remains an enigmatic figure. The number of oral traditions deeply critical of him is evidence of the widespread animosity of people who saw themselves as his victims; in stark contrast, others hailed him as a hero and founder of the Zulu nation. So, before we begin to untangle the circumstances that culminated in the successful attempt on his life, it is time to ask: what can we know of Shaka the man?

How even to pronounce his name? *Amalala* speakers, such as Stuart's informant Ngidi (who came from the Cele chiefdom in the coastal lands south of the Thukela) said 'Tshaka', and not 'Shaka',[1] as the *amantungwa* would have. This explains why the early Port Natal settlers, such as Isaacs, living in *amalala* country, always wrote 'Chaka' since that spelling indicated the 'Tsh' sound.

The very meaning of Shaka's name reflects how perceptions of him differed. There is a beetle that in the early days the Zulu called an *inkambi*, and which they later referred to as an *itshaka*. The Zulu believed it caused intestinal disorders and made the stomach swell out.[2] When Nandi became pregnant by Senzangakhona, the story goes that she was at first said to be suffering from this ailment.[3] Jantshi, who insisted that he had 'carefully questioned' his father about the name, confirms this tale. But this does not mean that Shaka was named after an intestinal beetle, as is so often maintained. As we have seen, King Cetshwayo remarked that Shaka's name indicated that he was a 'bastard'. Jantshi explained to Stuart that the expression *'itshaka'* was used to describe a girl who became pregnant before marriage, and that the illegitimate child she bore was also spoken of as *itshaka*.[4]

An alternative tradition gives a much more positive spin to Shaka's name than 'bastard'. Magema Fuze, the pioneering Zulu historian, wrote that it meant that Shaka would 'violently disturb [*shakazisa*] all the tribes'.[5] More convincing is Ngidi's explanation that, while Senzangakhona's name for his son – and which he used among his own people – was Mandlesilo, 'strength of the wild animal', Shaka was his additional praise-name. Dingiswayo had bestowed it on him in recognition of his heroic military prowess, and it means '"He who beats but is not beaten" (*uSitshaka ka sitshayeki*)'.[6] Whatever the truth of the matter, it is certainly the last meaning that perhaps best reflects Shaka's character.

'He was always talking of war,' Stuart was informed by Mayinga, a member of the Gaza chiefdom in northern Zululand connected to Shaka's prime enemies, the Ndwandwe, and conquered by him.[7] Isaacs was equally explicit: 'War and dominion were the ruling passions of Chaka.'[8] Of course, as the ruler of a militarily expansive state with a dominant warrior culture, it is hardly surprising that Shaka was bellicose. Melapi, born in 1814, when still a small child saw Shaka during a visit to emDlazi, the *umuzi* of his father, Magaye kaDibandlela, the trusted tributary *inkosi* of the Cele people through whom Shaka administered his lands south of the Thukela River. He told Stuart that 'Tshaka made up songs for himself', and the one he heard included these vaunting words:

> I am not a goat to be made terrified in the kraals,
> I am not a gate-keeper such as is selected by kraal-owners [the headman of an *umuzi* chooses the gatekeeper],
> I am a great warrior there in the Zulu country,
> I am foremost in the place of headrings [in the *isibaya* where affairs are discussed].[9]

Besides his being warlike, what else can we know of Shaka's character? Isaacs, determined to denigrate Shaka in order to strengthen his own colonising agenda, was unequivocally negative: 'Chaka seems to have inherited no redeeming quality; in war he was an insatiable and exterminating savage, in peace an unrelenting and a ferocious despot, who kept his subjects in awe by his monstrous executions.'[10] In contrast, Charles Maclean, who spent nearly three years at Shaka's court and, as a child, was permitted a degree of intimacy with Shaka that would have been denied an adult, summed him up more equitably. 'Shaka', he later wrote, 'was a man of great natural ability, but he was cruel and capricious.'[11] James Young Gibson, a Zululand magistrate at the end of the nineteenth century whose pioneering history of the Zulu people was based partially on oral testimony, wrote that Shaka's character, as known to the descendants of the people he had ruled, was made up of two contradictory qualities: 'generosity and wanton cruelty'. While 'liberal' to those who earned his favour, to others it appeared 'that he derived a kind of amusement from seeing them killed'.[12] Indeed, Mayinga related that Shaka 'killed off frequently. We used to think the king was having sport and we thought but little of it. He never seemed in earnest.'[13]

Gibson noted that Zulu tradition was 'vague' when accounting for Shaka's apparently insouciant cruelty,[14] yet there was purpose behind it. Unpredictable violence was a most effective means whereby Shaka maintained a degree of control over his *izikhulu*. By destroying some of the great men of his kingdom in an apparently indiscriminate and arbitrary fashion, the rest were intimidated – for the time being, at least – into toeing the line. And when he eliminated an *inkosi*, Maclean recorded with a shudder, Shaka also made sure to destroy his wives and his whole family so that none would be left alive to avenge him.[15]

While seemingly arbitrary executions were thus an instrument of policy, not all of Shaka's subjects were willing to accept it with a submissive shrug. Baleka was a woman of the dissident Qwabe who suffered under Shaka's inveterate suspicion. She passed on their traditions of Shaka's callous bloodthirstiness, which she had learned from her grandmother: 'Seeing vultures flying above, he [Shaka] cried, "Wo! The birds of the king are hungry!" People were then killed and put out on a hill to be eaten by the vultures. And wu! The vultures were all out on the hill!'[16]

The 'hill' refers to the place of execution always within a short distance of the *ikhanda* where the king was holding court, and where the corpses were left for the birds of prey to feed upon. The Zulu form of execution was a grisly business, so that Maclean marvelled at the 'fortitude and dignified calmness' of people facing it. Men, he recorded, were killed by a blow from a heavy *iwisa*. But if they were only stunned and fell to the ground 'a sharp pointed stake (which is already prepared) ... is thrust up the abdomen. Being thus skewered, he is thrown into the nearest thicket or jungle.'[17] Women were not clubbed to death like men. Instead, a rope with a slipknot was tied around their neck and this was struck with a heavy stick 'and the person throttled till the eyes came out of her head'.[18]

Besides wincing memories of executions, people also preserved tales of Shaka's other purported atrocities. Like all anecdotes of wanton cruelty, these should be accepted only with careful reservations. Indeed, as Ndhlovu reflected, people regularly concocted horror stories about Shaka, such as impaling children on posts.[19] So when Baleka of the Qwabe said that 'Tshaka did many evil things to people, like cutting open a pregnant woman to see how her child lay',[20] we are tempted to discount the tale. Except that, in this case, it was repeated by several other informants.[21] Ndhlovu contributed the convincing anecdote that Kutshwayo kaNswakele reproved Shaka, saying: 'It is evil to cut open a person as if he were a beast. If a person has done wrong, and the king does not put him to death, he should be sent into the wilderness to disappear.'[22]

It is perhaps enough, when trying to understand why Shaka was eventually assassinated, to take these stories of arbitrary cruelty as indicators of popular fear and dislike among certain of his subjects. His purported cutting open of a pregnant woman, which seemingly took place at kwaDukuza at the very end of his reign, was particularly notorious, and Melapi believed that this capricious and cruel deed 'was one of the reasons why Dingana put Tshaka to death'.[23]

Nevertheless, Shaka the cruel and wicked despot was only part of the picture, and like any human being he had other, more vulnerable sides to his character. From talking to Zulu people during King Dingane's reign, Andrew Smith gained the impression that 'Chaka was a man of great feeling and used frequently from grief or excessive joy to burst into a crying fit'. In an access of artless vanity while watching his army ford the Mzimkhulu River to invade Mpondo territory, he apparently turned to Fynn in a characteristic fit of tears and asked if he 'ever saw so great a man as he was'.[24] We also learn that Shaka was 'very fond of going about visiting places. He sat very little indoors.' Late in his reign, once he had settled at kwaDukuza, about ten kilometres from the seashore, he is said to have enjoyed sitting for hours watching the waves of the Indian Ocean. At sunset, he would energetically start off home 'at a run' with his courtiers – many of them plump and stately like most Zulu men of high status – scurrying and panting to keep up with him.[25] Such physical activity was not surprising, though, in a man who Isaacs noted was considered 'the best pedestrian in the country', and who in the dance 'exhibited the most astonishing activity'.[26]

In his social relations with the white traders in his kingdom, Shaka showed flexibility and a willingness to be informal with them in private and to let down his guard. As Maclean recollected, 'The pompous manner in which he always behaved to our party while in the presence of his chief captains and warriors to our amusement was altogether thrown aside in the retirement of his residence, where he conversed familiarly with Capt. King through Jacob the interpreter … While minutely examining the texture of a blanket, he held it to his face, and expressed his admiration for its warmth and softness.'[27]

Shaka exposed both his vulnerability and vanity to the traders in the matter of his white hairs. A Zulu king was shaved and shorn with much ceremony. Mbulo (born in the early 1850s), whose father, Mlahla, had dressed Shaka's hair, recalled that when he did so 'he would make a stroke and then duck down onto his elbow, then make a stroke again, only to duck back, and so and on, because afraid of him'.[28] The king was shaved while discussing public affairs with his councillors in the *isibaya*. During the performance, he was 'not touched with the hand' and the clippings were carefully dropped into a basket and safely disposed of lest an *umthakathi* employ the king's *insila* to bewitch him.[29]

The Zulu remembered that when Shaka 'got older he used to have the white hairs pulled out of his head. He always wanted to be regarded as quite young,'[30] doubtless fearing that if he were seen to be ageing his enemies would be tempted to take advantage. Indeed, his grey hairs, recalled Maclean, 'caused him great uneasiness' and he anxiously inquired if the white men possessed any remedy. He was thrilled when he learned they possessed the 'valuable preparation' – Macassar oil, a fashionable hair conditioner – necessary to restore his hair and beard to their full blackness.[31] Ironically, his intense desire for hair dye would (as we shall see) play a not inconsiderable part in the circumstances that led to his downfall.

Despite having an *isigodlo* of hundreds of young women at his disposal, 'Tshaka had absolutely no issue – male or female,' declared Melapi.[32] This lack of progeny has led a prurient modern age to question Shaka's sexuality. But there is no mystery here. The Zulu agreed that their kings were simply following the practice among leopards and lions for the mother to hide a male cub for fear the father would kill it.[33] Cetshwayo stated bluntly that Shaka simply did not wish to have progeny.[34] Dingane, Shaka's successor, had no child either. That was because both feared the consequences of raising an heir to become a competitor and possible usurper – as Mpande, the third Zulu king, would discover when forced to share power with Cetshwayo, his over-mighty son and *inkosana*.

Put another way, just because Shaka had no heir did not mean he avoided sexual intercourse with women. Andrew Smith lubriciously reported that 'Chaka used to sleep in company with four of his wives, one on each side and one across the feet and one at the head',[35] and it is unlikely he remained chaste in these tempting circumstances. Nor does lack of children necessarily mean Shaka was sterile. Like other Zulu men he doubtless practised *ukuhlobonga*, or external sexual intercourse, when he did not wish his partner to conceive.

Besides, is it true that he fathered absolutely no children? Tradition had it that whenever Shaka, while living under Dingiswayo, 'met a girl in the path he would catch her and make her pregnant' and that his indulgent patron would not punish him for the rape.[36] Some held that while Shaka was living in the Mthethwa country he had wives. This would explain why, when he seized the Zulu chiefdom, he was already wearing the *isicoco*, which signified he was a married man.[37] There was also the strong tradition that one of these Mthethwa women bore him a son, Zibizendlela. He was said to have fled from Shaka, no one knew quite where, perhaps south to

Faku, the Mpondo king, to whom he was said to have *khonza*'d, or far away to the north, to Ndebele country, where his descendants were said still to be living in the early twentieth century.[38]

Zibizendlela might well have survived in exile but, once Shaka was king, what then became of a woman he made pregnant and of her child? Andrew Smith asserted that, if any of Shaka's women fell pregnant, they were ordered to abort the fetus. If that did not work, they were put to death.[39] However, as Maclean noted, white settlers relished the notion that the savage king killed any concubine he made with child. From his observation while living at Shaka's court, any *umndlunkulu* or *isigqila* the king made pregnant was sent away to live 'in great retirement and obscurity'. These banished women kept their children but 'never hinted they were of royal blood'. Maclean added the revealing insight into the restricted nature of life in the royal *isigodlo* that pregnant women did not dread being banished, but instead looked forward to it 'with pleasure, as a relief from the dull monotony of their secluded life'.[40]

Maclean believed that Shaka had a 'compact' with Dingane to sire no heir that would interfere with his half-brother's eventual succession.[41] However, there was the matter of Monase, the woman from Shaka's *isigodlo* whom he gave in marriage to his half-brother, Mpande, along with a large number of cattle and a specially built *umuzi*. One tradition has it that Monase was already pregnant by Shaka, and that her son Mbuyazi was his, not Mpande's.[42] Another tradition insists that Shaka was deliberately invoking the custom of *ukuvuza* whereby the biological father – in this case Mpande – 'raised up seed' for Shaka, who feared any offspring of his own would be killed. That made Mpande and Monase's child Shaka's legitimate heir, and in 1856 Mbuyazi would die in battle at Ndondakusuka fighting Cetshwayo, Mpande's eldest son, for recognition as the heir to the kingdom.[43]

All we can truly say in the end of Shaka the man is that in many ways he will remain unknowable, the projection of conflicting adulatory and condemnatory traditions. Nevertheless, what does emerge about this person of such contradictory characteristics – at once vain and emotional, cruel and generous, bellicose and suspiciously fearful – was that he possessed extraordinary abilities. Had he not been skilful and aggressive, decisive and ruthless beyond ordinary measure, he would never have overcome his many rivals and bitter enemies to build the kingdom that was his monument. And, even though a scant fifty years after his death British imperialism would shatter his arduously constructed kingdom into pieces, the terror and mystique of his name lives on.

What did he look like, this ferociously determined kingdom-builder? As with his character, his physical appearance remains something of a conundrum. Once again we have to weigh up positive and hostile traditions. Then there is the problem that Zulu with first-hand recorded memories of him were children at the time, who, like Melapi, 'peeped at him through the hut-coverings while dancing was taking place', too far away to see his face well enough to describe it.[44] Others who spoke of Shaka's features were repeating the tales of their fathers – and just how well had these forebears actually seen him? Were they among those described by Maclean who, when they approached Shaka sitting 'elevated on a large roll of matting for a throne [*umqulu*]', did so in 'awful solemnity ... in a half-bent posture'? Or were they members of the large assembly, ranged before him in a semicircle, who 'squatted on the ground in a very humble posture, their elbows resting on their knees', who, at every pause in Shaka's conversation humbly responded, '"Yebo baba, yebo baba" (yes father, yes father)'?[45]

Other white hunter-traders besides Maclean saw Shaka close up and left descriptions. Isaacs described him as 'upwards of six feet in height, and well proportioned'.[46] But is that how the Zulu remembered him? Fuze, writing his history a century after Shaka's death, described him thus:

> Shaka as a grown man had a good, strong, well-built body; he had good buttocks, well-shaped but not large, unlike Mpande who had very large buttocks. He had a large body, but ... he was a man of war and not sedentary. He was brown in colour, unlike Mpande who was black, and as a king, glossy with good food. He did not get stout like Mpande, but remained muscular and powerful. Both Shaka and Mpande were of the same size as Dingane; the one who was tall was Mhlangana [another half-brother].[47]

Most recorded oral testimony is in general agreement regarding these physical characteristics,[48] his body being what Melapi described as 'dark-brown (*nsundu*) in colour'. Melapi also believed he was 'not tall ... of medium size',[49] although others thought that he was as tall as Mhlangana.[50] A few dissenting voices described him as 'slight' and light brown (like a lizard in colour).[51] Like Senzangakhona and Dingiswayo, he had not been circumcised.[52] Many of the family of Senzangakhona had patches of hair on their bodies, like spotted butterflies. Accordingly, in his *izibongo* Shaka is described as

> The butterfly of Phunga
> With round spots as though deliberately placed.[53]

It seems, then, that Shaka was physically well set up, strong and athletic – and hirsute. But how handsome was he? Mayinga was forthright. Shaka, he declared, 'had eyes always red, and a protruding forehead. He had a badly shaped head. His head came forward and then went back. He was not really ugly but his head was peculiar.'[54] Baleka of the Qwabe was even less equivocal. She told Stuart that her father said that Shaka had 'a large nose, and was ugly'.[55]

Indeed, Shaka's nose was clearly not his best feature. Senzangakhona's children were known for their prominent noses, and Shaka's was clearly large and wide.[56] Unattractively, 'Tshaka's nose used to perspire', said Mayinga. 'He used to take hold of his nose from above and give it a twist as if to blow it and get sweat off at the same time.' Even more attention was drawn to Shaka's nose, added Mayinga, because 'he snuffed a good deal', and snuffing was surrounded by considerable ceremony. If the king took a pinch of snuff from the boy holding the container, and then spoke before he sniffed it up, 'he had to throw it away as if useless and done with, and the boy would do the same and pour out more which the king then pinched once more'.[57]

To complete the picture, William Bazley, a Natal settler who in the mid-1850s often chatted to Fynn, learned that 'Tshaka was called Mpisinthonga because he had two prominent front teeth'.[58] These may have contributed to his widely reported speech defect. Baleka declared that he 'spoke with an impediment (i.e. mouthed his words, as if his tongue was too big for his mouth and pressed on his teeth)',[59] while Ngidi reported that Shaka 'seemed to have a defect in his speech; he mouthed his words'. This, suggested Ngidi, may have been on account of his 'having learnt the Mtetwa dialect'.[60] Indeed, Jantshi was certain that Shaka 'spoke the Mtetwa dialect when he became king. He consequently always *tefula*'d [spoke in Qwabe fashion]. He is said to have lisped or stuttered, or pretended to do so.'[61] It does seem ironic that Shaka spoke in the fashion of his Qwabe enemies rather than in the dialect of the ruling *amantungwa*. Menacingly, he is remembered to have laughed 'outside his mouth', meaning he had a hollow, artificial laugh.[62]

Shaka, then, was no film star in looks like Henry Cele, who portrayed him in the popular television series. Although he was all-powerful, Shaka seems to have accepted that he was not a handsome man. To his credit, he was able to make a wry joke of it. Mtshebwe, a son of Magaye kaDibandlela, the Cele *inkosi* and a great favourite of Shaka's, recalled that the king said to his father, who was a good deal younger than him:[63] 'Even though it is said I am in the habit of killing people, never will I kill you. Were I to do so ... the Zulus would laugh at me. They would say I had killed you simply for being handsome, and because I am *isinkontshela*, i.e. with a prominent, protruding forehead, and ugly.'[64]

CHAPTER 6

People of Our House

We have already encountered several white adventurers at Shaka's court. Their presence in his kingdom, inconsiderable as it was, would play a crucial part in determining his destiny.

Shaka and Zululand did not exist in an African void, untouched by the probing, grasping but deceptively desirable hand of colonialism. Shaka was very well aware of the Portuguese presence at Delagoa Bay and of the lucrative trade conducted through Lourenço Marques. In return for their ivory and cattle, the Zulu received those seductive, exotic wares that so gladdened the hearts of the king and his *izikhulu*: brass and copper beads, woollen and cotton blankets, cotton salempore and calico cloth from India, usually coloured blue. Shaka took active steps to secure this desirable commerce. By mid-1824 he had extended his sway over the chiefdoms living in the coastal plain as far north as the further side of Delagoa Bay, whose rulers paid him formal tribute by sending him elephant tusks.[1] Shaka's growing regional power had the desired effect of overawing the Portuguese at Lourenço Marques, and they dared not dispute his domination of the trade through their port.

But Lourenço Marques was far distant from the Zulu heartland, and Shaka was willing to welcome a less remote supplier of goods. But who? The British-ruled Cape Colony, of which Shaka was gradually becoming aware, was just as far away. Nor was it easy to make trading contact by land. Westwards over the Drakensberg, which marked the kingdom's western limits, the highveld of the interior was dominated by the emerging Sotho mountain kingdom and by Mzilikazi's roaming and belligerent Ndebele state, Shaka's inveterate foe.

More than that, the great plains of the interior were relentlessly plagued by *drosters* (or gangs of runaways) of mixed-race, semi-nomadic hunting communities that had moved north over the Orange River and out of the jurisdiction of the Cape Colony. These Griqua, Ooorlams, Bergenaars, Hartenaars and Basters were mounted on horses and armed with muskets, exactly like the formidable Boer commandos (or militia of farmers) on which their military style was based. Expert and ruthless fighters, they raided far and wide for captives and cattle, effectively challenging even the warlike Ndebele. The Zulu had no desire to confront them either – and when they did, as in 1826, they came off second best.

The Cape was in any case in much closer and easier reach overland southwards along the coast from Zululand than over the mountains. But the way was barred beyond the Mzimkhulu River by the powerful Mpondo chiefdom of which (as we shall see) Shaka was understandably wary. The most viable trade route to the Cape, therefore, seemed to be by sea. And that is where the Port Natal settlers provided Shaka with the means.

In the early nineteenth century, British traders and hunters from the Cape, with the backing of local commercial interests and the colonial authorities, had begun to take an interest in the economic possibilities of the region that was becoming the Zulu kingdom. They also knew from exploratory voyages up the east coast that the only good natural harbour between Algoa Bay in the Cape Colony and Delagoa Bay to the north was a great bay about halfway between the Thukela and Mzimkhulu rivers. A great, bush-covered bluff thrust into the sea on the southeastern side of this bay, which enclosed several small wooded islands. Deep channels between the sandy flats allowed passage for vessels. In these pristine days the bay abounded with flamingos, hippopotami, turtles and fish. The one drawback was a sandbar that impeded entrance to the bay to all but small vessels.

On 10 May 1824 the 21-year-old Henry Francis Fynn (known to the Zulu as Mbuyazi),[2] son of the owner of the British Hotel in Long Street,

'Durban, Port Natal from the Top of the Berea': a view of the bay with the Bluff in the distance.

(JOSEPH CHRISTOPHER, *NATAL, CAPE OF GOOD HOPE*, 1850)

Cape Town, landed in this bay with his five companions from the tiny, single-masted sloop *Julia*. They were the advance party of a bigger group of 26 prospective settlers who arrived on about 20 June 1824 aboard the fast-sailing, two-masted brig *Antelope* to swell the incipient community, which they dubbed Port Natal (and which would be renamed Durban in 1835). Their commander was Lieutenant Francis George Farewell, RN, whom the Zulu called Febana. Born in 1791 in the genteel obscurity of an English country rectory, Farewell was a naval veteran of the Napoleonic Wars. He had been severely wounded in action in the Adriatic in 1811 and was described as 'a brave and enterprising officer'.[3] Crucially, he had secured the support of JR Thompson & Co. of Cape Town for the establishment of a permanent trading post. He and Fynn were to act as agents for these merchants who wished to obtain ivory, hides and maize from the Zulu. They also planned to extend their operations north to capture some of the flourishing trade flowing through Delagoa Bay.

Fynn and Farewell hoped that the government of the Cape Colony would annex their settlement to bring them under the protection of British rule. To that end they directly went through the motions of raising the Union

Flag and firing salutes, and on 1 May 1824 petitioned the Governor of the Cape, Lord Charles Somerset. They were disappointed. It was made clear to them that no attempt to claim Port Natal for the Crown would be sanctioned, and that the traders were on their own.[4]

Left with no other option, in August 1824 Fynn and Farewell opened communications on their own account with Shaka. Magaye of the Cele, Shaka's manager in the south, sent an *induna*, Lucunge, to report their arrival to Shaka. Lucunge said to Shaka: 'Nkosi ... some people have arrived as if sprung from the earth. But I cannot tell you more; their speech is not understandable.' Curious, Shaka ordered them to be fetched to kwaBulawayo. On the way, Zulu children screamed with fright at the pale apparitions 'who had come out of the water' with blond hair 'like maize tassels'.[5] Horrified mothers gathered their offspring up in their arms and fled into the bush, while their menfolk required much persuading even to come close.[6]

The *amabutho* at Shaka's *ikhanda* were no less dismayed. Dinya (born in about 1827) told Stuart that when Fynn arrived he was 'mounted on a horse (itself a strange, unfamiliar beast in Zululand) with his hat on his head, gun in hand, hair like cattle tails ... All present were moved with wonder and awe, so much so that the regiments shuffled back as far as the fence.'[7] Shaka himself displayed more sang-froid, and when the white men came before him he 'walked round them ... surveying them. He was astonished at their colour.'[8]

Outlandish as they were, Shaka tentatively welcomed the traders and referred to them as *abakwethu*, or 'people of our house' – kinsmen. From the first he was able to communicate with them through their black interpreter from the eastern Cape, known as Jacob or Jakot Msimbithi. Shaka grasped how these strange men – initially known among the Zulu as *abalumbi*, or 'makers of wonderful things', in reference to their ships and guns – could supply him with the same goods as could the Portuguese at Delagoa Bay. But Port Natal was so much closer than Lourenço Marques, and lay within the southern marches of his domain. This meant Shaka could control these traders far more effectively than he could the distant Portuguese.

Besides their offering commercial advantages, Shaka saw immediately how these *abakwethu* might be the conduit through which he could foster relations with the British authorities at the Cape, whose power he was beginning to appreciate.[9] Furthermore, he saw that they carried muskets (of which more later) and that they could make useful allies against his enemies. With all these considerations in mind, and in recognition of Fynn's medical assistance after the failed attempt to assassinate him, on 8 August 1824 Shaka put his mark with due ceremony to a significant document that Farewell placed before him. Shaka granted Farewell & Co. permission to occupy the land surrounding Port Natal and extending 50 miles inland and 25 miles (respectively, 80 kilometres and 40 kilometres) along the coast. He also gave the settlers the right to exercise authority over this territory, as well as permission to trade.[10]

Like all such treaties entered into between colonisers and local rulers, the two sides doubtless had differing perceptions of what exactly it was they had agreed to. The settlers supposed they had been accorded a greater degree of independent control over the territory granted them than Shaka intended, but, since he was the greatly dominant party, they had to abide by his more restricted interpretation. As far as Shaka was concerned, he had neither ceded Port Natal to the settlers nor surrendered his ultimate authority over it. Rather, he looked upon the settlers as typical client chiefs, and expected them to render service to him as would other tributaries, including military support. And, without any overt backing from the British authorities, the traders had no choice but to abide by Shaka's terms, even when he confiscated their ivory after they trafficked in it without his express permission, and placed irksome restrictions on their commercial operations generally. Isaacs complained that Shaka 'had no feeling in favour of commerce', fearing that involvement in trade would 'enervate' his subjects and make them unfit for war.[11] Through it all, the hunter-traders suppressed their discontent and irritation with the way Shaka managed them. For on one thing the settlers were all agreed: it would be the utmost folly to annoy the king on whose goodwill their enterprise – and lives – depended. However, perhaps they would be able to manipulate him so that he served their interests rather than the other way around? Time and opportunity would tell.

Most of the initially hopeful Port Natal settlers who had arrived on the *Julia* and *Antelope* were quickly daunted by the hardships they

Henry Francis Fynn, Port Natal hunter-trader
(LOCAL HISTORY MUSEUMS' COLLECTION, DURBAN)

encountered and returned to Cape Town. By December 1824 the settlement had been reduced to only six men: Farewell, Fynn, John Cane (called Jana) – whom Dinya remembered as the 'tallest of all the Englishmen, and ... very strong and industrious'[12] – Henry Ogle (known as Wohlo or Hohlo), Joseph Powell and Thomas Halstead. They were reinforced by another small party whose brig, *Mary*, was driven onto the sandbar by a gale on 1 October 1825 and foundered on the beach. Their leader was James

Saunders King (dubbed Kamu Kengi), who had been born in Halifax, Nova Scotia, in 1795, and who had taken his discharge as a midshipman from the Royal Navy in 1815 (although he liked to pose as an ex-lieutenant). He had subsequently entered the Merchant Navy and had been vainly trying to drum up support in England for the Port Natal project. He brought with him his 17-year-old assistant, Nathaniel Isaacs (Mis Isisi), who had spent two years on St Helena in the counting house of his uncle, and the ten-year-old Charles Maclean.

Maclean recorded his first impressions of the little rudimentary settlement. Farewell's 'fort' on the north side of the bay was a 'very primitive, rude looking structure' consisting of a quadrangular palisaded enclosure protecting a barn-like wattle-and-daub structure of typical Khoekhoe design with two or three smaller clones. Ten years later, only one dwelling at Port Natal had even the semblance of a European house. As for European furniture, that was almost entirely lacking. Numerous beehive Zulu huts surrounded the 'fort'. Maclean described the inhabitants of Port Natal as a 'motley group' of whites, Khoekhoen from the Cape and local Africans. The first two groups Maclean found to be in an indescribably tattered condition. Their attire was characteristically a picturesque combination of local costume and garments sewn from skins, and with European touches such as Fynn's famous crownless straw hat. In Maclean's opinion, the practically nude Africans distinctly had 'the advantage of appearance'.[13]

Not that the little party of settlers would have cared about their appearance. Within a very few months they were adopting local customs. The traders took wives and concubines from the local people, as well as from the Khoekhoen brought with them from the Cape. One such was the formidable Rachel, who, in her European skirts, may have been a manumitted slave. When Farewell was up country she confidently exercised authority on his behalf.[14] Like any Zulu man, many traders legitimised their marriages through the payment of *ilobolo* and positioned their wives' huts around their residences in conformity with the layout of the *umuzi* of a local chief. Fynn and Ogle were remembered to have had the 'largest number of wives'.[15]

Speaking of chiefs, with Shaka's permission the traders rapidly set themselves up as *amakhosi* in the coastlands. Shaka (as King Cetshwayo later put it), 'finding his people very scattered' in the region of Port Natal, decided it would suit him if the settlers drew them in under their control and accepted their allegiance.[16] Some acknowledged one particular settler as their chief, some another. Consequently, as in typical Zulu political life, the power and fortunes of the various settler chiefs waxed and waned with the number of adherents they could attract to their banner.

The hunting, fishing and agricultural work of their subject people freed the settlers from spending too much of their time and energy on subsistence. Instead, they could give their full attention to trading and hunting ever further afield for commercial gain. And, although Britain had outlawed the slave trade in 1806, the likelihood cannot be entirely discounted that they sometimes also abducted people to sell covertly as slaves to American and Brazilian vessels calling at Port Natal.

To the hunter-traders' delight, the vicinity of Port Natal still absolutely teemed with game of every variety, although indiscriminate hunting would decimate it in remarkably short order. The settlers fanned out in hunting parties under Fynn, Cane and Ogle in search especially of elephant and hippopotamus ivory and of buffalo hides. Their Khoekhoe retainers and African adherents assisted them as guides, carriers and hunters. The Khoekhoen were already familiar with muskets, but the settlers also trained their African retainers in their use. The missionary Captain Allen Gardiner, RN, who arrived in Port Natal in 1835, observed that many of them were 'very tolerable marksmen'.[17] A decade earlier, Shaka had noticed that too.

CHAPTER 7

Fighting Stick of Thunder

Once he became king in 1828, Dingane decreed that the Mzimkhulu River must be regarded as the southern boundary of the Zulu kingdom because 'the land south of the river belonged to Faku, the Pondo king'.[1] Shaka would not accept such bounds to his sway, but the disastrous Mpondo campaign of 1824 graphically signalled the limits of his military reach.

Despite their many conquests, Shaka's *amabutho* were not invariably invincible. The further they operated away from their bases, the more their defective logistical arrangements diminished their chances of success. Essentially, warriors had to live off the countryside while on campaign. It is true that *izindibi*, or baggage-carriers, boys of between six and twelve, were attached to the senior men and principal warriors and toted their mats, headrests, tobacco and the like. They also helped drive the cattle accompanying the army. Some of the *izinduna* were accompanied by young women bearing beer, corn and milk. After a few days, these stocks would be exhausted and the girls would return home, as would those *izindibi* who could not keep up with the army. All the warriors carried iron rations in a skin sack, the favourite combination being a cooked cow's liver and maize grains. But these too would soon give out. The increasingly hungry *amabutho* tried to spare their own population while marching through Zulu-ruled territory, slaughtering the cattle they had brought with them, and bivouacking at *amakhanda* where stores of food had been amassed. But once the army entered enemy territory it began to forage ruthlessly.

If the actual conquest of a territory was the objective of a campaign, then the strategic goal was to bring the foe to a decisive battle. When the enemy avoided facing battle, or when the more limited goal was to raid for cattle and captives, then the strategy was to force the enemy to evacuate their territory or take refuge in its fastnesses. The idea was that as they fled they would relinquish at least some of their livestock and other goods, to be scooped up by the raiders. However, the raiders could easily become the victims of their own strategy. When unable to come to grips with the enemy warriors – or if defeated – and having comprehensively stripped the countryside of supplies and burned all forms of shelter, the raiders would be left with no option but to retire. But, hungry and weary, suffering from exposure, encumbered by their captured cattle and other loot, and eager to get home, that is when the raiders were most vulnerable to counterattack. Such was the Zulu fate in the Mpondo campaign of 1824.

The heart of the Mpondo kingdom was located near the coast along both sides of the Mzimvubu River, which flows through an impressive gorge with towering sandstone peaks on either side (the Heads) into a wide estuary. The town of Port St Johns is situated today at the river-mouth. By the late eighteenth century the Mpondo kingdom was expanding, and by Shaka's day ruled over vassal chiefdoms extending north along the coast to the Mzimkhulu River and south to the Mthatha River. Following a succession dispute, in about 1818 Faku succeeded his father, Ngqungqushe, as the Mpondo paramount. It was not long before he was challenged by Shaka's expanding kingdom.

In 1824, just before the settlers landed at Port Natal, Mdlaka kaNcidi, Shaka's foremost commander, led an army south along the foothills of the Drakensberg and into Mpondo territory. We should not imagine that this force was very large. At the time of the Anglo-Zulu War, in 1879, the population of the Zulu kingdom was somewhere around three hundred thousand people. Its army, when males in the age-band between their early twenties and late forties were fully mobilised, numbered no more than twenty-nine thousand.[2] Farewell, writing to Lord Charles Somerset in September 1824, reported that he found the 'large territory he [Shaka] was possessed of

... 'very thinly peopled' and that fourteen thousand men 'might be fighting men on a push'.³ Perhaps the strength of the *amabutho* fit for active service was somewhat higher than Farewell surmised, but Shaka's armies fell far, far short of the armed hordes conjured up by the fevered settler imagination.

So we must think of only several thousand warriors under Mdlaka entering Mpondoland in pursuit of Madzikane, a Bhaca chief who had fled south from the environs of the Mngeni River to avoid Zulu raids. Failing to catch up with the Bhaca, Mdlaka seized Mpondo cattle, since he did not dare to return to Shaka empty-handed.⁴ Faku refused to take this affront to his sovereignty lying down. His praises hailed him:

> You shall here remain great ...
> The milk is all the chief's, the shield also.
> Take the whole world under you,
> You shall not be wounded ...
> So as a rock remains a rock
> An axe shall continue an axe.⁵

Faku delegated command of his forces to his 25-year-old son, Ndamase, whom the Xhosa historian John Soga described as a man of 'courage and resource'.⁶ Ndamase intercepted the Zulu forces, and in the fierce fighting his warriors were initially successful, inflicting heavy casualties on three of the Zulu *amabutho* – which they 'cut up' and 'finished off', as Maziyana put it. Mdlaka sent in more warriors to support their comrades and the Mpondo were forced to break off the engagement. Mdlaka used the respite to begin an orderly withdrawal northwards along the coast. Maziyana told Stuart that 'Faku used supernatural powers to set hyenas of the forest on them. The hyenas ate the Zulu cattle as well as the members of the force, and followed the force until it got ... into Zululand.' Most likely, these 'hyenas' were symbolic of the Mpondo warriors who pursued and harassed the retiring Zulu. In any event, they were highly successful and the invaders, who lost all their cattle and were completely out of supplies, were 'obliged to eat melons (*amabece*) and wild plants' they found on abandoned homestead sites, not even waiting to cook them they were so famished.

This is why the Zulu dubbed this disastrous campaign the *amabece impi*, or 'melon campaign'.

That would not be the end of the story, however. Faku had fought off the Zulu incursion with some success, but the Mpondo ruler could not doubt that Shaka would at some future time be avenged for the humiliation he had suffered. So Faku cautiously moved his 'great place' further away from Shaka's reach into the steep hills between the Great and Little Mngazi rivers. Nor was he wrong to take this precaution. Once the experiences of the *amabece impi* had been diffidently related to him with many an excuse, Shaka immediately dispatched spies into the Mpondo territory so that his forces would have better intelligence when they attacked again.[7]

Meanwhile, this smarting humiliation rankled. As with any ruler whose reputation is built on exceptional success in war, Shaka knew perfectly well that a military reverse, even a fairly minor one, would damage his prestige and authority. This is why he decided he must employ the newly arrived *abakwethu* as auxiliaries. For he quickly came to appreciate that by harnessing the shock effect of the settlers' firearms he would be able in future campaigns to tip the military balance back in his favour.

The Zulu required some time to become accustomed to the whites' fearsome muskets. Makuza (born in the mid-1840s) vividly conveyed to Stuart a sense of the Zulu's initial wonderment:

> 'This stick which they carry, what is it for?' [This was said by the earliest Zulus of the gun that was carried, for they did not know it was a weapon.] Tshaka then wanted the carrier [a European] to aim at the vultures hovering above with this stick of theirs. The European did so, and fired, bang! The sound caused all round him to fall on hands and knees. The bird was brought down. Wonderful!'[8]

This vivid story – which was corroborated by Isaacs, who identified the interpreter Jacob as the marksman[9] – celebrated a rather lucky shot, because a muzzle-loading flintlock musket was a feeble firearm by later standards. It had an effective range of no more than a hundred metres and a rate of fire of about three rounds a minute. Moreover, without sights and with a smooth-bore barrel, its accuracy was low. Shaka was nevertheless quick to investigate the potential of this novel weapon,[10] known onomatopoeically to the Zulu as an *isibamu*.[11] Maclean recalled how Shaka put the courage of his warriors under gunfire to the test. At the first crack of the muskets aimed at them, they fell to the ground in fright, whereupon Shaka had them bludgeoned for cowardice.[12] Even so, their craven response showed satisfactorily how Shaka's enemies would also respond to the *izibamu*. Jantshi described how Shaka was remembered as testing the power of muskets by having the white traders aim at cattle at different distances. Indeed, it was reportedly Shaka's far-fetched intention 'to send a regiment of men to England who there would scatter in all directions in order to ascertain exactly how guns were made, and then return to construct some in Zululand'.[13]

Unsurprisingly, nothing came of this plan. The Zulu, with their deeply ingrained belief that only hand-to-hand combat was honourable conduct for a warrior, proved resistant to embracing a gun culture. In comparison, the Xhosa, for example, who between 1779 and 1878 fought nine Frontier Wars against colonisers bearing firearms, increasingly adopted firearms themselves and modified their tactics to make best use of them. The Zulu, on the other hand, never went beyond regarding them as mere ancillary weapons, a form of throwing-spear. They were generally far quicker to see the potential of firearms for hunting, especially of elephants for their ivory.[14]

Shaka was therefore ahead of his *amabutho* in appreciating the value of firearms, as was his brother Dingane. Indeed, in his *izibongo* Dingane was celebrated as 'Jonono who is like a fighting-stick of thunder [a musket]!'[15] Yet, even if their *amabutho* could have been persuaded to take up firearms, neither Shaka nor Dingane could obtain them in appreciable numbers. As late as 1837, near the end of Dingane's reign, Captain Gardiner reported that while 'muskets have been introduced as an article of barter with the Zulu by some of the European settlers at or near the port ... at present this traffic is in an incipient state'.[16] Therefore, if Shaka were to add muskets to his arsenal, they had to be carried by the Port Natal settlers and their trained black hunters.

Shaka first employed his white tributary chiefs against the Ndwandwe, his mortal enemies who were hovering menacingly just north across the Phongolo River, eager to recapture the territory the Zulu king had wrested from them. Shaka's old adversary Zwide, the Ndwandwe *inkosi*, died in early 1825, soon after the settlers had arrived at Port Natal. As was almost always the case in the chiefdoms of the region, the succession was disputed. Sikhunyana won the struggle in 1826 to succeed Zwide. He overconfidently imagined he could challenge Shaka and reclaim his lost lands south of the Phongolo. As he is supposed to have said to his father, Zwide, who could not be persuaded to fight Shaka again: 'Tshaka has, as you say, defeated you, because you are an old man. I am his own age, and mean to try and see what I can do.'[17]

But Shaka stole a march on Sikhunyana. The Zulu king grasped how he could seize the opportunity presented by the debilitating rivalry within the Ndwandwe ruling house to make a pre-emptive strike, especially as he now had the Port Natal traders and their firearms at his disposal. A combination of royal pressure and the promise of booty induced Fynn and several of the traders, along with their African retainers trained in firearms, to join the *amabutho* Shaka was concentrating at kwaBulawayo in September or October 1826 for the coming campaign.[18]

The army, this time under the direct command of Shaka himself, set out from kwaBulawayo for kwaNobamba in the emaKhosini valley. It then advanced northwest towards the Phongolo in a great cloud of dust as the packed formations moved forward, each *ibutho* led by its commander. The *izimbongi* in the van of the army loudly praised Shaka's heroic accomplishments as they went. The weather was hot and every man rolled up his great war-shield and carried it on his back.

The army advanced by easy stages, as it always did (despite the legends that it ran all day), and Fynn recorded that on one occasion it rested for two full days, and on another for a day and two nights. Finally, the army, which during the previous few days had been marching in several divisions to ease the problems of supply, converged on inqaba kaHawana, a mountain fastness near the source of the White Mfolozi. Scouts brought Shaka the intelligence while bivouacked there that Sikhunyana's army had concentrated in the wooded country just north of the Phongolo River. The Ndwandwe warriors were positioned on the slopes of the izinDolowane hills overlooking the Phongolo, with their cattle in their midst. Their women and children, who had accompanied them to war, were gathered in a body higher up the hillsides.

Shaka advanced to the attack and the ensuing battle did not last more than an hour and a half. It is not clear if the musketeers made much difference to the outcome or, indeed, if they were called on at all – Maclean thought not[19] – but their mere presence on the battlefield for the first time was fraught with huge significance for the military history of the region.

In any event, the battle was an overwhelming Zulu victory. There was pandemonium as the desperately shrieking Ndwandwe women and children were massacred along with their men. Zulu *amabutho* roamed the countryside, killing the enemy wounded and rounding up their great herds of cattle as the spoils of conquest. The fugitive Sikhunyana, Shaka told Fynn, hid from the victors in a deep pit in the woods before making his escape with a few followers.[20]

Following the battle, the *amabutho* went through days of rites to cleanse themselves of the evil effects of homicide. The Zulu believed that the death of a person by violence released an especially virulent form of *umnyama*, that contagious, mystical evil force that created misfortune. When a warrior pushed his *iklwa* into the victim's yielding flesh, or battered out his brains with his *iwisa*, the victim's blood that spurted over the killer and his clothing formed a fearsome bridge between the living and the world of the dead. All sorts of special ritual precautions then became essential to gain ascendancy over the vengeful spirits of the slain, and to ensure that their evil influence passed to nobody else, especially not to the king. Only once he was cleansed could the warrior appear in Shaka's presence to report on the battle and who had distinguished themselves.

With his victory at the izinDolowane hills, Shaka had at last removed the most powerful and persistent threat to his kingdom. For the Ndwandwe, this time their defeat was irreversible. Their kingdom collapsed into absolute ruin and the survivors scattered far and wide. Some transferred their allegiance to Shaka, some to Mzilikazi of the Ndebele or to other chiefs of the region. No wonder Shaka's *izimbongi* gloated:

> As for Zwide, you have made him a homeless criminal.
> And now today you have done the same to the son,
> The people of Zwide, Shaka, you have jumped over them.[21]

CHAPTER 8

The Elephant Took What Belonged to It

When Isaacs returned to Port Natal on 30 November 1826, after a trading foray for ivory, he noted that Shaka had recently constructed a new *ikhanda* near the mouth of the Mvoti River less than eighty kilometres north of the Port.¹ The colonial town of Stanger was later built over its site, and the magistracy erected on the very spot where the *isigodlo* had been.² Called kwaDukuza, the *ikhanda* was known playfully to the Zulu as the place where one loses one's way on account of its great size.³ Maclean, who inspected it closely, has left a detailed description. Its layout followed that of any other *ikhanda*, but it was a particularly large one containing some 1 500 huts to accommodate about 3 000 *amabutho*. The *isigodlo* impressed Maclean especially. Built on elevated ground overlooking the whole *ikhanda*, it was about 366 metres in length and 55 metres wide and housed between 150 and 200 women in about 50 huts. These huts, Maclean enthused, were of 'unusual size and neatness in their construction' and were tidily arranged around a series of oblong, semicircular and triangular enclosures. The 'exceedingly' smooth and even floors of the enclosures were made of the same material as that of hut floors – a blackish, dark-green mixture of earth from anthills compressed with cow dung – and were polished to 'a glassy smoothness ... that reflects the image like a mirror'. 'Everything', Maclean exclaimed, 'wears an air of neatness that elsewhere we had not witnessed.'⁴

THE ELEPHANT TOOK WHAT BELONGED TO IT

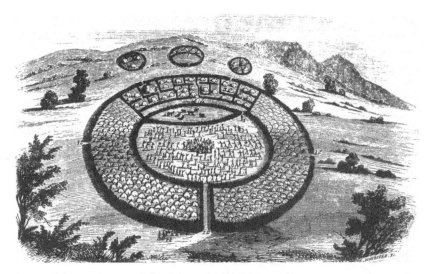

'View of the Kraal, or Capital, of the Kafir Chief Dingaan': an accurate representation of the layout of uMgungundlovu. That of kwaDukuza would have been very similar, including the small *imizi* outside the *isigodlo* at the top of the parade ground.

(REV WILLIAM C HOLDEN, *HISTORY OF THE COLONY OF NATAL*, SOUTH AFRICA, 1855)

KwaDukuza, Isaacs noted down, meant 'hide-away', deriving from Shaka's subjects' desire that he should sometimes retire from kwaBulawayo 'while they attacked his enemies'.[5] And certainly for a while kwaBulawayo remained Shaka's administrative centre and the king only visited kwaDukuza, as he regularly did his other *amakhanda*. Yet his purpose in building kwaDukuza was more complex than Isaacs would suggest.

Ngidi was closer to Shaka's motivation when he told Stuart that 'there is no doubt that T. wanted to go on building [*amakhanda*] until he came in touch with the Europeans, he being on friendly terms with them'.[6] And, indeed, it does seem that by the end of 1827 there were three new *amakhanda* in the vicinity of Port Natal besides kwaDukuza. Closer proximity to the Port would allow Shaka easier access to the trade going through it, and enable him to exert more effective supervision over his potentially dangerous tributary white chiefs.

However there was more to it than that. With the final elimination of the Ndwandwe threat, it was no longer necessary for Shaka to be within striking distance of the northern borders of the kingdom. Now was the moment to tighten his control over the client and tributary chiefdoms of the coastlands south of the Thukela River managed for him by his great favourite Magaye, the Cele *inkosi*. Magaye's son, Melapi, remembered that when Shaka built kwaDukuza he ordered his father to make up songs so that they could dance together. Magaye, fully understanding Shaka's new southern agenda, composed the following:

> With what nations are you going to make war?
> The elephant took what belonged to it ...
> For we took that [the assegai] of the Ndwandwe,
> Broke it in pieces, and drove it into the ground.[7]

Shaka had other reasons too for moving away from kwaBulawayo. He had deliberately built it in the heart of the Qwabe country after the attempt to assassinate him in 1824 so as to overawe the people of that disaffected chiefdom. It seems he was aware that the Qwabe remained as hostile as ever to his rule and he suspected they were planning to try again to kill him. Clearly, he would feel more secure once he had moved away from the Qwabe country.

Officials at the Cape were certain that reasons of security were fundamental to Shaka's shift towards Port Natal. A report of October 1828 put this conviction in a nutshell: 'Chaka's people are represented as dissatisfied and disposed to revolt in consequence of his cruelty and constant wars. Chaka is sensible to this disposition of his people to free themselves from his yoke and has removed his kraal within one day and a half's journey of Port Natal with the view of taking shelter with Farewell's party in the event of his people throwing off their allegiance.'[8]

It is probably true that Shaka did come increasingly to look to the traders' firepower to protect him, if necessary. But in late 1826 he was still thinking of harnessing it to his own aggressive agenda. In August 1828, Major General Richard Bourke, the Lieutenant Governor of the Cape, wrote to his superiors in London: 'I have been informed that since the arrival of English under Farewell and King at that place [Port Natal] in 1825 Chaca's forces have been accompanied on their marauding expeditions by one or more of these Englishmen who by their fire-arms contributed to the success of the plunderers and shared in the plunder as their reward.'⁹

And certainly, in early 1827, the settlers' firepower was crucial in subduing Bheje kaMagawuzi of the Khumalo in a campaign that was an offshoot of the victorious one against the Ndwandwe. Shaka had no hesitation in deploying his *amabutho* on one campaign after another with little or no chance for recuperation. Ndhlovu voiced the strong tradition that Shaka was overfond of sending out his army, 'so that that people did not sit still and did not rest'.¹⁰ The time would come when resentment at unremitting campaigning would spill over, but that point had not yet quite been reached.

On the way back from destroying the Ndwandwe at the battle of the izinDolowane hills, Shaka detached a division of his army to finish off Bheje. The Khumalo *inkosi* had been holding out for years in his nearby stronghold in the rugged Ngome region of the northern borderlands, with its dense forests and deep gorges. The defenders had not lost their long-standing advantage and handily repulsed the *amabutho* sent against them. Even when Shaka reinforced his men they remained bogged down for months before the Khumalo stronghold.¹¹

At the same time that Shaka sent his forces against Bheje, he dispatched another division from the army that had defeated the Ndwandwe on a different mission. These *amabutho* marched north towards the humid and malaria-infested bushveld of the Lepelle River, known to the Zulu as the Bhalule. Their objective was not conquest but to raid for cattle. They were no more successful in their mission than the *amabutho* tied down by the Khumalo. The Lepelle was too flooded to cross, the local Pedi people took to their strongholds, and dysentery gripped the raiders. When the army was already retiring, expertly harassed by Pedi warriors, it unexpectedly encountered a party of Griqua under Barend Barends on a long-distance hunting expedition in search of ivory. Despite being outnumbered, the Griqua, with their unfamiliar firearms and horses, badly mauled the *amabutho*.¹² As far as Shaka was concerned, no further evidence of the efficacy of firearms was required.

So, early in 1827, Shaka summoned the Port Natal traders to him and required them to lend him military assistance with their firearms against the Khumalo.[13] Shaka thought about ten musketeers would be enough to do the trick.[14] Duly, ten or eleven men volunteered. Isaacs and Cane were of their number, along with two Khoekhoen and several of the settlers' African hunters.[15]

There is more to this party of volunteers than meets the eye, however, for it represented the irreconcilable divisions that were beginning to pull the Port community apart. Most of the volunteers who marched against Bheje belonged to James King's settlement, whereas the traders who had been part of the Ndwandwe campaign were of Farewell's party. King, who had been away for several months in Cape Town drumming up business, had returned on 6 October 1826 with a newly chartered vessel, the schooner *Anne*, and was attempting to set up his own commercial operation in competition with Farewell's. There was already bad blood between the two over unpaid debts in their business partnership, and now there was a furious row. The settlers and their adherents divided, rallying behind either Farewell or King, each of whom tried to build up his following into a private army and to win Shaka's favour at the expense of the other.

Therefore, the involvement of King's partisans in the expedition against Bheje must be seen as part of King's vendetta against Farewell's party. He clearly intended to upstage his rival by responding to Shaka's call for military assistance against the Khumalo. And, besides courting Shaka's favour, King also anticipated securing the cattle and other loot that went with a successful campaign.

Even if the role of the gunmen at the izinDolowane hills was unclear, there is no doubt that they proved decisive in storming Bheje's stronghold on 7 February 1827. The battle that day appeared inconclusive, even though (as Isaacs recorded) 'the report of our muskets initially struck terror into the enemy'.[16] But the Khumalo soon recovered from their initial shock, and the fighting became fierce and man-to-man. Isaacs himself was wounded by a barbed spear in the back and suffered excruciating pain and much loss of blood. Yet, when the Zulu resumed the attack the next day, they found that the Khumalo had had enough. In token of their surrender, they gave up their half-starved cattle and goats as tribute to Shaka. The king subsequently presented King with 78 head of cattle and Isaacs' party also seized a number of young women and other captives from the

Khumalo. As for Isaacs himself, the Zulu praised the wounded 'Mis isisi' as 'the one who waddles; off he goes at speed', and (with reference to his musket fire) 'the echoes of the cliffs at Ngome'.[17]

Soon after the Bheje expedition, Fynn, who was a supporter of King in the dispute with Farewell, and who had been visiting Mpondoland regularly since 1826, established a station near the Mzimkhulu River with a party of his African hunters.[18] His presence attracted some two thousand new adherents and soon Fynn was deploying a private army that hunted elephant for ivory and raided local communities to capture cattle to exchange for more ivory. His intention seems to have been to develop an overland route through the Mpondo country by which he could export his ivory to the eastern Cape and thus be free of the Port Natal dominated by Farewell. Indeed, the conflict between King and Farewell had become so extreme that in January 1827 King abandoned Port Natal and annexed the mouth of the Mlazi River to the south with the idea of establishing a rival port there.[19]

It was hardly surprising that these disputes 'tended much to perplex' Shaka,[20] and made it difficult for him to know which faction to rely upon. This dilemma became increasingly important as Shaka became ever more anxious in 1827 to make contact with the British authorities in the Cape. This was a project that had been on his mind ever since the settlers first arrived on his shores. He had at that time approached Farewell, who reported in September 1824 that Shaka 'expressed a wish of sending two of his chiefs to the Cape for the purpose of being better acquainted with the English nation'.[21]

Why was Shaka eager to foster good relations with the British at the Cape? Besides matters of trade, he must have possessed some inkling of their great military success in the recent Fifth Frontier War of 1818–1819. Defeat had forced Hintsa, the Xhosa paramount whom Shaka acknowledged as being a powerful ruler in his own league, to sue for peace and accept the advance of British dominion eastwards from the Great Fish River to the Keiskamma River. It would seem that Shaka calculated that if he could make allies of the British he could use their support as a counterweight to continuing opposition to his rule at home.

Which of the fractious settlers could best assist Shaka in making diplomatic contact with the British? He had initially confided in Farewell, but no longer favoured him and turned instead to King. Indeed, as King had hoped it would, the participation of his adherents in the Bheje campaign had helped secure Shaka's esteem. King's trump card, though, was the small schooner his workmen were building at the Port. With its fore-and-aft sails on two masts, a schooner was designed for speed and good sailing even in shallow waters. This was the ideal vessel for transporting Shaka's emissaries to the Cape, and the monarch knew it. But, while the schooner languished not fully built, King realised this put him in a strong position to wrest favours and concessions from Shaka. It has been convincingly suggested that King deliberately dragged his heels completing the vessel – its construction took a dilatory two and a half years – until Shaka finally decided to support him over Farewell.[22]

The schooner was still unfinished when, on 24 July 1827, Shaka summoned King, Isaacs and Fynn into his presence. He dismissed his attendants, and in a 'peculiarly grave manner' and with 'a wily air' eventually confided that 'he should like to cross the water to see King George, but feared that he should not receive a welcome reception; he would therefore send a chief, under the charge of Lieutenant King, as soon as the vessel should be finished'. He then anxiously charged King to use the opportunity to obtain 'some stuff for turning white hairs black', which he pretended he wanted for his aged mother, Nandi, rather than himself. Shaka nevertheless was shy about this request and begged the trader 'in the most entreating manner' to keep it a 'profound secret'.[23]

The delighted King now knew he was firmly established in Shaka's favour and that Farewell was finally eclipsed. But before the 30-ton schooner, named the *Elizabeth and Susan*, could at long last be launched on 10 March 1828, an upheaval shook Zululand that cast a lurid light on the growing precariousness of Shaka's dominion.

PART III

A Wolf Without a Place to Hide His Head

CHAPTER 9

What Has Killed My Mother?

The death in August 1827 of Nandi, Shaka's mother, was the great rupture in Shaka's reign. Beforehand, he had cannily contained mounting discontent and had survived one assassination attempt, but afterwards he seemed ever more outrageous in his demands on his people, more extreme, more ruthless. Unfolding events began to slip his control as his diplomatic and military initiatives foundered and ran counter to each other. Resistance to his rule began to harden and new conspiracies to form. This time he would not escape the assassin's blade.

Nandi was held in enormous respect as the *iNdlovukazi*, the Great She-Elephant or Queen Mother. She presided over his *isigodlo*, dominating the other *amakhosikazi*, or royal female relations, and commanding the king's *umndlunkulu*, women from whose ranks he selected his concubines. With no royal wives to dispute her sway, Nandi was omnipotent in managing Shaka's domestic arrangements.

Nandi was described as 'dark-skinned, big, and strongly built' with small breasts,[1] but as usual oral tradition was divided over her character. Nandi means 'sweet' in Zulu, and Mtshapi recalled she was given that name because she was 'a good-tempered person who did not quarrel with her mother'. As Queen Mother, she was apparently renowned in the Zulu country for her good nature, and was 'well-liked'.[2] Was her name given her in hope of a pliant character rather than in recognition of one, and was her favourable reputation in Shaka's kingdom a matter of discretion rather than fact? Her praises present a very different picture and refer to her physical unattractiveness and sexual frigidity, as well as to her domineering personality:

> She whose thighs do not meet,
> They only meet on seeing her husband.
> Loud-voiced one ...[3]

Whatever her actual appearance and character, there is no doubting that she was a central figure in Shaka's life. We simply do not know the true nature of his emotional relationship with her – whether he revered or resented her, or was uncomfortably ambivalent in his feelings towards her. Even so, his mother's death detonated wild emotions in Shaka – whether of grief or guilt is a matter of debate – and sent out devastating seismic waves of hysteria and violence across the Zulu kingdom that took on a grim political character.

On 11 August 1827 Isaacs was at his camp at the mouth of the Mlazi River, about twenty kilometres south of Port Natal, extracting tusks from hippopotamus carcasses and preparing hides, when messengers arrived announcing the death of Nandi.[4] She had expired at the eMkhindini *umuzi*, situated on a ridge about five kilometres west of kwaBulawayo, presided over by Noncoba, her unmarried daughter.[5]

The day before Nandi died, Fynn was with Shaka and a large number of warriors in the vicinity of kwaDukuza, engaged in hunting elephant for ivory, when relays of messengers began to arrive with word that Nandi was ill. By nine o'clock that night they were reporting that Nandi was in danger of her life. Upon which, Fynn recorded, Shaka decided he must set off at once for kwaBulawayo despite the darkness, and arrived there at about three o'clock in the morning. Shaka begged Fynn to visit his mother at eMkhindini to see how she did. He found her smoke-filled hut crammed to bursting point with *izinyanga* and frantic attendants. The weather was exceedingly hot and Fynn could barely breathe in the suffocating atmosphere. After shooing out most of the crowd, he managed (as he put it) to seize the opportunity of 'seeing my patient'. He later recorded unambiguously in his diary: 'Her complaint was dysentery, and I reported at once to Shaka that her case was hopeless and that I did not expect that she would live through the day.'[6] Nor did she.

'No sooner did Nandi die,' recounted Ngidi, who, like Nandi, was of the Langeni people, 'than Tshaka was overcome with grief and said, "Alas for my mother, alas for my mother! What has killed my mother?"'[7]

This is a question that, despite Fynn's firm pronouncement that it was dysentery, has continued to perplex. Some Zulu interviewed by Stuart, such as Ngidi, Jantshi and Mkehlengana (born in about 1845), were convinced that Nandi 'died a natural death' – an opinion confirmed by Madhlebe, of the Khumalo people, who was born in about 1822 and who had grown up at kwaBulawayo. He declared that as a young child he 'was present' when the Queen Mother expired. However, it must be noted that all of the above were insisting on death by natural causes to rebut the strong and persistent tradition that Nandi was killed by Shaka, her own son.[8] Ngidi roundly declared that there 'is no evidence' that Shaka put her to death. Like the others interviewed, he alluded to the widespread whispers, hearsay and rumours that pointed the finger at Shaka, but would give these allegations no credit.[9]

Perhaps King Cetshwayo was being honest when he declared in 1881 to the Cape Government Commission on Native Laws and Customs: 'The king says he does not know what happened at the death of Tyaka's mother.'[10] Or, then again, Cetshwayo (who was highly intelligent and politically adroit) was probably being quite deliberately non-committal. He would have guessed just how gleefully his two colonial inquisitors would have pounced on an admission of matricide as damning proof of the inherent savagery of his people. Significantly, it seems that Fynn was motivated by the same consideration. He confided to the Natal settler William Bazley (whom the Zulu called Gwembeshe, or 'the bow-legged one') that when, in later life, he was an assistant resident magistrate in the Colony of Natal, and was called upon to give evidence before the Natal Native Commission of 1852, he had 'suppressed the fact that Nandi was killed (given her death wound) by Tshaka, for fear of what people would say in England'.[11]

Fynn, to be blunt, was reneging on the clear statement in his diary that Nandi had died of dysentery. But perhaps the 'dysentery' was always a diplomatic fabrication. As the Zulu historian Magema Fuze reflected, 'is it likely that the Zulus would have revealed to him, a white man, the secret of what actually happened?'[12] And we might wonder just how thoroughly Fynn could have investigated Nandi's ailment in the smoke and hysteria of her hut when he 'saw' her? Dysentery is caused by viral, bacterial or parasitic infestations through the ingestion of contaminated food or water. In its worst form, foul-smelling watery diarrhoea streaked with mucus and blood is accompanied by vomiting, fever and shock, sometimes leading to death. The infection requires several days to reach that fatal stage. Therefore, the five 'old natives' who discussed Nandi's death with Fynn and Bazley incredulously inquired, how could Nandi have contracted *intsheko* (which is what they termed a bloody flux of the bowels) and then died so rapidly after Shaka had left her in good health to go on his elephant hunt with Fynn? According to Bazley, Fynn did not demur.[13]

So, if Nandi did not die of *intsheko*, what are we to suppose killed her? Fuze was uncompromising in his conclusion: Shaka stabbed her.[14] If indeed so, what then were the circumstances? Although there were variants in the oral testimony, essentially the same story was repeated. It went like this: one of Shaka's *umndlunkulu*, reputedly a woman of the Cele people, gave birth to his child, a boy. It was Nandi's obligation, as mistress of the *isigodlo* and in obedience to Shaka's absolute injunction, that she quietly banish the mother and her child. In the past she had done as required, but this time – for reasons we can only guess at – she secretly kept the baby with her. Lunguza (born in about 1820) related that a jealous and malicious *umndlunkulu* betrayed her and whispered to Shaka: 'Go to your mother. You will find her with something beautiful.'[15] When Shaka stealthily entered her hut, he found his mother fondly nursing a child in her arms. According to Ngidi's account, she guiltily tried to hide it, but her son insisted on having the boy placed before him. He them ominously inquired, 'Mother, where does it come from?' With unwise bravado, the spirited Nandi shot back: 'You ask me where it comes from? Don't you have a penis, then?'[16] Bazley's informants offered an alternative version: 'Some say she denied it [hiding a child of his] and turned round to get some straws or wood to feed the fire with, the hut being dark, and he in his rage, stabbed her up the fundament with a sharp stick [which "must have been the shank of an assegai"] through her leather skirt. This penetrated some inches up the anus. He told her if she divulged it he would have her torn limb from limb and eaten by the dogs of the kraal.'[17]

Some alternative versions have Shaka leaving the hut in a towering rage to fetch a spear to stab his mother, some said in the armpit, which was the usual mode of execution; others have him stabbing her in the stomach with a sharp-pointed awl of a type used by women for sewing mats and which he must have snatched up in fury.[18]

While not refuting the tradition that Shaka was responsible for his mother's death, it is possible that he deputed others to commit the deed for him. Lunguza had heard that Shaka directed an *inceku*, or confidential body servant, 'to go and stab his mother and afterwards to tie up the wound so it could not be seen'. The wound, declared Lunguza, 'was a small one, and may have been caused with an awl or small assegai'.[19] The *inceku* was said also to have killed the baby boy along with his young mother.[20]

Mgidhlana, a son of King Mpande's born in about 1828, thought it unlikely that Shaka would have had his mother stabbed, let alone to have done it himself. But, if he had wanted to kill her for harbouring the child, he would have resorted to poison. He recounted another tradition that suggested that Shaka instructed an *inyanga* to brew a deadly decoction from the multi-stemmed umdlebe tree, with its dark-green, pear-shaped leaves marked with maroon that 'causes blood to flow from nostrils and ear'. While Shaka was conveniently away on his elephant hunt, the *inyanga* administered the poison by putting it in her food.[21] And, certainly, the branches of the umdlebe tree (*Synadenium cupulare*, commonly known as the deadman's or crying tree) were in the customary arsenal of an *umthakathi* intending to concoct an evil, occult medicine to cause death. But it is suggestive that the milky sap of the tree also causes diarrhoea. One way or the other, traditions of Nandi's being stabbed in the anus or given poison all explain the rectal bleeding that could be mistaken for dysentery.

Of course, in the final resort, it is not possible to be sure whether Nandi died of natural causes or whether Shaka was responsible for her death. Nevertheless, what the persistent and widespread rumours of matricide disclose – tales accompanied by telling and convincing circumstantial detail – is that by 1827 there was a deep swell of opposition to Shaka's rule and a readiness on the part of many of his subjects to believe the very worst of him. Moreover, Shaka's well-attested and grossly exaggerated reaction to Nandi's death smacked suspiciously of pathological remorse and guilt rather than simple grief at the death of a parent, and certainly would have fed public belief in his complicity, rather than allaying it.[22]

CHAPTER 10

I Am Lamenting Because of My Mother's Death

While his mother lay dying at eMkhindini, Shaka sat for several hours in front of his own hut in silent contemplation, Fynn recalled. He told Bazley that as soon as Shaka was finally brought news of Nandi's death he burst into tears, although this display did not convince some sceptical onlookers who murmured that 'the evil-doer cried like a little girl'.[1] Certainly, his grief was extreme.

After his first paroxysm of grief, Fynn recorded, Shaka donned his full war costume in honour of his mother. Accompanied by his principal *amakhosi*, all similarly attired, he strode to the hut where Nandi had breathed her last. The people, meanwhile, began flocking in the same direction, stripping off their beads and other ornaments in mourning. For some time Shaka stood silent before the hut, his tears, which he occasionally wiped away with his right hand, dropping onto his great shield before him. Then, wrote Fuze:

> There was a long silence while he sobbed, and then he suddenly gave a loud scream: '*Maye ngomane!*' ['Alas for my mother'] Wo! And there was heard a great death wail from all the people … crying out, '*Maye ngomane!*', while others cried, '*Maye babo!*' ['Alas! Indeed!'], and as they repeated it the homestead shook with emotion, which lasted throughout the night.

And the following day the death wail continued as people arrived from all directions to take part in the lamentations.[2]

Such crying and lamentation was not normal even on the death of a king, and in Baleni's memory Nandi was the only royal personage to be mourned in such a way.[3] James Gibson, a magistrate in late nineteenth-century Zululand, believed he knew what was behind the extraordinary display of grief. In his experience, 'a Zulu's tears flow most freely when induced by desire for revenge'. The assembled throng thus fully comprehended that by his weeping Shaka was telling them that he attributed Nandi's death to witchcraft by those who wished her ill, and that he had been personally deeply wounded by such audacity. So everyone there understood they had to establish their innocence of this terrible offence against the king and his mother, and that this included demonstrating their loyalty by their exigent desire to destroy those guilty.[4] People gave themselves over to extravagant displays of weeping, for if they did not, others might accuse them of being defiant or, even worse, of not crying because they believed Shaka was the real culprit. To keep on crying, people put snuff in their eyes, but to be found out doing so also carried the penalty of death for dissembling.[5] In mounting frenzy, people turned on each other, beating the insufficiently sorrowful to death.

At the end of the third day, Shaka put an end to the killing in the environs of kwaBulawayo. But his *amakhosi*, to demonstrate their devotion and to express their overwhelming sorrow, sent out war parties across the land to kill people who had not proved their innocence by instantly presenting themselves at kwaBulawayo to join in the mourning.[6] Isaacs was horrified on 14 August when he witnessed such a party attacking an *umuzi*, setting it alight and killing and mutilating the homestead head and slaughtering his wives and children while his servant fled into the bush.[7] Desperate to prove the intensity of their grief, people from all over the kingdom drove herds of cattle to kwaBulawayo to condole with Shaka with their lowing.[8]

Once he had brought the first intense spasm of public mourning to an end, Shaka set about burying his mother. A boot-shaped grave was dug in the hut where she had died, and on the second day after her death Nandi was placed in it on a mat propped up in the usual sitting posture, and

A photograph taken in the 1920s of Nandi's grave site, marked by the uMlahlankosi tree on the left

(REV A T BRYANT, *OLDEN TIMES IN ZULULAND AND NATAL*, 1929)

covered with another mat. Personal articles she had last used, such as clothing, jewellery, blankets and eating utensils, would have been placed beside her. The grave was filled in and covered with stones and the hut allowed to decay and fall to pieces around it. Fynn stated that a grove of trees was planted on the site, although it seems it was the custom to allow trees to spring up naturally around it.[9] In the 1920s, Bryant photographed a decayed uMlahlankosi tree (*Ziziphus mucronata*, or buffalo thorn) still standing there.[10] The branches of this tree are used in the ceremony to bring home the spirit of the deceased.

King Cetshwayo professed not to know if anything especial occurred at Nandi's burial, except that the identical ceremony was always observed at the interment of a great personage as at that of a commoner, the only difference being that the grave of the former was made into 'a nicer shape'. After the burial, he explained to the Cape Commissioners, 'a wooden fencing is erected round the grave, and every year when the grass is being burnt, there are men to see that the grass on or near the grave is not burnt'.[11] ('To burn the thicket of trees and thick mat of grass on the grave would have been tantamount to burning the Queen Mother herself.)

But, here again, Cetshwayo had his reasons for being cagey. He knew full well that at the burial of his father, King Mpande, in 1872, the old king's *inceku* and two of his wives had followed him into the spirit world with broken necks. There they would continue to serve him as they had in life. Cetshwayo had assured the British then that the age-old custom which they totally abhorred had not been adhered to, but he lied.[12] Fynn was not present when they buried Nandi, but he later learned with horror that 'ten of the best-looking girls' of her *umuzi* were thrown into the grave with her, alive.[13] Zulu oral testimony does not dispute that her servants – 'three old women, three women, *izinceku*, as well as girls to cook for her down below' – were interred with her, only whether they were buried alive or strangled beforehand. But none seemed shocked that a person of Nandi's exalted rank should be accompanied in death by those familiar to her. Otherwise, asked Ndukwana, 'Whom would she be with down below?'[15]

For three months Nandi's grave was watched over by members of her Langeni people and others selected by Shaka, including a large contingent of warriors.[15] Meanwhile, Ngomane kaMqomboli, Shaka's trusted Mthethwa mentor, whom he had appointed his chief *induna*, announced a year-long programme of mourning abstinence for Shaka's beleaguered people. Young calves, it was said, were killed so that the lowing of their bereaved mothers made it seem that the very cattle had joined in the general mourning.[16] Everywhere people were forbidden to eat their staple of sour clotted milk, or *amasi*, because Shaka no longer had a mother and all must stop having milk. People were permitted to eat only the watery sour maize *incumbe* porridge intended for young children, and were forbidden to consume their normal *amabele* (sorghum) porridge.[17] Mini, who was born in the mid-1820s and was a tiny child at the time, remembered that people used to defecate into holes and cover them up to hide their faeces so it could not be seen that they had been consuming the prohibited *amabele* and face execution.[18] For Shaka said of those who continued to eat *amabele* porridge: '"So he is living in a state of contentment"' – i.e. he is satisfied with life, he is in a condition of prosperity and comfort, living in a state of enjoyment – '"whereas I am lamenting because of my mother's death!'"[19] Restrictions were also placed on sleeping indoors, and no woman (according to some sources) was permitted to cohabit with her husband and conceive.[20]

Yet it appears there were other reasons for the tribulations of Shaka's subjects during the intense period of mourning for Nandi. There was clearly a political aspect at play that reflected the deep tensions within the kingdom. King Cetshwayo commented that during this time 'very many people that had grudges against one another, killed each other without any more provocation'.[21] Indeed, there are suggestions that Shaka exploited the mass hysteria he had whipped up over Nandi's death to rouse popular animosity against his old enemies so that he could purge them. Fynn sagely deduced that behind the 'memorable lamentation' lay 'state policy'. He strongly suspected that Shaka wished his people – and especially anyone contemplating his assassination – to absorb the lesson that, if such an effusion of blood followed on the death of his mother, 'how frightfully terrific' must be that which his own would require.[22]

Once again, the deeply mistrusted Qwabe people fell victim, suffering mass killings and loss of cattle.[23] Nor was their *inkosi* excepted. During the mourning period when solid food was prohibited, a supply was delivered to Masawuzana, who was resident at kwaBulawayo. He was a son of Mteli kaLufuta, who had been a Qwabe chief. When Shaka inquired who had dared to order the food, Masawuzana fell over himself to inform Shaka that the food was not intended for him, but for his elder brother, Mnongose. Shaka had appointed Mnongose *inkosi* of the Qwabe, and was only too happy to use the excuse to have him put to death.[24]

But, at the same time as he was conveniently ridding himself of perceived enemies, Shaka's murderous and manipulative behaviour was eliciting grave alarm among other subjects who feared their turn would be next. This was not lost on Shaka, who began to suspect that all he had achieved in his ruthless mourning purge was to make new foes and conjure up fresh conspiracies. On 8 September 1827 Shaka rather desperately confided to Isaacs: 'I am like a wolf on a flat, that is at a loss for a place to hide his head in.' He then went on to complain that 'the Zoolas had killed all his principal people and his mother',[25] thereby blaming unnamed plotters and their agents rather than himself for the recent orgy of killings.

And, certainly, there are indications that a conspiracy was beginning to coalesce in the royal house. Ngidi recalled an incident very suggestive of this. An *impaka* is a wild cat possessed as a familiar by an *umthakathi*, who sends it on errands to carry out his villainous intentions against an individual. Soon after his mother's death, a wild cat taken to be an *impaka* made its way into kwaBulawayo, and Shaka used its uncanny visitation to lay a trap for those he believed were conspiring against him. He sprinkled the blood of a slaughtered beast on the doorways of the *isigodlo* and then summoned *izangoma* to 'smell out' the perpetrator of this evil act – and, while they were at it, to explain the presence of the *impaka*.

Only *izangoma* had the ability to detect the invisible and intangible force of witchcraft, and to 'smell it out' by identifying the supposed evildoers. This potentially gave them enormous powers over even the greatest of the land, whom they could finger as *abathakathi* and so deserving of death. But Shaka had already reduced their power by executing *izangoma* who displeased him, and by doing so with impunity had proved that his supernatural powers were supreme in the land. Consequently, *izangoma* now had to tread with extreme care. In this case, those summoned unwisely believed they knew which way the wind was blowing and 'smelled out' in order of seniority Dingane, Mhlangana, Ngqojana, Sophane and Mfihlo, all of them *abantwana* and Shaka's half-brothers. Doubtless, they were correct in exposing the *abantwana* as potential, if not actual, conspirators. Shaka would have welcomed the finger pointed at them since it would serve as a dire warning and perhaps put a halt to their scheming, but he was not ready to act against them openly.

So he summoned another set of *izangoma*, who endorsed his ultimate supernatural authority by declaring that 'the heavens above' (that is, Shaka) had himself sprinkled the blood. Moreover, they verified that the wild cat was not bewitched but simply a mother catching rats for its young in the royal *ikhanda*. A posse of warriors sent to find its nest and brood duly confirmed this. Shaka thereupon executed all the *izangoma* who had given him the 'wrong' answer.[26] But the *abantwana* had been warned that the king's eye was fiercely on them.

Nevertheless, Shaka was increasingly uncomfortable continuing to reside at kwaBulawayo, right in the very heart of the Qwabe country, which he venomously described as 'the place of the *impaka*'.²⁷ So, during the last months of 1827, Shaka quit kwaBulawayo. Taking his *amakhosi*, women, warriors and great herds of cattle with him, he progressed in great state to kwaDukuza, where, to shouted praises, ululations and the bellowing of cattle, he fixed his new capital.²⁸

As was usually the case with an *ikhanda* where the king resided, a small, separate *umuzi* was built on a slight rise about fifty metres from the *isigodlo* where he could relax in privacy with his intimates and women, or hold more exclusive meetings with councillors or petitioners. At kwaDukuza it was known as kwaNyakamubi (or Ugly Year) and had first been built at kwaBulawayo before being reconstructed at the new *ikhanda*.²⁹ Shaka was not to know, but it was where he would be killed within the year.

CHAPTER 11

Splasher of Water With an Oxtail

As soon as the period of official mourning for his mother came to an end, in September 1827, Shaka vigorously took up the stalled issue of sending a diplomatic mission to the Cape.¹ Under his urging, James King's workmen made hurried strides towards completing the schooner that was to carry the envoys there.² Shaka, clearly satisfied with their progress, made his 'scrawling, fishbone' mark through the last few lines of a document that King put before him in February 1828. Jacob the interpreter and Isaacs were the witnesses (although Isaacs edited out his participation in his memoirs). The document that King had drawn up superseded the grant Shaka had made to Farewell in 1824 and effectively recognised King as paramount among the Port Natal traders. It not only granted him 'free and full possession' of Port Natal and surrounding territories, but also accorded him 'the free and exclusive trade' of all of Shaka's domains. Moreover, it signally honoured him with the appointment as 'chief' (*induna*) of kwaDukuza, which gave Shaka's new capital into his charge. Finally, it placed him in command of the embassy soon to set off for the Cape and commissioned him to 'negotiate a treaty of friendly alliance' between his kingdom and that of King George IV, known to the Zulu as Mjojo.³

It was not lost on Farewell that he had entirely forfeited Shaka's favour and that King's faction had won the day.⁴ As for King, he was cock-a-hoop.

His great objective now, as his manoeuvrings once he reached the Cape would reveal, was to present Shaka's grant of February 1828 to the colonial authorities and to lay claim to the territories it specified. However, he realised that, for the claim to be effective and for him to exploit his exclusive trading rights in Zululand to the full, he needed some measure of British protection. And that in turn meant he must persuade the Cape government to establish some sort of authority over Port Natal.

With the *Elizabeth and Susan* successfully launched on 10 March 1828, the embassy, which was under King's full charge, was at last ready to depart. Shaka entrusted King with 50 tusks of elephant ivory to cover expenses and to be disbursed as gifts. The schooner sailed on 30 April 1828 with King, Jacob the interpreter, Shaka's two emissaries and the six Zulu of their suite on board. Also taking passage were Isaacs (without shoes and wearing a barbarous cap made of civet cat fur),[5] young Charles Maclean, and Farewell and his wife, Elizabeth, whom he had married in 1822. Farewell had brought her to Port Natal in 1826, and she had her own consignment of hippopotamus ivory to sell. For Farewell, who needed urgently to obtain fresh trade goods from the Cape, being beholden to his successful rival, King, for his passage must have been a bitter pill to swallow. After an uneventful voyage, the *Elizabeth and Susan* entered Algoa Bay and on 4 May docked in Port Elizabeth, still a nascent settlement hardly calculated to impress the Zulu on board, who were expecting unimaginable wonders.[6]

The leader of the Zulu embassy was Sothobe kaMpangalala of the Sibiya people, a senior *induna*. His aide was Mbozamboza, a lesser *induna* who held a confidential post as one of Shaka's official intelligence-gatherers. Sothobe was permitted the comfort of taking two of his wives with him, one of whom was Mafokose, the mother of his heir, Nobiya.[7] It seems that Shaka had selected Sothobe as his ambassador for occult reasons. According to Makuza, who had his information from his father, Mkomoyi, who had served as one of Shaka's warriors, Shaka had himself seriously contemplated crossing the sea to the Cape. Cautiously, though, he wanted to find out first what the ocean intended to do with one who wished to sail upon it. So, when standing one day on the Durban Bluff with his *amabutho*, Shaka and all his warriors threw their *amawisa* into the sea. The belief was that, if an individual's stick was carried away, it would be clear that he would not return if he ventured over the ocean. The waves duly cast back most of the sticks, but not Shaka's. Obeying the omen, Shaka asked for volunteers to take his place. But no one dared to cross the mighty sea that bled away on the horizon into the limitless sky. So Shaka selected a man of influence at his court whose *iwisa* had returned to the beach, and that was Sothobe.[8]

Mayinga and Melapi, who grew up with Sothobe as their *inkosi*, and who knew him when he was an old man, described him as an extremely arrogant, deep-chested giant of a man with a sloping forehead who wore his *isicoco* on the back of his head. As one of Shaka's acknowledged favourites, he was permitted to sport a bunch of the red lourie (*gwalagwala*) feathers that none but Shaka, *abantwana* and a few *izikhulu* could wear. He was renowned, in a culture centred on cattle, for being able to estimate the number of livestock in a herd correctly at a glance.[9] Sothobe was subsequently celebrated in his praises for his heroism in sailing out to sea in a ship:

> Splasher of water with an oxtail,
> Great ship of the ocean,
> The uncrossable sea,
> Which is crossed only by swallows and white people ...[10]

Although (as we have seen) an embassy to the Cape had been brewing in Shaka's mind since the first arrival of the Port Natal traders, it is difficult to divine exactly what his purpose was in dispatching it at the moment he did. The most explicit statement we have concerning Shaka's intentions is the report King submitted to the colonial authorities soon after his arrival in Port Elizabeth. Ambassador Sothobe, he wrote, was to 'proceed to England for the purpose of explaining to our government the friendly disposition of Chaka towards our nation'. He was also to ascertain whether the British authorities would oppose Shaka's intention of making an attack on the chiefdoms near the Cape's eastern frontier. Mbozamboza was to return from Port Elizabeth as soon as possible with a report on how the embassy had been received at the Cape.[11] Some six weeks later, Sothobe – who when interviewed by Cape officials always donned full dancing dress and his headdress with its tall crane feather, and carried his spear and shield[12] – eventually made clear to Deputy Quartermaster General Major AJ Cloete, the government representative dispatched to negotiate with him and to circumvent King's machinations, that another aim of the embassy was to open up 'fair dealings' and trading relations between Zululand and the Cape.[13]

In fairness to the Cape authorities, how were they to view this unexpected and undeniably odd embassy? In particular, how should they react to King's bland but alarming statement that Shaka was intending a military campaign in the direction of the Cape that threatened upheavals along its borders? Historians have been quick to damn the Cape officials' reception of the embassy as a typical case of colonial arrogance and racial prejudice, exacerbated by the worst sort of bureaucratic bumbling and red tape. Isaacs' own very partisan version of what befell the mission and why it foundered started this particular hare.[14] He pulled no punches in his memoirs and categorically declared that the 'the chiefs were subjected to annoyance, and by insignificant display of paltry authority and petty power, which ... excited feelings of no ordinary indignation'.[15] However, the voluminous official correspondence paints a rather different picture.

If at first dubious about the status of the emissaries,[16] the Cape government soon took Shaka's mission entirely seriously, but was always somewhat at a loss as how best to deal with the parties they were negotiating with. What were they to make of the bumptious, shady pseudo-lieutenant King, with his obvious personal agenda centred on gaining official recognition of his control of Port Natal? And to what extent was he honestly representing Shaka's interests and intentions? Yet it proved impossible to exclude him from the negotiations because the two suspicious and prickly Zulu representatives would not commit themselves to anything without first asking his advice and securing his approval. So whose mission was it really? King's or Shaka's?

King became ever more frustrated as the officials refused to swallow his agenda, while they became increasingly suspicious of his motives and standing. As Major General Richard Bourke, the Acting Governor, expressed it, 'the conduct of Mr. King has been so extraordinary throughout the business I feel it is difficult to place any reliance on him'.[17] The unsatisfactory negotiations foundered once and for all when the colonial government finally ordered Cloete to break off all communication with King because it had resolved not to 'recognise him in any official capacity whatever'.[18]

For their part, as talks stalled, the Zulu emissaries were becoming rapidly disillusioned. They were never taken to Cape Town as they supposed they would be, and visited only Port Elizabeth and Grahamstown, then still very insignificant settlements. As Maclean later commented, 'from what he had seen' Sothobe could not have gained 'any very high notions of the white men's country or the greatness of their cities'[19] — even if the water that came 'out of a hole' (that is, a pump) clearly did make some impression.[20] King, for all his deviousness, was certainly correct when he complained that the Zulu emissaries were 'dissatisfied' with their treatment and insulted by the authorities' failure to bestow gifts on them as courtesy required. Nor is it surprising that they were justifiably beginning to fear how Shaka would receive them if their mission failed.[21]

Even so, they were becoming increasingly keen to return home. In early July, Mbozamboza packed up his war dress and started out overland for Zululand before being apprehended and turned back. Mbozamboza's attempt to abscond decided the authorities to send the whole embassy home by sea. However, because they refused to permit them to embark on King's schooner, they detained them in Port Elizabeth until a warship from the Cape Station could be readied to convey them back to Port Natal.[22]

CHAPTER 12

Buffalo That Stood Glaring with a Spear

Many as the reasons were for the failure of the Zulu embassy to the Cape, the greatest was the grossly inopportune raid Shaka launched against the Mpondo while discussions between the parties were taking place. As we have seen, when King first arrived in Port Elizabeth he made mention of Shaka's intention to attack chiefdoms close to the Cape's eastern frontier. Duly, from mid-June 1828 strong rumours started reaching officials that a great Zulu army was marching south towards the borders of the colony.

Why Shaka mounted this campaign at such a delicate diplomatic moment remains a conundrum. From the perspective of King and other traders, there were advantages to be gained. Upheavals on the Cape frontier might draw the British up the coast towards Port Natal. It was in the interests of the traders that Britain become increasingly involved in the affairs of the Port and eventually extend its protection over it. The traders had been pursuing that goal ever since they first landed in the bay because it would rescue them from Shaka's unpredictable and often highly alarming control. Then again, King thought he saw how he could exploit the threat of the approaching Zulu army to strengthen his bargaining hand. Throughout the negotiations he consequently sought to project himself as the person best positioned and equipped to act as an intermediary between the British and the Zulu.[1]

THE ASSASSINATION OF KING SHAKA

Despite Farewell's loud protestations to the contrary,[2] the Governor of the Cape did indeed come to believe firmly that Shaka's attack on the Mpondo had been 'fomented and encouraged' by King and his associates.[3] Yet it must be questioned to what extent they could manipulate Shaka to suit their purposes. Undoubtedly, the activities and schemes of the traders complicated Shaka's management of affairs of state, but he nevertheless pursued his own very definite political objectives. The best the traders could do was to take advantage of Shaka's initiatives if they were able to. In this case they probably did just that by persuading Shaka that he would win the approval of the British, and enhance the prospects of his embassy to the Cape, if he attacked their apparent enemies on the Cape frontier. That at least was the conclusion of Major General Richard Bourke, the Acting Governor.[4]

Still, if we turn our attention away from how the traders believed they could exploit Shaka's Mpondo raid to their advantage, and concentrate instead on Zulu thinking about the matter, we come up with a rather different picture.

Once Shaka had settled in kwaDukuza in early September 1827, the official mourning for Nandi came to an end. It was now time to bring her spirit home (*ukubuyisa*) and to ritually purify Shaka of the dark powers of *umnyama* associated with her death.[5] Droves of calves were slashed open on the right side for the gall bladder to be ripped out of the living beast, which was left to die in agony, its cries summoning the royal *amadlozi*. One by one the *amabutho* paraded before Shaka and each man sprinkled him with gall. The *amabutho* then performed a war dance, oxen were sacrificed and the *izinyanga* washed Shaka with *intelezi* to ward off evil.

According to Fynn, Ngomane, Shaka's chief *induna*, now addressed the great throng. To conclude the mourning ritual for Nandi, it was necessary to make war against neighbouring peoples who had not come forward to lament Nandi's death. This was the final act in the *ihlambo* (washing, or cleansing) ceremonies that marked the end of a period of mourning. 'As tears could not be forced from these distant nations,' Ngomane declared, 'war should be made against them, and the cattle taken should be the tears shed upon her grave.'[6] In this way, the *umnyama* associated with Nandi's death would be cast into the enemy's country.[7]

Shaka immediately entered into discussions with his military commanders as to who should be the target of the great raid. They selected the Mpondo, with whom there was unfinished business. Shaka had not forgotten the humiliation of the *amabece impi* – the melon campaign of 1824 – and what could be more appropriate than to secure delayed revenge in honour of Nandi's shade? This time, nothing was to be left to chance in planning the campaign, and Shaka sent out spies to gather military intelligence of the country through which the *ihlambo impi* (or cleansing army) would pass. Among the intelligence-gatherers was Mbozamboza, subsequently Sothobe's associate in the embassy to the Cape. He spent several months reconnoitring Mpondoland, and penetrated as far south as the Cape border.[8]

Mourning ritual and revenge aside, what other motives might Shaka have had for attacking the Mpondo? It is likely he calculated that a campaign had become politically necessary. After the unprecedented excesses of the mourning for Nandi, it would refocus the attention of his alarmed and fearful subjects on fresh military glories. And, if great herds of cattle were captured, he could reward his *amabutho* and *amakhosi* – insatiably eager as ever for plunder – and so damp down simmering discontent and mounting internal opposition to his rule. Quite possibly, he might also have reflected that a show of military strength in the region of Port Natal and the lands to the south would remind the presumptuous traders that he, and not they, held the whip hand.

In May 1828, shortly after the embassy to the Cape had sailed, and once the rivers had become easily fordable at the beginning of the dry season, a Zulu army began its march southwards under Mdlaka kaNcidi, Shaka's most senior and seasoned commander.[9] The strength of the *ihlambo impi* is unknown, although Cape border officials estimated the size of the force that entered Mpondo territory at between two and three thousand men.[10] Shaka himself went with his army as far south as Fynn's post on the banks of the Mzimkhulu River. His *izibongo* hailed him as

> Buffalo that stood glaring with a spear on the banks of the Mzimvubu,
> And the Pondo feared to come down to it.[11]

But, in fact, Shaka did not accompany his army deep into Mpondo territory as his praises suggest. As Farewell explained, Shaka 'never goes with the army himself but remains generally five or six days in the rear ... so that he never incurs any personal risk and he is quite careless with his people's lives'.[12] In this case, Shaka remained at Fynn's settlement guarded by an *ibutho* and in the company of a number of his *umndlunkulu* girls under the supervision of Mnkabi, one of Senzangakhona's more influential widows.[13]

Shaka had learned in military operations, since the failure of the *amabece impi*, to appreciate the effectiveness of the traders' supporting firepower. He required it again for the *ihlambo impi*, and on its way south it was duly joined by contingents of Farewell's retainers from Port Natal and musketeers from Fynn's post on the Mzimkhulu. According to Fynn, he and Farewell remained at his residence near the Mzimkhulu with Shaka, and took no part in the raid.[14] However, the Cape frontier officials learned otherwise. On 17 July there was word of 'a white man who directs the movements of his [Shaka's] army and makes use of firearms'.[15] Faku himself reported that 'a party of armed Englishmen', including Fynn, Farewell and Henry Ogle, had joined in the attack on him.[16]

When the *ihlambo impi*, with Farewell, Fynn and other musket-bearing auxiliaries in its ranks, crossed the Mzimkhulu it advanced southwestwards through the Mpondo country. According to Fynn, Shaka instructed his cousin Maphitha, his influential viceroy in northeastern Zululand, who was with the army, to ensure that it did not come into conflict with any whites.[17] By mid-June a section of the army had penetrated the Bomvana country, south of the Mthatha River.[18] It seems that Faku drove the royal herds to the sanctuary of the Drakensberg and cynically allowed the marauding Zulu to seize the cattle of his subordinate chiefs instead.[19] According to some accounts, the Mpondo put up stout resistance, ambushing the Zulu in the forests and flinging volleys of their small spears, black on one side and white on the other, with poisoned blades. Shaka had those warriors whom the Mpondo had bested executed for cowardice when they returned.[20] Others recalled, however, that 'there had been no actual fighting with the Pondos, only a seizure of their cattle'.[21]

Then, on 18 June reports reached Cape officials that Shaka's forces had turned back. It was not until mid-July, though, that they were certain the

Zulu had retired across the Mzimkhulu with their considerable booty in cattle, which Isaacs numbered at about ten thousand.[22]

Even so, the Cape authorities remained extremely nervous of a Zulu incursion. They were determined to warn Shaka to stay north of the Mzimkhulu, since they considered all the country to its south to be in the Cape's sphere of interest.[23] Military preparations were accordingly put in motion in late June and a burgher commando assembled on 10 July.[24] In late July, Major WB Dundas, with 50 burghers and a force of Thembu auxiliaries, ventured deep into Mpondo territory. Near the upper Mthatha River on 26 July they attacked a large group of warriors who, from their dress and military style, they presumed were Zulu and captured cattle and women in great numbers.[25] However, it eventually dawned on the border officials that these people were not Zulu but the Ngwane people of Matiwane kaMasumpa.[26] The Ndwandwe had dislodged the unfortunate Ngwane from their original home at the headwaters of the White Mfolozi, and then Shaka had driven them southwest beyond the Mzimkhulu.

The unhappy fate of the Ngwane crypto-Zulu was of no immediate concern to Shaka. In the longer run it would have been, though, because it signalled a shift in Cape policy towards greater involvement in the affairs of African states north of its border.[27] However, from Shaka's immediate perspective the *ihlambo impi* had been a successful operation, despite its potentially adverse impact on relations with the Cape. Once again, the Port Natal traders had been constrained to bow to his will and offer him military service. His show of military force had reasserted Zulu predominance over his African neighbours. And, although the Mpondo kingdom had not been too seriously damaged in the raid, Faku hastened to stave off any further attacks by sending peace envoys to Shaka with a few cattle as tribute.[28] The captured Mpondo herds were sent to Shaka's cattle posts near kwaDukuza from where they would be distributed as largesse to the *amakhosi* and other clients whose loyalty Shaka was anxious to secure.[29] Whether that would be enough to dispel maturing opposition to his regime remained to be seen.

CHAPTER 13

This Is King Chaka's Name

After many delays on account of bad weather, the sloop-of-war HMS *Helicon* finally arrived in Algoa Bay from Simon's Town to take off James King and the Zulu delegation. They embarked on 7 August, the Zulu at any rate being 'in high good humour'.[1] The *Helicon* sailed on 9 August, accompanied by the *Elizabeth and Susan*, which carried Isaacs, Farewell (who sensibly left his wife behind in Port Elizabeth) and Maclean.[2] Both ships arrived at Port Natal on 17 August.

Fynn recorded that at about this time Shaka dreamed that the vessel in which his ambassadors sailed had a broken mast. The *amadlozi* spoke through dreams, so he deduced that something had gone seriously amiss with the mission.[3] Nor was he mistaken. The embassy had been a miserable failure for King as well as for Shaka. King had not succeeded in obtaining British recognition either of the Port Natal settlement or of himself as its sole leader. He complained bitterly that he had been 'received as an object of suspicion' by the Cape authorities, and that all his hopes 'of effecting a friendly and mutually beneficial treaty' had been dashed.[4] He landed in Port Natal a humiliated and broken man, too ill to report to Shaka in person. He died at his house on the Bluff in early September of what his companions termed a 'liver complaint'.[5] Isaacs and Fynn were with him to the end, but the embittered Farewell refused to be reconciled with King or even to visit him as he lay dying.[6]

For his part, Shaka had gained nothing concrete from the embassy. All he got back was the exasperating statement that, while the Cape government was anxious to be on good terms with him, it would oppose by force any Zulu movement southwards that disturbed the Cape's eastern frontier.[7] It is likely that Isaacs made this known to him, because it was more than Sothobe's life was worth to do so. In any event, Shaka did not take at all kindly to the rebuff. According to Isaacs, he furiously insisted that the whites had no right whatsoever to interfere with him, and that he would destroy all the frontier tribes unless they became tributary to him.[8]

In a terrifying interview on 26 August, Shaka violently accused Isaacs and King of plundering the chest of unacceptably paltry gifts the Cape government had dispatched to him on the *Helicon*.[9] He was enraged beyond measure that Isaacs had not brought him the fabulous Rowland's Macassar Oil necessary to restore his youthful looks. He scorned utterly the unsolicited patent medicines chosen by the Cape authorities that were delivered in its place. Shaka was also deeply suspicious that King had kept for himself the ivory tusks he had entrusted to him as a gift to King George.[10] Matters were not made any easier for Isaacs when Sothobe and Jacob did their urgently persuasive best, through what he termed their 'shameful misrepresentations', to pin the chief blame for the failure of the mission on King and him.[11] Throughout the ordeal the trembling Isaacs was 'incessantly abused' by Shaka and 'often threatened with execution'.[12]

Enraged as he was, Shaka did his best to ensure that the humiliating and politically dangerous failure of his mission to the Cape was not widely known. James Gibson wrote that in the early twentieth century the popular tradition persisted that Sothobe had 'crossed the water and entered into a treaty of friendship with the English king'.[13] It was doubtless to put a positive spin on the diplomatic debacle that Shaka awarded Sothobe a great herd of cattle instead of executing him. Even so, Shaka could not disguise from his inner circle his unmistakable dismay at the failure of the embassy.[14]

Despite the sorry end of his first attempt to treat with the British, Shaka would not have been the ruler he was if he had not acted immediately to retrieve the situation. He would reopen negotiations. King's faction had failed him, but he knew he remained as dependent as ever on the traders to facilitate relations with the Cape authorities. He had no option, therefore, but to turn to Farewell's discredited party. They, of course, were only too happy to comply and to hope it presaged a return to Shaka's favour.

Shaka's choice of a new emissary fell on John Cane, a London-born carpenter by trade who had arrived at Port Natal with Farewell in 1824. Cape officials quickly identified him as 'the principal agent of Farewell' whose prejudicial characterisation of King's embassy should be taken with a large grain of salt.[15] On his own reckoning, Cane left kwaDukuza on foot on about 6 or 7 September 1828 with Mbozamboza, another *induna*, two warriors and two *izindibi* to carry their baggage. An Mpondo guide led them overland through Faku's territory to the Cape, an arduous journey that took 23 days in all.[16] As accreditation, Cane carried with him a scrap of paper with a brief note in pencil to which Shaka had scribbled his 'signature'.[17]

When interviewed by Cape officials in Grahamstown on 7 October and again in Cape Town on 10 November, Cane elaborated on Shaka's new terms. Besides reiterating his desire for good relations and peace, having now 'set aside his shield', Shaka wanted to open regular communications overland with the Cape. Cane was also charged to request the colonial government to send an emissary to Shaka to make known its wishes. In a politic ploy (doubtless suggested by the traders playing up to the strong evangelical Christian lobby in the Cape) he requested that a missionary be sent to live among the Zulu. And as a final incentive – which reflected the traders' urgent desire for the extension of British protection over them – Shaka undertook that if the British wished to establish a settlement at Port Natal he would allocate to it a strip of territory ten miles (16 kilometres) inland from the Port stretching right down the coast as far as the Mpondo country.[18]

A leitmotif that ran through Cane's statements, and also those made by the Zulu of his party, was Shaka's angry concern with the whereabouts of the ivory he had entrusted to King on the first embassy, and which he believed he had purloined.[19] And, to make good the defective gifts from the Cape government that King had brought back with him, Shaka specifically requested 'blankets, medicine of a simple kind, dogs of the large breed, hatchets and knives, a cloth cloak, a brass plate to wear on his arm to extend from the wrist to the elbow and to fasten with a clasp, and also some sealing wax' to go with a seal (doubtless suggested by Cane) to authenticate his future communications. And, once again, there was the urgent request, to be kept strictly private, for the Macassar oil.[20]

Having dispatched Cane's embassy, and in a move typical of his long-standing endeavour to pick his way between the irreconcilable Port Natal factions, Shaka set about mending fences with the recently deceased King's followers. When Isaacs reported King's death to him, Shaka jumped to the conclusion that he had been poisoned and performed the proper rites to propitiate his shade. He lamented an old friend, even if nothing shook his conviction that King was guilty of mishandling the embassy to the Cape and of defrauding him. Even so, he endowed Isaacs with the lands he had previously granted King. Isaacs drew up a document specifying the details of the grant, upon which Shaka made his mark on 17 September 1828. Irritated that Jacob's signature as witness was larger than his, Shaka trumped this act of *lèse-majesté* by scribbling all over the blank part of the page and declaring, with satisfaction, 'there, anyone can see that is a king's name, because it is a great one. King George will also see that this is King Chaka's name.'[21]

Meanwhile, in the Cape, Cane's embassy was enjoying considerably more success than had King's. Colonial policy had undergone a change in the previous few months following Shaka's alarming Mpondo raid. There was now a commitment to a more active diplomatic engagement with the African polities bordering the Cape. Consequently, from their first arrival in the colony Cane and his party were received courteously, and Captain RS Aitchison of the Cape Mounted Riflemen was detailed to escort the party to Cape Town.[22] There, after interviewing Cane, the new Governor of the Cape, Sir Lowry Cole, found him to be both 'shrewd and intelligent' and took his mission entirely seriously.[23]

On 26 November 1828 Cane was informed that he was to return to Shaka with Captain Aitchison and an armed escort.[24] Two days previously, Aitchison had been issued his instructions for the Zulu Mission. He was to assure Shaka of Cole's 'friendly disposition' and of 'his wish to preserve a good understanding with him'. However, and doubtless to Cane's disappointment, he abjured any British responsibility for the Port Natal traders and consigned their wellbeing to Shaka's care. Moreover, he reiterated the previous injunction to King's embassy that any Zulu incursions that threatened the stability of the colony's border regions would be resisted with force.[25]

Aitchison and his party had only just reached the Cape's eastern frontier when, on 26 December 1828, Cole formally countermanded the Zulu Mission under his charge.[26] Cane and the Zulu envoys languished in Grahamstown until March 1829, when they were finally allowed to depart for Zululand.[27] What had happened to derail this promising diplomatic mission so completely? On 15 December Farewell arrived in Port Elizabeth on the *Elizabeth and Susan* with all of the other residents of Port Natal on board with the exception of Fynn and Ogle. He brought the startling news that Shaka had been assassinated on 23 September 1828, a full two months before the Zulu Mission had set out to visit him.[28]

PART IV

Are You Stabbing Me, the King of the Earth?

CHAPTER 14

They Hate Him

The day before John Cane left kwaDukuza in early September 1828 on Shaka's second embassy to the Cape, a messenger arrived from far to the north. He carried confirmation that the Zulu army had reached the vicinity of Soshangane kaZikode of the Gaza kingdom, situated nearly 700 kilometres away, south of the Lepelle River – known to the Zulu as the Bhalule – in the hill country 130 kilometres to the northwest of Delagoa Bay.[1] The army, the messenger reported, was obeying Shaka's orders not to engage the enemy until it had exhausted all its provisions. It was now waiting to consume the last of its cattle before it attacked.[2]

Shaka had dispatched his army northwards only a few days after it returned from the *ihlambo impi* against the Mpondo.[3] 'An ox bellowed,' recounted Mtshapi, 'whereupon Tshaka there and then summoned his army in the night. He then gave the order, "Let it arm, and make for the Balule. Let it fetch the red cattle of the *umkhandli* (the cattle which were eaten by the women of the *isigodhlo* when they had washed [menstruated])."'[4] Launching a fresh campaign right on the heels of one that had just been brought to a close was unprecedented. Shaka's *amabutho* were dismayed, indignantly questioning, 'Why are we being sent away on another campaign? We shall not have time to build our own kraals.'[5] Indeed, Shaka was later widely said 'to have *bunguleka*'d, i.e. gone mad by giving such an order'.[6]

THE ASSASSINATION OF KING SHAKA

Of course, Shaka was neither mad nor irrationally impulsive, and there was coherent purpose behind his launching of the *Bhalule impi*, even though the campaign was to prove a military disaster. There were several elements to his decision to send his army north without reasonable time for recuperation. Some are readily identifiable and superficially explicable. But others, lurking potently beneath the surface, are more conjectural.

At the most superficial level, there is some indication that Shaka was dissatisfied with the performance of his army in the *ihlambo impi* and wanted it to prove itself in more serious fighting.[7] He also deemed that several tributary chiefs to the west of the Swazi kingdom had not obeyed nearly rigorously enough his injunctions concerning the mourning to be followed for Nandi, and needed to be taught a lesson.[8] Operationally, these miscreants were within normal range of the Zulu army. But it was hardly a matter of urgency that they should be 'eaten up' before the army had rested.

Further intelligence that Shaka received straight after the return of the *ihlambo impi* was certainly more pressing. He learned that Hlangabeza kaMabedla of the Ntshali people, who lived along the upper reaches of the Black Mfolozi River in what had once been Ndwandwe territory, in northern Zululand, had fled the kingdom with all his people and cattle. Hlangabeza clearly was in fear of Shaka's retribution since he was one of those who had not respected the mourning for Nandi; moreover, he had held back from taking part in the *ihlambo impi*.[9] However, what apparently impelled Shaka to react was the knowledge that Hlangabeza was making for Soshangane's territory.

Soshangane's migratory kingdom was one of the Ndwandwe fragments making their way northwards after Shaka's victory over Zwide in 1819. Shaka knew that it was Soshangane's policy to entice Ndwandwe remnants and other disaffected elements away from Zululand with offers of cattle, ivory and wives.[10] An attack on Soshangane would kill two birds with one stone. Not only would Shaka's army punish the disloyal subjects and tributaries it overtook on the way, but defeating Soshangane would also put an end to his constant draining away of Zulu subjects.[11]

But – and these are weighty reservations – Soshangane's kingdom was more than twice as far away as Faku's and was situated in unfamiliar and difficult country. The Zulu army would be operating well beyond the limits of its logistical support and campaigning without adequate prior intelligence. Since Shaka had carefully looked into these selfsame matters before launching his raid into Mpondoland, his failure to do so for the Gaza campaign is, at first sight, all the more perplexing. And the Zulu army duly suffered the dire consequences of its lack of adequate planning.

Unlike the *ihlambo impi*, where Shaka had accompanied his army as far south as the Mzimkhulu River, he did not leave kwaDukuza for the *Bhalule impi*. However, he made sure that all his senior brothers marched with the army.[12] He was content to entrust the command once again to Mdlaka, his senior and most trusted general. It was a daunting assignment. When Mdlaka led the *amabutho* north, the men were in an ugly mood and became increasingly disaffected as they passed close by their homes without being able to rest. The army divided into two divisions at the Mkhomazi River, just south of Port Natal. One body went up the coast and the other inland through central Zululand, rendezvousing just north of the Phongolo River.[13] The army then followed the line of the Drakensberg northwards. It caught up with Hlangabeza and the Ntshali near the Assegaai River in southwestern Swaziland, about fifty kilometres north of the Phongolo, where they had erected temporary homesteads on the margins of a forest. Mdlaka divided his force, with one part advancing during the hours of night to the far side of the forest while the other made a frontal attack before daylight. Surrounded and surprised, the Ntshali were annihilated and their cattle seized. Hlangabeza tried to escape by hiding in water up to his neck, but the reserve of younger warriors who were following up behind the older *amabutho* discovered him and put him to death.[14]

While the intimidated Swazi took to their caves and mountain strongholds, the Zulu army pushed on northwards through the Pedi Maroteng paramountcy up the Tubatse (Steelpoort) River valley to its confluence with the Bhalule River. It then swung southeastwards around the headwaters of the Sabi River, and on through 150 kilometres of lethal, malaria-infested bushveld towards Soshangane's territory in the hills between the Matola and Nkomazi (Komati) rivers northwest of Lourenço Marques. This was unknown territory, and the Zulu often lost their way. Aware that the Zulu army was out of supply, the Gaza drove their cattle away to safety and remained holed up in their caverns in the hills. There the main Zulu army encamped while some parties raided cattle from the Tsonga people living to the north between the Limpopo River and Inhambane, a Portuguese trading post and settlement founded in the early sixteenth century, a little further up the coast.[15]

That much Shaka knew from the messenger who arrived just before Cane left on his diplomatic mission to the Cape, and it was probably the last news he ever received of his distant army. King Sobhuza I of Swaziland cut off his communications with the army, patrolling the paths, intercepting messengers and killing all Zulu who tried to pass.[16] What Shaka never learned before his death was that his great army had already met with disaster. The men were being laid low with malaria (*imbo*),[17] and many were suffering badly from dysentery. Tradition ascribes their crippling stomach cramps and diarrhoea to roasting their meat on fires made of the wood of umdlebe trees they came upon in a verdant valley. That they did so seems unaccountable, for this was the selfsame tree from which the poison that was said to have killed Nandi had been brewed, and its milky sap was known to cause diarrhoea. The Zulu believed moreover that its evil exhalations were deadly, and that if you breathed in its scent you developed a terrible headache, passed blood and died.[18] Indeed, recounted Mtshapi, when the army entered the valley 'the umdhlebe tree was crying out, "Meh!" like a goat. As it cried out it exuded blood, like that of a person who is bleeding.'[19]

With his men stricken with illness and dropping from lack of food and exhaustion, Mdlaka understood it was essential to storm the Gaza strongholds and terminate the campaign. But Soshangane was familiar with Zulu tactics and knew they would make their assault at dawn. So he attacked first, at night, when the Zulu were unprepared. Weakened by illness and hunger, demoralised and taken by surprise, the Zulu were cut to pieces and one *ibutho* was entirely destroyed. Mdlaka appreciated that the game was up. He could not ask his badly mauled army, ill, famished and reduced to eating locusts, to renew the offensive. It was time to withdraw as best he could to Zululand. He would have known only too well what reception he could expect to receive from Shaka when he returned without having defeated Soshangane and without any cattle as booty. But he had no choice.[20]

The most singular thing about the Zulu army that perished in the Delagoa Bay hinterland was its sheer size. The *Bhalule impi* was evidently much larger than the army that had campaigned in Mpondoland, and there is ample evidence that Shaka considerably reinforced the *ihlambo impi* as it proceeded on its way against Soshangane.

Shaka ordered that the *Bhalule impi* be joined by a force raked together indiscriminately from the entire male population. 'Call up all the riff-raff,' he commanded, 'let no one remain behind, not even the old men with bad knees.'[21] The directive that every stay-at-home should be swept up (or *ukhukhulelangoqo*) targeted every *ngoqo*, or inferior person, the despised nobody who never appeared at the king's *ikhanda*, never assisted in building it and never attended hunting parties.[22] Fifty years later, in the reign of King Cetshwayo, the war song composed for this general mobilisation was still remembered:

> Go every one to war!
> Old birds and young!
> He says this –
> Who is as big as the whole country.
> You who stayed at home yesterday
> Won't stay at home today.[23]

Naturally, despite Shaka's orders 'a large number did remain behind', with some taking to the bush to avoid the call-up.[24] And, in any case, Shaka quickly realised that the mobilisation had been too sweeping. When the old men bearing the white shields of the older *amabutho* assembled with the *Bhalule impi*, Shaka exclaimed: 'But how far will these old men get? Let them remain here with me.'[25] However, the army had scarcely been gone for two days when he decided that the 'white shields' were too old to guard him effectively. So he recalled all the *izindibi*, leaving the disgruntled warriors to carry their baggage themselves, and formed these boys into a young *ibutho* known as the iziNyosi, or the Bees.[26]

So, where does this leave us? A major campaign launched without respite immediately after the previous one had ended against an enemy well beyond the army's logistical range; a campaign, moreover, accompanied by the most comprehensive mobilisation in anyone's experience. There simply must have been more to this than Shaka's desire to punish disobedient adherents and chastise Soshangane for abetting them. And, indeed, it seems that what was driving Shaka in his extreme decision to send his army as far away as he could was a second, but aborted, conspiracy to assassinate him.

After the attempt to kill him in 1824, Shaka had fastened the blame on the Qwabe, and had exploited the opportunity to attack the Ndwandwe. He had shrunk from pinning the conspiracy on his royal brothers, though they were (as we have seen) likely culprits. More recently, in August 1827, while still at kwaBulawayo, he had suspected them of conspiring against him, but had again drawn back from openly accusing them. Nevertheless, the *abantwana* must have known that Shaka was highly suspicious of them. They obviously feared that he would strike before they did and waited for an opportunity to anticipate him.

As the *ihlambo impi* came to an end and the army began to withdraw from Mpondoland, the princes decided that the moment was ripe. When they resolved to act they clearly did so with the knowledge, and probable connivance, of the Port Natal traders, who were hoping to benefit from 'regime change'. Isaacs stated in his memoirs that 'the death of Chaka had long been premeditated by his brothers'.[27] Fynn was more specific. He recorded: 'There is little doubt that the intention of killing Shaka had long been in contemplation. As I have since understood, it was intended to have taken place at my residence [at the Mzimkhulu River] during the attack on the amaMpondos, at which time both brothers [Dingane and Mhlangana] remained behind with Shaka feigning illness, when an opportunity was wanting to effect their purpose.'[28]

Dinya succinctly told Stuart what transpired: 'On the troops' coming from Pondoland to the Mkomazi, the princes wanted to kill Tshaka. Dingane and Mhlangana wanted to kill Tshaka, but were afraid of the forces.'[29] One account has Shaka stabbed slightly in the back during a night-time hunting dance with his army while bivouacked at Nyenyezini, 'a low-lying place south of the Mzimkulu'.[30] However, this sounds rather too much like a garbled version of the assassination attempt in 1824. The telling of the event by Mcotoyi, the *inkosi* of the Thuli, who had been born in 1828, rings far more true.

On way back from Pondoland, recounted Mcotoyi, Shaka came to the lower drift of the Mkhomazi where he went to sit on a flat rock by the river. The army was crossing by a higher drift, so Shaka was unattended except by his brothers Dingane and Mhlangana, his trusted *inceku* Mbopha kaSitayi (who was in on the plot) and other members of his household. The conspirators decided to seize the fleeting opportunity to kill him. 'It is said the princes knelt,' continued Mcotoyi, 'leaning on the butt-ends of their assegais as if in a position of humiliation.' Unfortunately for them, a man called Lucunge, who was an *induna* of Magaye kaDibandlela, Shaka's loyal Cele *inkosi*, chose that moment to wander into sight with his companions. Abashed at the sight of his king, he tried to withdraw, but Shaka called him back and made him kneel in front of him. Shaka then ordered those present – including his would-be assassins – to sharpen their spears on Lucunge's forehead as if it were a grindstone to teach him to be more circumspect in future. While they did so as carefully as they could and his forehead nevertheless streamed blood, Lucunge gamely carried on declaiming Shaka's *izibongo*.

This 'simple incident', as Mcotoyi described the whole sadistic episode, was exactly the sort of unexpected diversion that unhinges plots at the last moment. It threw the plotters off balance, and they decided to find another moment to do the deed. In any case – and this was a vital consideration for the future – they were afraid on reflection of how the warriors would react once they discovered that they had killed their king.[31] Next time they would wait to act until no *amabutho* were in the vicinity.

It must be supposed that Shaka was only too conscious of the conspiracy closing in around him. While on his mission to the Cape, John Cane reported that 'Shaka's people are ... dissatisfied and disposed to revolt in consequence of his cruelty and constant wars. Chaka is sensible of this disposition of his people to free themselves from his yoke.'[32] Indeed, the loyalty of even such a one as Sothobe, who had been his ambassador to the Cape, must be in doubt. After Shaka's death, when the assassins purged almost all of his close confederates, Sothobe alone prospered. Dingane put him in charge of building his new *ikhanda*, made him an *induna* of the newly raised uHlomendlini *ibutho*, and elevated him to be the principal *inkosi* south of the Thukela.[33] Clearly, Sothobe was of the princes' party. And, although it cannot be proved, it is likely that after his return from the Cape

Sothobe kept the conspirators abreast of developments at kwaDukuza and encouraged them to act. Surrounded by hidden enemies, distrusting those closest to him, is it any wonder that at this time (according to Fynn) Shaka composed this song?

> Why do they not kill him as they did his father?
> Why do they not kill him as they did his father?
> They hate him.
>
> The calf of the hated one, like his father,
> The calf of the hated one, like his father,
> They hate him.[34]

If we accept that Shaka lived in real fear of a conspiracy to kill him, this would go some way to elucidate what lay behind the extraordinary *Bhalule impi* and to explain its connection to the two embassies to the Cape.

Farewell stated in December 1828 that Shaka had sent his 'fighting men' to Mozambique 'for the express purpose of weakening his tribe with a view to his punishing them with greater brutality'.[35] That seems an obtuse and improbable objective. More likely, was it not an attempt to put the members of the royal house he suspected were conspiring against him at a safe distance by ordering them to serve with the *Bhalule impi*? And what should he do about the traders, whose loyalty was at best dubious? It is suggestive that Shaka summoned a company of King's African retainers and another of Farewell's to join the *Bhalule impi* under the command of the *induna* Ndangane. The traders themselves stayed safely behind in Zululand under Shaka's eye, bereft of their armed men.[36]

Yet sending his enemies temporarily out of the way could only be a short-term solution. Behind it must have been a longer-term calculation. Unfortunately, we do not know for certain what it was. Quite likely, though, Shaka was awaiting the successful return of his first embassy to the Cape. Armed by a powerful British alliance, his hand would be greatly strengthened against his internal enemies. That consideration would help explain his unrestrained fury at the failure of King's mission and his instant dispatch of Cane's to repair the damage. As we have seen, Cane was successful.

But it was too late. The British mission was on its way to kwaDukuza to discuss the terms of the treaty Shaka so desired when it turned back on news of his death.

Meanwhile, the fiasco of the first mission would have reached the ears of the conspirators serving with the *Bhalule impi* and encouraged them to make a fresh move. If they left the *Bhalule impi* and sped south, Shaka would not have his loyal army around him as on the previous occasion when the conspirators pulled back at the last moment on the banks of Mkhomazi.[37] This time, Shaka would be dead before the army returned from campaign. The assassins would also have had time to determine how best to placate the *amabutho* and to persuade them to acknowledge the new king – whichever of the royal brothers he might turn out to be.

CHAPTER 15

Are You Not Going to Stab Him?

In his *izibongo* Dingane was saluted as

>   Restless one,
>   One who left his regiment!¹

But the prince was not alone in deserting from the *Bhalule impi*, which was shedding large numbers of unwilling conscripts as it advanced.² Before the army could make contact with the fugitive Hlangabeza and his Ntshali people, and when it was still in the vicinity of Ceza – a great, looming, flat-topped mountain that dominated the Sikhwebezi River basin in north-western Zululand – Dingane decided that he too would go no further.³ However, he was not simply reporting sick as an excuse to home. He was intending to kill his brother Shaka.

Fynn wrote that 'Dingane's pretext for putting Shaka to death was the latter's having unnecessarily kept the nation in a state of perpetual warfare'.⁴ His real motive, though, would have been his accelerating fear that Shaka (who clearly distrusted him) would likely execute him should he survive the campaign against Soshangane. Certainly, if one excludes Sigujana, whom Shaka had killed to become ruler, there was truth in the last words ascribed to Shaka, in which he protested that since becoming

ARE YOU NOT GOING TO STAB HIM?

king he had never put any of his brothers to death.[5] Yet there was nothing in the increasing intemperance of his rule to persuade his royal brothers that he would flinch from starting to do so. Consequently, several of Dingane's brothers — Farewell thought six or seven, Isaacs three or four — felt equally threatened and resolved they must join him in plotting Shaka's death.[6]

Isaacs believed that what finally spurred them to action were reports that during the army's absence Shaka was going to 'greater lengths in acts of cruelty' than ever before, as Farewell expressed it.[7] Tales abounded of his atrocities against womenfolk left behind while their menfolk were campaigning with the army. Fynn was being considerably more restrained in his reporting than either Farewell or Cane when he declared that 'Dead bodies were to be seen in every direction, not less than 400 or 500 [women] being killed during the absence of their husbands at war.'[8]

Despite these compelling reasons for contemplating regicide, Dingane was not a man to act either hastily or imprudently. Later in his reign he earned a notorious and abiding reputation as being self-indulgent, treacherous and bloodthirsty, thanks to the horrified disapproval of missionaries and the furious denunciations of the Voortrekkers, who went to war with him in 1838. The Port Natal traders who knew him at the time of Shaka's assassination and soon after were more ambivalent, much depending on how they fared under his rule. Cane immediately characterised him as 'as weak, cruel, indolent, capricious and even more prone to shed human blood than the monster [Shaka] that has been put to death'.[9] However, almost exactly a year later, on 12 December 1829, Isaacs would write of him: 'Chaka was born and nurtured in war, which was his darling aim, but Dingān cultivates the repose of peace, and only wields his spear when necessity compels him: he is no warrior — he is a man whose soul seems devoted to ease and pleasure.'[10]

Nevertheless, Isaacs also recognised that Dingane was 'deliberative and calculating, though bold and energetic'[11] — characteristics that proved indispensable in plotting Shaka's death. The Zulu recognised his deep, unfathomable nature, calling him in his *izibongo* 'Deep one, like pools of the sea!'[12] and

> The black one which is the rich growth of the Mkhumbane [a little stream at Port Natal]
> Where growth becomes so thick that no foot can be put in.[13]

They also saw that he was habitually prudent – 'He who peers into gullies before crossing'[14] – and knew how to keep his mouth shut, an essential quality in a conspirator:

> The reserved one he doesn't speak, he has no mouth
> He is not like Shaka
> Who used to finish a kraal speaking.[15]

Indeed, Isaacs noted that Dingane was 'reserved, even to the extreme, and in speaking seems to weigh every word before he utters it'.[16] The Zulu said he was 'sweet breathed by smelling meat', which meant that his external appearance was deceptive, like the smell of meat which temporarily suppresses bad breath.[17] But underneath his deliberately bland exterior he was unpredictable and dangerous:

> Ox that encircles the homesteads with tears;
> Mamba who when he was down he was up.[18]

Isaacs noted on 1 May 1829 that Dingane's fierce glance was 'keen, quick, and always engaged, nothing escaping him, but every movement and gesture of his people was readily caught, and immediately noticed'. He was quelled by Dingane's exceedingly 'piercing and penetrating eye', which he rolled 'in moments of anger with surprising rapidity'.[19]

Appropriately for a habitual dissembler, Dingane never laughed out loud, but merely gave an amused grunt and nodded his head to and fro. It could be, though, that he did not wish to show his ugly teeth, which were unusually small.[20] When he spoke, it was in the *amalala* style because as a young man he had given his allegiance to the Qwabe (as Shaka had to the Mthethwa) and had lived many years among them. Thus he himself would have pronounced his name as 'Dingane', rather than as 'Dingana', as the *amantungwa* would have done.[21] Like Shaka, he had patches of hair on his body, and was hailed in his praises as

'Dingarn [Dingane] in his ordinary and dancing dresses.' In the central image, he is wearing a cloak of the blue salempore cotton cloth imported from India and favoured by the Zulu elite.

(CAPTAIN ALLEN F GARDINER, *NARRATIVE OF A JOURNEY TO THE ZOOLOO COUNTRY IN SOUTH AFRICA, UNDERTAKEN IN 1835*, 1836)

Hairy-One with hair like a lion's,

Having hair even on the legs.'[22]

Lunguza, who as a child had often seen him, remembered that he had 'the slightest show of whiskers, and a small beard', that he was 'dark brown in colour' and wore the headring. Like many of Senzangakhona's descendants, Dingane had what Lunguza described as 'very large fat thighs and a large neck' but was not flabby, being 'solidly built ... firm and tough'.[23] His '[p]rominent buttocks, handsome posterior!' were acclaimed in his *izibongo*.[24] He had a large, fleshy chin that always sweated. He used to scrape off the drops with his snuff spoon, which was carried by his *inceku* in a basket along with his capacious snuff box fashioned out of a large gourd.[25] Despite Dingane's heavy frame, Isaacs observed with some surprise that he 'exhibited his skill and agility' at dancing, which, Isaacs sourly observed, went with his 'habitual propensity for corporeal pleasures' in the company of the women of his household.[26]

It is to be doubted, however, that Dingane had dancing and singing on his mind when he conferred with his brothers near Ceza Mountain on how they should proceed against Shaka. As Mcotoyi recounted, 'Dingana and the other princes said, "When shall we rule and enjoy peace and contentment? This man Tshaka after all appointed himself. He is not the true or hereditary king."'[27] But, who then was? And who, if the conspirators succeeded in killing Shaka, should succeed him? It seems that when Shaka moved his capital south of the Thukela he entrusted the country to the north of the river to Dingane as his effective viceroy, and that by doing so he was effectively establishing Dingane as his successor. Maclean, as we have seen, believed that Shaka had a 'compact' with Dingane as his inheritor.[28]

However, Dingane had a serious rival. Not only was Mhlangana the tallest of the half-brothers,[29] but, in the view of both Jantshi and Ndongeni (a collateral of the royal house), he was genealogically Shaka's rightful heir. Here again, nothing is as straightforward as it seems, and Ndongeni was biased because his father, Xoki, had been killed by Dingane for supporting Mhlangana's claim. Even so, Mhlangana was probably the rightful *inkosana* because he was born of Mzondwase, Senzangakhona's fifth wife, and was his second-born legitimate son. When Shaka killed Sigujana, the first-born son of Bhibhi, Senzangakhona's eighth but 'great wife', it was Mhlangana who should have succeeded him as the Zulu *inkosi*, and not Shaka.[30] Dingane was the son of Mphikase, Senzangakhona's sixth wife.[31]

Seemingly, Dingane and Mhlangana decided to put the matter of the succession aside until after they had dealt with Shaka. Besides not wishing to open a rift in the ranks of the princely conspirators at this delicate and dangerous moment, they were used to working as a team. Fynn understood this, and alluded to their 'apparent fondness' for each other that was 'so great that one was seldom seen without the other'.[32] But, if Dingane and Mhlangana were willing to work hand in hand along with several others of their brothers, they were not willing to trust all of the *abantwana* serving with the *Bhalule impi*. They left Mpande, son of Songiya, Senzangakhona's ninth wife,[33] whom it seems they considered too weak-spirited to be an effective assassin,[34] to continue north with the army, along with his full brother Nzibe, who was still a stripling. Nzibe subsequently died of *imbo* (malaria) on the campaign. Mpande, who must have been very fond of his promising young sibling, later raised seed for his spirit through the *ukuvuza* custom whereby his eldest son, Hamu, became Nzibe's heir rather than his own.[35] King Cetshwayo, when angry, used to exclaim, '"By the bones of Nzibe in Sotshangana's country!" No one would dare answer and the sky would cloud over.'[36]

Their compact made and their plan formed, the royal conspirators abandoned the army and made their way back towards kwaDukuza. Once in the vicinity of the *ikhanda*, Dingane and Mhlangana entrusted a herd boy they encountered on the veld with a message to Mbopha kaSitayi of the eGazini people, who was Shaka's *inceku*.[37] It was he who had been in on the plot with the princes during their aborted attempt to assassinate Shaka at the Mkhomazi River at the end of the Mpondo campaign, and they needed him again. As Shaka's confidential body servant and one who was in constant personal contact with him, even sharing his food, it was essential to have his support if they were to gain ready access to the king.[38] Even more crucially, Maclean explained, as Shaka's trusted *inceku*, Mbopha was 'the only individual in the Zulu nation who was permitted to carry a spear in the presence of and within a limited distance of the king'.[39]

Here we must reintroduce the formidable figure of Mnkabayi, Shaka's redoubtable aunt, who had twice previously acted as Zulu regent, and who had secured the throne for Shaka. With Nandi's death, this practised kingmaker had become indisputably the matriarch of the Zulu royal house, the Great She-Elephant, or *iNdlovukazi*. Mnkabayi and her twin sister, Mmama, had been Nandi's friends and were convinced that Shaka was responsible for her death. Moreover, they believed that his incessant campaigns and repeated acts of violence were destroying the kingdom. Having once been Shaka's most ardent supporters, it seems that they had now become his covert and malevolent enemies. Her *izibongo* describe Mnkabayi as

> The cunning one
> The cunning one of Hotshoza
> Who destroys one deceiving him with gossip.[40]

She had become a consistent and manipulative voice in Dingane's ear, whispering rebellion, working on his and Mhlangana's well-grounded fears that they would be Shaka's next victims. She also must have woven Mbopha into her plot with effective blandishments. Otherwise, unless he had already been primed, he would surely not have been prepared to sneak out of kwaDukuza and meet the princes clandestinely on the veld,[41] even though, as Fynn recorded, Mbopha was already on very friendly terms with them,[42] and (as we have seen) had stood by them at the Mkhomazi River when for a moment Shaka's life had been in their hands.

Magidigidi, who was born in about 1823 and as a child saw Mbopha, described him as about six foot tall, dark and stout.[43] Maclean remembered him with loathing, 'a cringing and cowardly scoundrel' who abused his confidential position with Shaka to urge the execution of many innocent victims.[44] Now, when he joined the princes, he is reputed to have said:

> 'Hau! So you are here, children of the king? You are troubled by the madman. As soon as you returned from Pondoland the order was given to move on. Are you not going to stab him?' They said, 'What should we do to him?' To which he replied, 'Stab him to death. He is a madman.'[45]

It seems Mnkabayi had already promised Mbopha that if he joined the conspiracy his reward would be a large chiefdom of his own. Overcome by greed and ambition, Mbopha was foolishly taken in.[46] Yet, in being prepared to kill Shaka, it seems he harboured a more personal motive too. Mbopha may have served Shaka dutifully and to his great personal advantage, but, Makewu told Stuart, he was also intent on 'avenging his mother's death at the hands of, or by the direction of, Tshaka'.[47]

So, having confirmed their pact with Mbopha, with Mnkabayi's blessing, Dingane and Mhlangana entered kwaDukuza. Unsurprisingly, Shaka was not best pleased to see them. 'So you are returning on your own?' he asked them sourly.[48] Beset by the profoundest misgivings, deeply suspicious of the princes' motives for leaving the army, and mistrustful of all those in close proximity to him, Shaka's accumulating fears manifested themselves in a dream while he took his habitual nap at midday. According to Fynn, Shaka dreamed he had been killed and that Mbopha was serving another king. The Zulu did not scoff at dreams, since the *amadlozi* communicated through them and warned people against unsuspected enemies and coming dangers. So, when Shaka awoke he confided his dream to the women of his *isigodlo* attending him. By an evil chance for the king, one of them happened to be Mbopha's sister. Knowing that the dream spelled her brother's death, she left Shaka's presence as soon as she was able and hurried to warn her brother that his hours were numbered. There was nothing for it now. Mbopha and the two *abantwana* must strike immediately or suffer their own deaths.[49]

CHAPTER 16

What Is the Matter My Father's Children?

The circumstances surrounding Shaka's assassination are difficult to reconstruct with any unambiguous precision. Writing in the late 1920s, the Rev Alfred Bryant drew attention to the fact that there were no white witnesses to Shaka's death, and that whatever Fynn and other Port Natal traders wrote about it was based entirely on hearsay. The Zulu oral testimony Bryant employed (and that collected by James Stuart) was drawn from those who had been very young at the time, or who had learned about the killing of Shaka from the older generation. Unsurprisingly, Bryant found their testimony conflicting and divergent in details. There was no unanimity, for example, about who actually stabbed Shaka, where he was precisely when attacked and where he fell.[1]

Not even the date of the assassination is certain. Shaka Day, which was subsumed into Heritage Day in South Africa in 1995, is celebrated annually on 24 September. Fynn wrote in his diary that Shaka was killed on that date.[2] Yet Isaacs recorded that a distraught messenger from kwaDukuza brought him the news just after breakfast on 24 September that Shaka had been killed the previous evening, that is, on 23 September.[3] Farewell corroborated that date, twice reporting to the Cape authorities in December 1828 that Shaka had died on 23 September.[4] But, to confuse the picture, on 15 March 1829 he wrote to John Barrow of the Admiralty Office that

'Chaka was murdered by his brothers on 21st September last'.[5] On balance, though, it seems most likely that Shaka was assassinated on Tuesday, 23 September 1828, but we can never be entirely sure.

There is much more certainty about where the assassination took place. It was in the environs of kwaDukuza in the *umuzi* called kwaNyakamubi, built about fifty metres outside the *isigodlo*. At what time of day did the deed take place? Mkehlengana, whose father was at kwaDukuza when Shaka was killed, said it was 'early in the day, before the time at which the assembly usually went up to the king'.[6] Likewise, Dinya said it was in the morning.[7] On the other hand, Maziyana insisted it was at night-time and that torches were alight.[8] The preponderant body of evidence, however, points to the time's being towards sundown, when Shaka was complacently watching his immense herds of cattle being driven homewards for the night, wrapped snugly against the evening chill in one of his woven blankets obtained from the Port Natal traders.[9]

We should not imagine him alone in his pleasant contemplation of his bovine wealth. Serving women from the *isigodlo* were in attendance, and numbers of courtiers were keeping him company. They included Nxazonke kaMbhengi, an elderly uncle of Nandi's, along with several of his Langeni kinsmen, as well as Mxamana kaNtandeka of the Sibisi people. Like Mbopha, Mxamana was one of Shaka's *izinceku* and was also his principal *imbongi*. He was the one who, when he saw vultures overhead, would praise Shaka and say in bloodthirsty anticipation of an execution: 'Your birds are hungry and desire food.'[10]

That evening, Shaka, seated on rolled mats in the open space outside his hut, was routinely receiving a delegation of about ten men. Who exactly were these people? Some (including King Cetshwayo) said they were Mpondo who had come from Faku with a small drove of oxen to pay tribute to Shaka.[11] Others insisted that they were hunters bringing Shaka the crane feathers he had commissioned for his ceremonial garb, along with monkey, genet and otter skins. They were either Tswana from the interior or iziYendane (tributaries from south of the Thukela River) who had arrived from the Mpondoland marches. Whoever they were exactly, Shaka believed they had taken an unconscionable time to fulfil his commission and began to take them to task severely as they cowered before him.[12]

THE ASSASSINATION OF KING SHAKA

It seems that during this hubbub Dingane and Mhlangana approached the king and greeted him, pretending they had just returned from the hunt. King Cetshwayo later declared that four more of their brothers were also in their company, and this is corroborated by the testimony of Matingwana, a boy at the time serving at kwaNyakamubi.[13] Their intention had been to kill Shaka on the spot, but, finding him so surrounded by people, they withdrew to confer anxiously with Mbopha. The *inceku* was up to the occasion.

He directed Dingane and Mhlangana to take up their positions behind the fence of the calf byre in the *umuzi*, their spears held at the ready under their karosses (blankets of animal skins sewn together), while he set about creating a diversion. Carrying a spear of the type usually reserved for killing oxen, Mbopha burst in unexpectedly upon the assembly. He began to belabour the members of the delegation with its shaft, loudly taking over from Shaka in berating them and stridently reproving his courtiers for pestering their master.[14] The members of the delegation crouched before Shaka knew enough of royal courts to suppose that Mbopha was acting at the king's behest, and that Shaka had given him his secret signal ordering their deaths. They leapt up and scattered, running for their lives, leaving uneaten the meat cooking for them.[15] There was general consternation as elderly courtiers struggled to their feet to remonstrate and others began to scatter. Andrew Smith, during his visit to Dingane on 30–31 March 1832, took down notes about what happened next. Shaka, who by now was standing leaning against the calf byre, was rather enjoying the commotion. Nevertheless, he sternly asked Mbopha why he had intervened and taken it upon himself to drive people out of his presence.[16]

There are divergent versions as to what happened next, all strongly coloured by the subsequent apportionment of blame based on clashing political agendas. Who actually killed Shaka: Mbopha, Mhlangana, Dingane or all three? And were they joined, as Matingwana attested, by two more of the princes, Ngqojana and Sophane?[17] It is ducking the issue to go along with Maziyana and say that they all 'hurled assegais at him. He was not stabbed at close quarters.'[18]

There were those who pinned the major role on Mbopha. Maclean was convinced that because Mbopha alone carried a spear he 'stole behind and assassinated his master'.¹⁹ Despite the active participation of the two *abantwana*, Isaacs had no doubt that it was Mbopha who actually 'speared him to death'.²⁰ Some oral traditions similarly pointed the finger at Mbopha. Makewu related that when Shaka turned his back on Mbopha the *inceku* threw a spear, which struck him,²¹ while Ndukwana stated it was Mbopha who 'actually stabbed'.²² Likewise, Jantshi declared that it was Mbopha who stabbed Shaka, though he had the integrity to admit that he was not in a position to 'speak accurately on this matter'.²³

Others believed it was Mhlangana who stabbed first, including Jantshi, thus contradicting his assertion that it was Mbopha.²⁴ It was said the brothers had agreed that Mhlangana would strike first because Dingane was sickened of killing after witnessing Shaka's constant executions. Mhlangana undertook to stab Shaka in the armpit, which would cause instant death, but on account of the blanket he was wearing only succeeded in piercing him through the arm or, alternatively, the back of his left shoulder.²⁵ Andrew Smith heard that Mhlangana stabbed his brother twice in the back.²⁶

What, then, of Dingane, who had masterminded the conspiracy? Fynn and Isaacs believed that, as soon as Mhlangana had struck Shaka, Dingane also closed in and stabbed him too.²⁷ Alternatively, Makewu was told that Shaka pulled out Mbopha's spear and tried to run out of the *umuzi*, past where another man was lying in wait for him at the gateway.²⁸ Andrew Smith identified that person as Dingane, who gave Shaka another wound and followed him for about twenty metres until he fell, whereupon he stabbed his dying brother again.²⁹ However, there was also a strong tradition that Dingane did not actually shed his brother's blood. When Shaka cast off the blanket wrapped around him in his attempt to escape his assassins' spears,³⁰ Dingane is supposed merely to have laid hold of him to prevent his flight.³¹

How did Shaka comport himself as the conspirators fell upon him with their spears? Mbopha had ensured that Shaka would not be able to defend himself by hiding away the spears in the king's hut while he was outside washing.³² But, when first stabbed, Shaka was in any case in the open, away from his hut. Unarmed, his only option was to attempt to break loose from his killers and escape out of the kwaNyakamubi *umuzi* towards the shelter of the *isigodlo* in nearby kwaDukuza. He never gained this sanctuary and died a short way outside kwaNyakamubi. But are we to believe it was in his character to beg his assassins for mercy, whimpering, 'Leave me alone, sons of my father, and I shall be your menial'?[33] In any case, it was the firm Zulu belief that, if you happened to be fighting your brother and he called out for mercy, you would not live long and misfortune would overcome you should you spare him.[34] So the assassins were remorseless with 'the evildoer who kills the wives of men who are away [with the *Bhalule impi*]',[35] finishing him off with more spear thrusts.

However, we can be fairly certain that they did not keep on stabbing his corpse, as was done ritually (*ukuhlomula*) with an enemy who had died courageously or with a ferocious wild beast such as a lion. Nor would they have observed the ritual of slitting open his belly so that the evil influence of *umnyama* would not make them swell up like the dead. For, in the case of killing a near relation, these rituals were not observed. Instead, their spears were not withdrawn and were left sticking into the body.[36]

The accounts closest to the time of his death are in agreement that Shaka only had time to gasp, incredulously, 'What is the matter my father's children?'[37] before choking on his blood and collapsing to the ground as he tried to break free. However, the temptation to ascribe significant last words to celebrities is universal, especially if they can be interpreted retrospectively as prophetic. And that in turn means they must be formulated long enough afterwards to ring true. That was certainly so in Shaka's case. The most succinct, and those that most immediately came to pass, were the ones purportedly addressed to Dingane and Mhlangana, and repeated by King Mpande's grandson, Mkebeni kaDabulamanzi (born in the 1860s): 'Are you stabbing me, the king of the earth? You will come to an end through killing one another.'[38] Otherwise, Shaka's prophetic last words all refer to the impending rule of the white men.[39] They are frequently referred to as 'swallows' because they 'come up from the sea' like those migratory birds, and because swallows also build their houses of mud.[40] In 1902, Mkando, who was born in about 1827, gave voice to the fulfilment of Shaka's dying prophecy in the bitterest of terms: 'When Tshaka died he said the white men would overrun the land; the whole land would be white with the light of the stars; it would be overrun by "swallows". We are your dogs.'[41]

CHAPTER 17

You Were Warned

Pandemonium broke out at kwaNyakamubi when the assassins fell upon Shaka with their spears. Courtiers scrambled to make their escape into the surrounding bush, because they knew it was customary for a ruler's closest associates to be killed on his death lest they oppose his successor.¹ Indeed, it does seem that the assassins and their associates quickly killed Nandi's uncle, Nxazonke. They also did away with Shaka's notorious and voluble *imbongi*, Mxamana kaNtandeka, who rushed to the dying king's aid and tried to help him up while heaping the vilest curses he could muster on the heads of his killers.² It seems a few courtiers did stand firm, including Sothobe. They seized their spears and contemplated attacking the three assassins. But the killers succeeded in talking them over and they withdrew to kwaDukuza or, like Sothobe, made for home.³

Left almost alone at the scene of the killing, the assassins rounded up a few men to raise the *ihubo*, a sacred ballad honouring the mighty deeds of the ancestors. They then sacrificed a black ox from the kwaNyakamubi herd in thanksgiving to Senzangakhona's mighty shade and to those of the other royal ancestors. All the *umndlunkulu* sallied out of the *isigodlo* and joined in the ceremony, some happily enough, others crying in fright, if not grief. While they danced, they sang: "'You were warned in the Mtetwa country, at the place of Ndiminde'" (at the place of those of the long tongue, those who tefula).⁴

THE ASSASSINATION OF KING SHAKA

After the sacrifice, Dingane and Mhlangana became involved in a dispute that laid bare the smouldering rivalry they had succeeded in damping down while Shaka still lived. The gall of the sacrificed beast, mixed with the contents of its paunch, was drunk by those who had killed it and the remainder was sprinkled over the bodies of those present to ward off the evil taint of *umnyama*. The depleted bladder was then worn on the arm of the chief man who had performed the sacrifice. Each of the two brothers angrily insisted on his superior right to do so. Mbopha quickly intervened and pacified the pair by suggesting a temporary expedient. Until the *Bhalule impi* returned and made known which of the princes it favoured as Shaka's successor, he, Mbopha, would act as an interim regent. The few people still lingering at kwaNyakamubi then dutifully acclaimed him, although it remained to be seen whether this scrambled arrangement would long pass muster.[5]

There was no mourning for Shaka.[6] His body was left all night where it had fallen. Scavenging hyenas did not trouble it because, the Zulu believed, they never touched the corpse of a king.[7] When morning came, a decision had to be taken concerning the disposal of the bloodied and already stiff cadaver. Mhlangana is said to have proposed that it be dragged to a pool in the nearby river and fed to the crocodiles. However, those of Shaka's attendants who had not yet fled insisted it must be buried properly as custom demanded, and Dingane concurred.[8]

The sanitised version of Shaka's interment – which draws essentially on Fynn's second-hand account – would have us believe that Shaka was entombed without all the ceremony that normally attended a royal burial. If this were so, no close companion would have been killed (as was customary) to follow Shaka into the spirit world to wait upon him there and keep him company. Nor would a special royal grave have been prepared. We are to believe that Shaka's body was unceremoniously lowered into an empty grain pit in the *isibaya* at kwaNyakamubi and his blanket laid over him.[9]

Zulu testimony, however, tells it rather differently. The spears were removed from Shaka's corpse and it was wrapped up in the skin of the black ox the brothers had previously sacrificed. It was then removed to a hut in the *umuzi*. Following the ancient custom, the body was placed in a sitting position tied to the central pole of the hut. Relatives kept it company at night and the inhabitants of kwaNyakamubi performed the funeral rites.

The corpse remained putrefying in the funeral hut and was not finally buried until all his personal belongings and the private things that had ever touched him – his loin-covers, dancing dress, beads and brass ornaments, food dishes and utensils – had been collected up from across the kingdom to join him in the grave. Most were probably burned beforehand, and others (in accordance to custom) placed up against both sides of the body, but not in front of or behind it.[10]

However, Shaka's spears were not laid in the grave with him. No Zulu would ever put a spear 'in the hands of a dead man' lest his *idlozi* be angry – and Shaka's had every reason to be so – and mystically stab living people, causing them to bleed from the mouth and die.[11] Certainly, Shaka's killers were in fear of his malevolent spirit, and ordered that all the surrounding empty grain pits be thoroughly closed up so that the *idlozi* could not find a channel of escape and wreak his vengeance on them.[12] Fynn recorded that, as an extra precaution, a piece of his buttock covering was placed in Shaka's mouth to repress his *idlozi*'s anger.[13]

When Shaka came to be buried, certainly in the customary sitting position, he was accompanied – as his royal status demanded – by a number of attendants of elite status. This *umgando*, as the group of victims was called, included Nandi's uncle, Nxazonke, and his *imbongi*, Mxamana, both of whom the assassins had killed immediately after Shaka. Ntendeka, the *induna* of kwaDlangezwa, joined them. Several others, through wounded, managed to make good their escape. Ngunuza kaNsiyana, one of Nxazonke's Langeni companions, realising he was about to be killed, scrambled up onto Shaka's hut and started praising him. This brought his assailants to a surprised halt. Ngunuza then suddenly leapt down, and broke through them, stabbing some as he went. He was said to have escaped to Faku.[14]

A heap of stones was raised over Shaka's grave and a hut built over it. As was customary, the inmates of the *umuzi* where he had perished and the people employed at his burial were posted there as guards. They were supplied with cattle and grain for their subsistence, since they were forbidden to abandon their watch on pain of death. Their isolation did not last for too long. The Zulu believed that after a few months the spirit of the dead ruler, who was buried in the *umuzi* where he had died, should be brought back (*buyisa*) at a great feast, propitiated with copious sacrifices and then requested to permit itself to be conveyed to a new spirit home, or *umuzi wedlozi*. Dingane, who was extremely anxious to evade the ravening fury of his brother's *idlozi*, performed this ceremony as soon as was appropriate.

In 1829, when Dingane established his new chief *ikhanda*, uMgungundlovu, in the emaKhosini valley, he rebuilt kwaDukuza close by as the abode for Shaka's spirit. When in 1843 King Mpande subsequently built his principal *ikhanda*, kwaNodwengu, in the Mahlabathini plain across the White Mfolozi from the emaKhosini valley, he made sure to rebuild kwaDukuza nearby as Shaka's new *umuzi wedlozi*.[15] On 26 June 1879 the British burned kwaDukuza during the final stages of the Anglo-Zulu War. It was never rebuilt, and Shaka's *idlozi* no longer had a spirit home.

As for the grave where Shaka's body lay buried at the abandoned kwaNyakamubi, a small *umuzi* was built close by so that its inhabitants would be on hand to care for the site.[16] In February 1829, JC Chase, on an overland expedition to Delagoa Bay, passed 'Chaka's sepulchre, which is built up with stones and protected by a mimosa fence, renewed monthly'.[17] The grave continued to be tended regularly until 1844, only sixteen years after Shaka's death. In that year, the British, who had annexed Natal on 12 May 1843, with its northern boundary fixed at the Thukela,[18] began allocating the land as farms to colonists. Shaka's grave was situated in the grant parcelled out to one T Potgieter. In 1873, the Surveyor General of Natal, William Stanger, laid out a village (named Stanger after him) on the site of kwaDukuza.[19] The whereabouts of the grave were largely forgotten, although not by all. Makewu told Stuart in 1899 that the abandoned grave still had a thorn tree growing out of it. It was situated at the side of the house built by WD Wheelwright, who had been the resident magistrate of the Lower Tugela division from 1887 to 1889, close to the magistracy that had been erected on the site of the *isigodlo* at kwaDukuza.[20]

PART V

The Wild Beasts of Jama Have Killed One Another

CHAPTER 18

The One With the Red Assegai Shall Not Rule

The Port Natal traders fell into a panic when word reached them, on 24 September 1828, that Shaka had been assassinated by his brothers. Anticipating that Shaka's violent death would unleash a civil war and that they would be caught up in the ensuing mayhem, they hurried in from their scattered settlements and prepared to make a desperate defence of the Port. The schooner *Elizabeth and Susan* was drawn up on the beach being caulked, but they rushed to make it ready for sailing. On 25 September they bundled their effects on board for fear that they would have to evacuate Port Natal. Isaacs recorded that for several days the traders hunkered down in 'a state of unpleasant suspense and alarm'.[1] Then, on 28 September, messengers arrived from Dingane and Mhlangana with soothing words. The princes, they said, trusted 'the white people would not be displeased' and would 'not mourn the death of a tyrant' who intended to attack Port Natal once the *Bhalule impi* returned, and then to go on to invade the Cape Colony. The princes, the messengers continued, assured the traders of their friendship and protection, and undertook that they would treat them better than Shaka had ever done. Above all, they entreated them not to leave.[2]

But over the next two months the situation failed to stabilise. The traders knew that the succession remained undecided, that there were many disaffected members of the royal house and Shaka's court who had to be mollified or dealt with, and that the compliance of the *Bhalule impi*, which had not yet returned, had to be secured. So, deciding that a temporary withdrawal was prudent, most of the traders took passage on the *Elizabeth and Susan*, which sailed on 1 December 1828 for Port Elizabeth. Before they left, Dingane and Mhlangana entrusted Farewell with a verbal message for the Cape officials, which he passed on the moment the schooner arrived on 15 December.³ The princes were anxious to appease the British, being well aware that they were 'offended' by Shaka's attack on Faku and the Mpondo. Their message therefore assured the Cape officials that 'now Chaka was dead, they wished to live on friendly terms with every nation and by no means would do anything to displease them'.⁴

When the two *abantwana* declared to the Cape officials that their intentions were entirely pacific, they did so in the knowledge that, with the *Bhalule impi* still away, their military resources were very limited. The only military force they had at their disposal was the *ibutho* of untried youths, the iziNyosi, or Bees, that Shaka had recently raised. To augment the iziNyosi they immediately formed a new *ibutho*, the uHlomendlini, or Home Guards, divided by age into two companies of older and younger men. As their commander, they appointed Nongalaza kaNondela, the Nyandwini *inkosi* who would later rise to become one of Dingane's leading generals. The uHlomendlini was a scratch force made up of men who had evaded joining the *Bhalule impi* and several hundred iziYendane, the 'mop-headed' menials and cattle guards serving in the *amakhanda* and cattle posts south of the Thukela. Fearing that the Mpondo, Bhaca and other neighbours would be tempted to raid Zulu territory for cattle now that Shaka was dead, the princes deployed uHlomendlini to round up and bring northwards all the royal herds from as far south as the Mzimkhulu River.⁵

Dingane and Mhlangana had each taken up residence in his own *ikhanda*. They were abiding by the agreement reached, as soon as Shaka was dead, that Mbopha would function as an interim regent until the *izikhulu*, people and the returned army formally recognised one or the other of them as king. But, while they nervously trod water, the two princes eyed each other with increasing distrust and antagonism, their old intimacy shrivelling in the heat of mutual suspicion and intensifying ambition. It was inevitable, therefore, that they fell out over small matters of protocol and over the greater issue of how to dispose of the cattle the uHlomendlini brought north with them. For cattle were wealth and power, which each increasingly wished to deny the other.[6]

On one matter, though, they quickly agreed. Isaacs noted on 6 October 1828 that Ngwadi kaNgendeyana, Shaka's half-brother by Nandi, had mourned for Shaka and seemed to be disposed to challenge the two princes for the royal *umqulu*.[7] Shaka had allowed Ngwadi to rule in a semi-independent manner in the country around the Mkhumbane River, just inland from Port Natal, where he had amassed great herds of cattle and even had his own little army, which had been exempted from the mobilisation for the *Bhalule impi*. Dingane and Mhlangana realised that Ngwadi posed a real threat to their aspirations, and feared that he might be favoured by the army when it returned, even if it seemed that he was likely to perpetuate Shaka's repressive mode of rule.[8] Ngwadi's immediate elimination was therefore deemed essential.[9]

The news reached Isaacs on 2 November 1828 that Ngwadi had been defeated and killed.[10] The two princes had placed Mbopha in command of a joint force of the uHlomendlini and iziNyosi. Since Ngwadi's private army was supposed to be of greater strength than Mbopha's combined force, he determined to take it by surprise. He led his men inland and then swung around to invade Ngwadi's domain from an unexpected direction. During the night, he stealthily surrounded Ngwadi's kwaWambaza *umuzi*, which had been turned into a veritable fortress with a thick, high fence of tree trunks and thorns. Mbopha attacked at dawn with the uHlomendlini. Not nearly as many warriors as expected were within kwaWambaza, but they defended it with such verve that they repulsed the uHlomendlini again and again. Mbopha then sent in his iziNyosi reserves and they finally swarmed over the palisade into the *isigodlo*.

The defenders fought stoutly to the death, and their womenfolk died with them. Ngwadi is said to have cut down eight of his assailants before being stabbed in the back by one of the iziNyosi lads. Ngwadi and his following were eliminated, but the attackers also suffered crippling casualties, especially the iziNyosi, and the princes were left with a severely reduced armed force of their own.[11] In a carefully considered gesture, therefore, they sent the cattle they had captured from Ngwadi to the starving *Bhalule impi*, still making its way home and deliberately loitering for fear of reporting back to Shaka without any booty.[12] At the same time they informed the army that Shaka had been killed.[13]

Still the days passed without the choice of a successor to Shaka. Mbopha continued to rule '*pro tempore*' as Farewell expressed it on his arrival in Port Elizabeth in mid-December, and the Zulu kingdom remained unsettled and dangerously on edge.[14] However, Farewell was confident that with Ngwadi's death the way was open for Dingane to be chosen as king.[15] As early as 28 September Isaacs had 'ascertained that Dingān's proceedings were quite acceptable to the people, and that there was little doubt of his being pronounced king on the arrival of the commando [*Bhalule impi*]'.[16]

Mhlangana did not see it that way and continued to insist he had a better claim than Dingane, not least because he insisted he had taken the most active part in killing Shaka. He had jumped over Shaka's corpse as Shaka himself had leapt over Phakathwayo, thus proclaiming that he was the murdered king's conqueror and successor.[17] However, it was this vaunting assertion that finally undid him when, in late November, the senior members of the royal house and the great nobles of the realm were summoned to meet and discuss the succession.[18]

The consultation took place before one of the first men of the country, Ngqengelele kaMvulana. He had been a confidant of Shaka's, and the king had raised his protégé to great heights and appointed him *inkosi* of the Buthelezi people. Also present were Noncoba, Shaka's half-sister by Nandi, and his aunt Mnkabayi. The last-mentioned's formidable presence dominated the meeting and, in Jantshi's words, 'Dingana was made king by Mkabayi'.[19] She successfully brought Mhlangana's genealogical claim into question, waspishly inquiring: 'Is the child of Myiyeya's [that is, Mphikase, Dingane's mother] not the child of someone of importance?'[20] Of even greater weight, though, was the argument formulated by Mnkabayi and seconded by Noncoba that a man who had killed his king was not fit to rule. Ngqengelele weightily agreed, and it was decreed that 'The one with the red assegai shall not rule'.[21]

What, then, about Dingane and his undeniable part in the assassination? It was decided, through an act of legalistic legerdemain, that he was fit to rule because he had only caught hold of his brother while the other two stabbed him, and was therefore not guilty of shedding Shaka's blood.[22] Not unnaturally, Dingane *giya*'d (performed a war dance) in triumph on learning of this decision, for the way was now clear for him to be declared king.[23]

But what was to be done with Mhlangana? He had a large body of support, and it was likely that when he learned he had been passed over in favour of Dingane he would spark a civil war. It was to stave off this eventuality that Mnkabayi and Ngqengelele resolved that Mhlangana must be put to death, the justification being that he had instigated Shaka's murder and carried it out.[24] Yet to act openly against Mhlangana also carried the risk that he and his followers would resort to arms. Moreover, although rivals, Dingane and Mhlangana had long been very close, and it was not certain that Dingane would tamely acquiesce in his brother's execution.

So Mnkabayi devised a cunning stratagem. Mbopha, who now knew which one of the two *abantwana* was to be declared king, played his nefarious part. He set about deliberately whipping up discord between the brothers, convincing each of them that the other was plotting his death. Dingane at length decided on a pre-emptive strike, egged on and assisted by his aunt. In a treacherous show of reconciliation, Dingane invited Mhlangana to go bathing with him in the Mavivane, a stream close by kwaDukuza. Mhlangana would have done well to recall that this was precisely the ploy Ngwadi had adopted when he murdered Sigujana to clear the way for Shaka. As on that occasion, Dingane and Mhlangana had agreed not to bring their armed followers with them. But Mnkabayi's men were concealed at the spot, and sprang out to drown Mhlangana. It is said that the *umntwana*, realising too late that he had been betrayed, cried out, 'Nhi! Son of Sitayi [Mbopha], have you done this to me?'[25] Dingane's *izibongo* recalled the deed in these chilling words:

> Deep river pool at Mavivane, Dingana,
> The Pool is silent, and overpowering,
> It drowned someone intending to wash
> And he vanished, headring and all.[26]

CHAPTER 19

Wizard Whose Liver Is Black

A week or so after Mhlangana's death, and some two months after Shaka's assassination, the *Bhalule impi* began drifting home in small, dispirited groups. It would be several months more before the last stragglers came in.[1] Since abandoning its offensive against Soshangane, it had withdrawn towards Zululand through the malarial coastal lands, pursued by the Gaza, who killed all those unable to keep up.[2] The defeated army was out of supply, and so desperate was their privation that the warriors 'had no shields, for most of them, having no food, had been obliged to soak them in water and eat them!'[3] They had few effective spears either, for they had been driven to gnawing away the bullock sinews by which the blades were fastened to the hafts.[4] Eventually they reached the lands of the Tsonga, tributaries of the Zulu king, who were able to supply them. But by then their condition was pitiful and their losses had been catastrophic, reducing the army 'to a mere nominal force'.[5]

It is impossible to say just how many men the *Bhalule impi* lost. The assertion of the Port Natal traders, that the army had been 30 000 men strong, probably more than doubled its actual size, but their estimate that casualties added up to two-thirds of the original number is not unrealistic.[6] Isaacs was probably also close to the mark when he calculated that, for every man who had died in the fighting, three had perished from sickness, starvation and exhaustion. In all, it was, as Isaacs reflected, 'the most signal defeat of the Zoolas had ever sustained'.[7]

The army arrived back to find that Shaka was dead, and that Dingane, with the support of the *izikhulu*, had stepped into his place. He was calling himself Malamulela (Intervener) because he had intervened between the people and the madness of Shaka.[8] Indeed, he had moved very cannily and swiftly to win popular approval. Isaacs noted as early as 21 October 1828 that Dingane had already abolished most of Shaka's 'ferocious customs' and, most importantly, he had decreed that he would allow unmarried *amabutho* freely to enjoy premarital sex and would permit several of the older *amabutho* to assume the headring, take wives and set up as adult homestead heads. He also relaxed military discipline and ensured that warriors serving at the *amakhanda* were well supplied with meat.[9] Consequently, Dingane did not find it difficult to win over the dispirited remnants of the *Bhalule impi* and persuade them to accept – or, at least, not to oppose – his succession.

With that assurance, the day of *ukubuzana* could be held. This, King Cetshwayo explained to the Cape Commissioners in 1883, was the day of ceremonial questioning when 'all the great men of the country assemble and talk to one another about the heir, whom they look upon as king already'. They say to each other, continued Cetshwayo, '"You must take care of this king and not act out of an evil heart against him."' Having agreed among themselves, they would then send a deputation to the *inkosana*, inviting him to leave the *ikhanda* where he had been living as prince and to transfer to the former king's chief *ikhanda* 'as king'.[10] And so it was with Dingane, at about forty years of age the undisputed *inkosana* chosen (it must be said) by Mnkabayi and acclaimed as king by the nation.

Isaacs wrote of Dingane only a few months later, on 29 April 1829: 'He never sought to gratify the feelings of revenge from the mere love of cruelty, though at times he was implacable, and perhaps unrelenting.'[11] Dingane's innate cruelty is debatable but, be that as it may, for a Zulu king killing was a necessary act of state. Nzobo kaSobadli, the portly and notoriously ill-tempered personage whom Dingane raised to be one of the principal men in the kingdom,[12] and who seemed adept at strengthening Dingane's resolve whenever he was inclined to mercy or compromise, stated the case uncompromisingly: 'The killing of people is a proper practice, for if no killing is done there will be no fear.'[13] Dingane took Nzobo's admonition to heart, and it was not long before he was emulating Shaka and declaring that 'vultures had come to attend the men's assembly and must therefore be given food (i.e. corpses of human beings)'.[14]

As King Cetshwayo bleakly put it, his uncle 'Dingaan commenced his career as king by killing all his brothers, except Panda [Mpande, Cetshwayo's father], also his brothers' principal chiefs and friends, with all their women and children … At least eighty people thus perished.'[15] Unabashed, Dingane's praises crowed:

> Hornless calf of the daughter of Donda, [ancestor of Mphikase,
> Dingane's mother]
> That went and kicked the other calves,
> And blood flowed from their nostrils.[16]

In some Zulu eyes, extensive fratricide might have made Dingane 'a bad king'.[17] Nevertheless, most Zulu subsequently understood that Dingane, having already had a hand in killing both Shaka and Mhlangana, naturally feared his surviving brothers would conspire in turn to assassinate him.[18] In his *izibongo* Dingane is called 'Wizard whose liver is black, even among his father's children'. An actual *umthakathi*, or wizard, was loathed and feared, but in metaphorical terms a 'wizard' denoted a person with amazing powers, while a 'black liver' meant profound courage. Dingane was therefore being lauded for his resolve in purging his brothers, whom his praises go on to list in order of seniority: Mhlangana, Ngqojana, Mdungazwe, Somajuba, Sophane and Mfihlo.[19]

Ngqojana, an *umntwana* whom the missionary Captain Allen Gardiner described as an engaging and intelligent man with unassuming manners, evaded execution until 1835. His crime, Dingane being childless, was that he stood next in line to the succession after the drowned Mhlangana.[20] Of his remaining brothers, Dingane spared Gqugqu, Senzangakhona's youngest, who was still a small boy and no threat as yet.[21] Mpande also escaped execution, and for his survival was subsequently hailed in his praises as 'The brass rod which remained from the other sticks'.[22]

Mpande, it will be remembered, had not been brought into the conspiracy to kill Shaka, and had instead continued to serve with the *Bhalule impi* throughout the disastrous campaign. Why Dingane did not now kill the 30-year-old prince along with his brothers is not entirely clear. One likely reason is that he was not considered eligible to succeed Shaka because he was 'of the *umsizi* hut'.[23] During the annual *umkhosi* festival, the king was daubed with *umsizi* (powdered ritual medicines) and had sex with one of the women of his *isigodlo* in a specially prepared hut. Any child born of this intercourse was accepted as a member of the royal house, but of inferior rank. Otherwise, it seems that there was consensus that Mpande was a simpleton (*isitutana*), and Dingane's councillors persuaded him that there was little point in killing him since he could never be a danger. So Dingane gave him a hundred cattle and ordered him to build his own *ikhanda* in the country between the Mhlathuze and Thukela rivers.[24]

Having disposed of his brothers, Dingane next turned his lethal attention to Shaka's henchmen. He did not act immediately, however. Fynn explained that many Zulu believed Shaka still to be alive, and regarded Dingane's succession merely as a cunning ruse to test their loyalty, as in the horrific days after Nandi's death. Knowing this, and aware that many Zulu who did accept that Shaka was really dead nevertheless 'deeply deplored' his assassination, Dingane decided to allow Shaka's officers to retain their positions until he believed his grasp on power was secure. Then it would be time enough to purge them and bring in his own loyalists. Most notable among these was the renowned warrior Ndlela kaSompisi, the brother of Bhibhi, the mother of Sigujana, whom Shaka had killed on his way to the kingship. A kindly and temperate man, he became Dingane's chief councillor and commander-in-chief.[25]

Dingane did not hesitate long in ridding himself of Shaka's close associates, or of some prominent *amakhosi* simply because they were too powerful and might resist his rule. Mdlaka, Shaka's seasoned military commander, had to go. According to one tradition, Mdlaka, secure in his prestigious reputation, had the temerity, once he returned with the remnants of the army, to tax Dingane with Shaka's murder. He was even arrogant enough to make known that he favoured Mpande over Dingane as king. But, according to King Cetshwayo, Mpande frantically distanced himself, saying, 'Let Dingaan, who killed him, be king.'[26] Dingane could not allow Mdlaka's challenge to go unanswered, especially since he wielded such influence in the army. So the general found himself one of the new king's earliest victims. On the other hand, there is an alternative but unlikely tradition maintaining that Dingane allowed Mdlaka to retire into obscurity.[27] Either way, he was quickly out of the picture. The same went for Ngomane, Shaka's chief councillor. He had been absent from kwaDukuza at the moment of Shaka's assassination, and had then fled for his life. Perhaps believing him too prestigious to kill, Dingane permitted him to live out his days in retirement.[28]

Many other prominent confederates of Shaka's were not so fortunate and were soon feeding the vultures.[29] Perhaps the unluckiest of all was Magaye, the Cele *inkosi* and Shaka's powerful viceroy south of the Thukela. He was probably a marked man in any case, but his misfortune was to be drawn into the final debacle of the Qwabe, Shaka's longstanding antagonists and victims.

Nqetho kaKhondlo, the younger brother of Phakathwayo, the Qwabe *inkosi* whom Shaka had killed, was (as we have seen) a great favourite of the king's. His situation under Dingane was likely to be uncomfortable at the very least, and he and a large section of the Qwabe revolted in early 1829 against the still insecurely established new monarch. Driving their great herds of cattle with them, including many royal cattle, the Qwabe migrated southwards out of the Zulu realm to the lands between the Mzimkhulu and Mzimvubu rivers. This was Mpondo and Bhaca territory, and in 1830 they eventually destroyed and scattered the destructive Qwabe host. Dingane was enraged by the loss of so many subjects and their wealth in cattle, and feared others might be encouraged to break free of Zulu rule. He blamed Magaye for not doing enough to prevent the defection of the Qwabe through his domain. In about February 1829, he dispatched the uHlomendlini to execute him, along with his brothers, near his ekuKekezeni *umuzi* on the banks of the iNanda River.[30]

Dingane replaced Magaye with his son Mkhonto, but soon executed him in turn. He then entrusted the region south of the Thukela to Sothobe, the one great survivor from Shaka's reign, who had so astutely thrown his hand in with the conspirators. Until the invasion of the Voortrekkers in 1838,

Sothobe governed his domain from kwaNobamba, his *umuzi* just south of the middle reaches of the Thukela.[31]

As had been promised him when Mnkabayi first drew him into the plot against Shaka, Mbopha was raised to be an *inkosi* south of the Mhlathuze. But, as a regicide who had betrayed his position of trust as Shaka's *inceku*, he could not be allowed to live and prosper. Dingane had additional cause to distrust him. He remembered just how effectively Mbopha had manipulated him and Mhlangana during the few months he had held the balance between them, and that he had played his reprehensible part in Mhlangana's death. Conveniently, Mbopha also made the perfect scapegoat for Shaka's death, and the returning army was satisfied by his execution.[32]

What of the Port Natal traders, with whose affairs Shaka had been so closely connected and they with his, perhaps even to the extent of being complicit in the conspiracy against him? Dingane understood that the traders were not faithful subjects, and that their objective was to establish Port Natal and the surrounding region as an autonomous base for their commercial activities. However, he valued their trade goods and connections with the Cape too much to try to evict them from his domain. And, even more than Shaka, he respected the military value of firearms. He began procuring them in increasing numbers through the Port and regularly called on the traders (as had Shaka) to provide military support during his campaigns.

As a consequence, the traders remained ensconced at Port Natal during Dingane's reign, even if relations with the Zulu monarch were often strained to breaking point. Twice, in 1831 and 1833, the traders evacuated the Port for fear of their lives, only for Dingane to lure them back with soft words and assurances. The settlement continued to grow, now that Cape merchants were increasingly eager to open up trade with Zululand, so that by 1838 there were about forty white traders at the Port. But most of these were new people, and almost all the original hunter-traders who had been there at the time of Shaka's assassination had left the scene.

Farewell was bringing trade goods overland from the Cape when he was killed in late September 1829 by Nqetho of the Qwabe, who believed he was spying for the Zulu. Cane and Henry Ogle (one of the original Port Natal traders) appropriated his cattle. Isaacs quit the Port for the last time in 1831 and became a clandestine slave dealer in West Africa. He died in

England in 1872. Fynn gave up his business connections in Port Natal in 1834 and entered the Cape colonial service. Between 1849 and 1852 he was British Resident with Faku. He then moved to British Natal and served as a resident magistrate, dying in his house on the Bluff at Durban (formerly Port Natal) in 1861. Cane, who remained at Port Natal through thick and thin, was with the traders who allied with the Voortrekkers in their war against Dingane, and was killed in battle in April 1838.

CHAPTER 20

Did You Not Bring Harm to Yourself?

Dingane was temperamentally a very different man from Shaka, and had seemed to hold out the promise for a reign of quite another sort. But once he was king he found himself following closely in his assassinated brother's footsteps. It was simply not possible for the ruler of the Zulu kingdom to do otherwise, since its structure and situation had not changed with Shaka's death. Dingane may have deplored Shaka's intemperate slaughter of his subjects, but, as we have seen, he had no option but to follow Nzobo's stern admonition that killing remained essential for a ruler. And, as it was with the bloody purge of his brothers and Shaka's close associates, so was it with many other matters.

Dingane had been uneasy with Shaka's centring of the kingdom in such close proximity to Port Natal, because it gave the traders an inordinate degree of influence over Zulu policy. Consequently, on becoming king he immediately moved the hub of the kingdom away from kwaDukuza and back north across the Thukela River to its traditional core in the emaKhosini valley. There, in 1829, he built his new great place, uMgungundlovu, where he kept up precisely the same royal state as had Shaka, down to kwaNkatha, the dread place of execution just outside the main gate into the *ikhanda*. At the very beginning of his reign he had expressed his intention to abolish his *isigodlo*, explaining that it was 'a bad institution' because it 'was the cause of people being put to death'. But his powerful *induna*, Nzobo, quickly poured water on that unroyal foible, briskly inquiring, 'How, without one, can you be a king?'[1]

Settled at uMgungundlovu, then, where everything was as it had been at kwaDukuza, Dingane very soon realised that he could not afford to relax his hold on the southern marches of his kingdom as he had initially intended. Port Natal remained the key to the region, and it was disturbing that the traders were eagerly attracting refugees from Dingane's realm to build up their following. As a consequence, not only was Port Natal fast becoming a troublesome nest of Zulu malcontents but also, even more alarmingly, the traders were training many of them as musketeers.

To put a stop to this haemorrhaging away of his subjects, Dingane had to reverse his initial policy. The redoubtable Sothobe brought the people of the southern reaches of the middle Thukela under his close supervision, and the inhabitants of the coastal lands were ordered to withdraw north of the Thukela. The uHlomendlini were stationed in southern Zululand to guard the heartland from Port Natal and to prevent the seeping away of any more refugees there. As with Shaka, Dingane also attempted to control the traders – much to their shrill indignation – by periodically imposing trade restrictions to keep them in line.

Like Shaka, Dingane wished to open diplomatic relations with the British at the Cape. He desired to reassure them of his pacific intentions and to facilitate trade. Taking a leaf out of Shaka's book, he added the bait of requesting a missionary to instruct him. He chose John Cane to convey this message. As he had when leading Shaka's second embassy in 1828, Cane and his party travelled overland to the Cape. They reached Grahamstown on 21 November 1830, but got no further. This time, the Civil Commissioner of Albany and Somerset refused to treat with Cane or to accept the 'four elephant's teeth' Dingane had sent as a present.[2] The humiliating failure of this mission infuriated Dingane, who did not attempt to negotiate with the Cape again.

In his spurned message to the Cape authorities, Dingane had expressed his intention of living 'in peace and harmony' with his neighbours, but he was no more able to do that than was Shaka. In 1830, he dispatched a military expedition south against the Bhaca to recover the cattle (including

DID YOU NOT BRING HARM TO YOURSELF?

royal herds) they had captured from Nqetho's fugitive Qwabe. The raid was unsuccessful, and a second attempt in 1833 fared no better. But Dingane required – no less than Shaka – to keep his *amabutho* employed and well rewarded, and his *izikhulu* contented with the redistribution of booty. So attacks on other neighbours continued. To the west, in 1830 and 1832 he campaigned against Mzilikazi and the Ndebele on the highveld, and again in 1837, when his *amabutho* captured much livestock. To the north, in 1836 he mounted a major campaign against the Swazi kingdom; and, when his *amabutho* stalled before the Swazi mountain fastnesses, he called in mercenaries from Port Natal. They defeated the Swazi, who surrendered some fifteen thousand head of cattle.

In short, it was rapidly apparent that nothing had fundamentally changed in Zululand under Dingane. He ruled the Zulu people in much the same way as had Shaka, not because of some dreadful character flaw but because the nature of the kingdom Shaka had created allowed for no alternative. The irony – as King Mpande was to point out on that famous day at kwaNodwengu when the *amadlozi* of Shaka and Dingane battled it out again as snakes – was that Dingane 'used to say he had killed Tshaka for troubling the people; in fact it was he who finished off the Zulu house'.[3]

And from one perspective it is true that, while Shaka grossly 'troubled' his subjects, it was in Dingane's reign – not Shaka's – that the Zulu kingdom was almost brought crashing down. Dingane has been much blamed for this. When Mpande was king, he liked to hear Dingane's praises. The royal *imbongi*, Magolwana kaMkhathini, would stamp hard on the ground so that his festival dress tossed to and fro, then draw himself erect, look towards Mpande and declaim: 'Hail now, bewhiskered one from Mgungundhlovu [Dingane]! You killed the Boers and brought harm to the Zulu country! You brought harm; did you not bring harm to yourself? This great boldness? Boldness as great as this?' Mpande 'would then whistle, and point his finger, arm raised up, at him three or four times quickly in approval'.[4]

It was all very well for Mpande to applaud, because his alliance on 27 October 1839 with the invading Boers had culminated in a joint attack on Dingane that led to Mpande's becoming king in his stead. But just how culpable was Dingane in his apparently disastrous handling of the Boers? No answer is possible, but would Shaka have been more successful in staving off the Boers from the Cape who were migrating with all their livestock and chattels in search of new lands to settle? After all, the Boers presented an entirely unprecedented challenge, while the structure of the Zulu kingdom and its military establishment was the same under Dingane as it had been under Shaka.

In October 1837, the Boers streamed over the Drakensberg passes and encamped along the headwaters of the Thukela. They came with firearms, horses and wagons that they laagered as mobile fortresses. Their military threat to the kingdom was only too apparent, and the Zulu leadership was dismayed when they rapidly established friendly relations with the Port Natal traders. In November 1837, Boer emissaries made known to Dingane their desire to settle in his territory south of the Thukela. Faced with this formidable challenge to the integrity of his kingdom, and to his own position as ruler, Dingane was persuaded by his *ibandla* to employ guile against an enemy he despaired of overcoming in battle. When a well-armed Boer deputation under Piet Retief arrived aggressively at uMgungundlovu to discuss terms with him, Dingane struck. On 6 February 1838 he ordered their execution – an act of treachery the Boers never forgave or forgot – and dispatched his armies to eliminate the rest of the Boers in their scattered encampments in the foothills of the Drakensberg.

Despite being taken completely by surprise, the Boers succeeded with some difficulty on 16–17 February 1838 in beating off the Zulu forces. An indecisive campaign then ensued. When the Zulu caught the Boers outside their laager and were able to employ their habitual man-to-man tactics with the stabbing-spear (*ikhwa*), they won, as they did at eThaleni on 10 April 1838. The Zulu also thoroughly routed the Boers' Port Natal allies at the battle of the Thukela, on 17 April 1838. The traders evacuated the Port and watched despairingly from their ship in the bay as the Zulu comprehensively and gleefully sacked the settlement between 17 and 24 April 1838.

However, when the Zulu army attacked the Boers at the battle of Veglaer, between 13 and 15 August, they were unable to penetrate the laagered Boers' all-round defence and proved vulnerable to steady musket fire and mounted sorties. The same scenario was repeated on 16 December 1838 when the Boers convincingly routed the Zulu army at the battle of Ncome, or Blood River. Worsted, but not destroyed, the

Zulu army retreated northwards, abandoning uMgungundlovu and the other *amakhanda* in the emaKhosini valley to the invaders. But the Boers had reached their limit. After the Zulu again caught them in the open and bested them at the battle of the White Mfolozi on 27 December 1838, the Boers withdrew to their bases and the two sides opened negotiations. On 25 March 1839 Dingane, who had retired north across the Black Mfolozi, undertook to allow the Boers to settle south of the Thukela. There they established their Republiek Natalia and commenced dividing the land up into farms.

Dingane tried to pick up the pieces. His first impulse was to put space between himself and the Boers by relocating the focus of his kingdom further north. To this end he invaded the Swazi kingdom. But a stinging defeat at Lubuye in the winter of 1839 thwarted that plan and weakened Dingane's prestige, already shaken, still further. Yet it was neither the Boers nor the Swazi who finally brought Dingane down. It was his half-brother, Mpande, he whom Dingane had so unwisely spared when he eliminated all his other rivals in the royal house following the assassination of Shaka.

Mpande, fearing with good reason that the increasingly suspicious Dingane was at last preparing to have him killed, fled south in September 1839 with a considerable following to take refuge in the Republiek Natalia. The canny Boers saw the advantage of forging an alliance with Mpande, and on 27 October 1839 they agreed to make him king in return for his leaving them in control of the lands south of the Thukela, and ceding them St Lucia Bay and its potential harbour.

On 29 January 1840 the armies of Mpande and Dingane, both about five thousand men strong, clashed at the fiercely contested battle of the Maqongqo hills. The Boers played no part in the fighting. Mpande was victorious, and the defeated Dingane fled across the Phongolo, abandoning the women of his *isigodlo* to his enemies, including his old mother, Mphikase. It was a Zulu saying that 'a king who left his home and went to the mountains was finished'.[5] So it was with Dingane. With the remnants of his army he made his way northeast towards the Lubombo Mountains. On reaching their sanctuary, his followers built him a makeshift *umuzi* in the dense bush on the slopes of Hlathikhulu hill. Dingane called it eSankoleni, or 'the secluded spot'. There he attempted to keep up the reduced observances of his royal state while he negotiated with Silevana, the regent of the Nyawo people in whose territory he found himself.

While the bulk of his remaining *amabutho* dispersed to forage, Dingane retained only the iziToyatoyi, an *ibutho* of young lads – not unlike the iziNyosi whom Shaka had kept by him at the last – to act as his guards. Silevana, who was a tributary of Dingane's inveterate foe, King Mswati II of the Swazi, found the fugitive Zulu king a most unwelcome guest. So he alerted a Swazi patrol under Sonyezane Dlamini to Dingane's whereabouts and they planned his death together.

A picked force of Swazi and Nyawo surrounded eSankoleni at night and some crept into the *isigodlo* section where Dingane slept. Woken by a barking dog, Dingane strode resolutely out of his hut, spear in hand. Silevana reacted first and cast a spear that passed through Dingane's thigh and pierced his lower intestines. Wounded as he was, Dingane managed to escape into the bush, protected by a few attendants, and his assailants melted away before the surprised iziToyatoyi could rally to his defence.

The iziToyatoyi finally found Dingane as dawn was breaking. His attendants were vainly attempting to staunch his deep wound. How, we might wonder, had Dingane fared that awful night as his lifeblood seeped painfully away? Had his thoughts gone back to the assassination of Shaka, and did he feel remorse? Or did he experience only regret and anger that his ambitions had been crushed, and that he was dying in such an inglorious way? He must surely have reflected, though, that Shaka's *idlozi* was finally exacting its revenge. Truly, as Dingane's *izibongo* lamented of the two brothers, 'The wild beasts of Jama have killed one another.'[6]

Dingane was carried back to eSankoleni where the iziToyatoyi inspected his wound and saw it was fatal. Rather than prolong his agony, they enlarged the wound with a spear so that he quickly died. His faithful attendants buried their king at eSankoleni. The site of the grave was known to the members of the Nyawo ruling house, who courteously placed stones on top of it. But, fearful that the Zulu might exact revenge for their part in killing Dingane, for more than a century they kept it a closely guarded secret, known only to a few.[7]

With Dingane dead and their ally Mpande now the Zulu king, Boer ambitions waxed. On 14 February 1840 they induced Mpande to cede them not only the lands south of the Thukela, as previously agreed, but those to the north between the Thukela and Black Mfolozi as well. This would have left Mpande with only a fraction of his kingdom, but the Boers did not have the capacity to occupy this great territory. Besides, the British were at last prepared to intervene in the region to prevent the Boers from gaining control over all of southeastern Africa. On 5 July 1842 the Republiek Natalia submitted to British authority, and on 5 October 1843 the British and Mpande formally recognised the boundary between British Natal and the Zulu kingdom. In effect, Mpande had surrendered his sovereignty over those parts of the kingdom south of the Thukela to the British. But he had secured the continued independence of the historic heart of Zululand, and could reign securely in the knowledge that the British recognised him as the Zulu king.

Unlike Shaka and Dingane, Mpande was spared the spear blade. He died a natural death in September 1872 in the *isigodlo* of kwaNodwengu and was buried with all the rites appropriate to a royal funeral. Of the three brothers who had been king, he, the most unlikely, had proved the most successful survivor. Despite his kingdom's being wedged uncomfortably between British Natal to the south and the Boers' South African Republic to the northwest, Mpande succeeded in maintaining its integrity against the encroaching forces of colonialism. Cetshwayo, his successor, was not so fortunate. He fell victim to British imperialism, and the Zulu kingdom was shattered beyond repair in the Anglo-Zulu War of 1879, only half a century after Shaka's assassination. The territory was wracked by devastating civil war and its colonial neighbours duly divided up the fragments. By 1887 the Boers of the New Republic had occupied the northwestern third of Zululand and the British had established their Colony of Zululand over the rest. Shaka's kingdom was no more.

Inkatha, the Zulu cultural and nationalist movement, was inaugurated in October 1920. It resolved to erect a stone monument over the presumed site of Shaka's grave at kwaDukuza. Topped by a carved funerary urn, the monument was ready for unveiling by 1932. The project was bedevilled by poor financial management, but renascent Zulu nationalism had nevertheless acquired its potent rallying point. During the years when the revived Inkatha Freedom Party ruled over the KwaZulu

Shaka's grave and monument in kwaDukuza (Stanger)
(COURTESY OF WIKIMEDIA CREATIVE COMMONS)

'homeland', the Shaka memorial was the focal point of the annual Shaka Day celebrations.

Inkatha consistently projected Shaka, the founder of the Zulu kingdom, as its hero. By contrast, Dingane, his wicked assassin who was also perceived as the treacherous king who had brought Boer vengeance down on the Zulu people, was generally written out of the story. Even so, as part of Inkatha's self-conscious determination to celebrate Zulu heritage, the KwaZulu Monuments Council erected a monument over the supposed location of Dingane's grave. The site is remote and difficult to reach and, like so many other monuments in Zululand, has been vandalised for its metal. Mpande's grave was also given its granite funerary monument. Yet it cannot be absolutely certain that the king lies there. There are reports that at the end of the Anglo-Zulu War British soldiers dug up the grave and carried away bones in a wooden biscuit box. But, since Mpande was buried (as royal custom required) with his *inceku* and two wives to attend him in the afterlife, who can know precisely whose bones were taken?

In more recent years, the African National Congress has rehabilitated Dingane in order to counter Shaka, who has come to symbolise Inkatha's exclusive Zulu nationalism. Dingane is now celebrated as a freedom fighter against white colonialism, and his role as Shaka's assassin is downplayed. And that is perhaps only right. Dingane was hardly unique in the Zulu royal house in killing his brother to gain the throne. Nor did his usurpation change the nature of the Zulu kingdom in any appreciable way. What was different about Dingane, and what puts him on a par with Cetshwayo, who grimly resisted the British invasion of 1879, was his valiant struggle against the Boers in 1838. In the long perspective of colonial aggression and African resistance, could that indeed be considered of more lasting significance than his admittedly dramatic assassination of Shaka?

Glossary of Zulu Words

In accordance with modern practice, Zulu words are entered under the stem and not under the prefix.

isAngoma (pl *izAngoma*) diviner inspired by ancestral spirits

iBandla (pl *amaBandla*) council of state

isiBaya (pl *iziBaya*) enclosure for livestock

imBongi (pl *izimBongi*) praise singer

iziBongo (pl only) praises

iButho (pl *amaButho*) age-grade regiment of men or women; warrior

uDibi (pl *izinDibi*) baggage boy

iDlozi (pl *amaDlozi*) ancestral spirit

inDuna (pl *izinDuna*) appointed officer of state, headman, councillor

isiGodlo (pl *iziGodlo*) king's private enclosure at upper end of homestead; women of the king's establishment

iHlambo (pl *amaHlambo*) ritual cleansing ceremony

ukuHlobonga to practise external sexual intercourse

iHubo (pl *amaHubo*) anthem

isiJula (pl *iziJula*) throwing-spear

iKhanda (pl *amaKhanda*) royal military homestead where *amabutho* were stationed

umKhandlu (pl *imiKhandlu*) council, assembly

ukuKhonza to pay allegiance to king or chief

umKhosi (pl *imiKhosi*) annual 'first-fruits' ceremony

isiKhulu (pl *iziKhulu*) great one of the realm, nobleman

iKlwa (pl *amaKlwa*) stabbing-spear (assegai)

inKosana (pl *amaKhosana*) king's heir by chief wife

inKosi (pl *amaKhosi*) chief

inKosikazi (pl *amaKhosikazi*) woman of status, principal wife

iLobolo (sing. only) goods or cattle handed over by man's family to formalise marriage transaction

uMnyama (sing only) spiritual force of darkness or evil influence

iMpi (pl *iziMpi*) military force, army, battle, campaign

iNceku (pl *iziNceku*) king's personal domestic attendant and advisor

iNdlovukazi Great She-Elephant, Queen Mother

umNdlunkulu (sing only) maids-of-honour

iNkatha (pl *iziNkatha*) sacred grass coil, symbol of the nation

iNtelezi (pl only) ritual medicines to counteract evil influence or sorcery

iNtungwa (pl *amaNtungwa*) person of common Zulu ethnicity and identity; Zulu insider

GLOSSARY OF ZULU WORDS

umNtwana (pl *abaNtwana*) prince of the royal house

iNyanga (pl *iziNyanga*) traditional healer, herbalist

umQulu (pl *imiQulu*) rolled-up mat

inSila (pl *izinSila*) body dirt

umThakathi (pl *abaThakathi*) witch or wizard

ukuThefula Zulu dialect spoken by Qwabe and other people of eastern seaboard

ukuThetha to go through the ceremony of giving praise to the ancestors

umuThi (pl *imiThi*) occult medicine

ukuVuza to 'raise seed' for another man

iWisa (pl *amaWisa*) knobbed stick (knobkerrie)

isiYendane (pl *iziYendane*) person with strange hairstyle; tributary from south of the Thukela River

umuZi (pl *imiZi*) homestead of huts under a headman

Timeline

c 1781/1787
Birth of Shaka

1787
Portuguese fort and trading post established at Lourenço Marques

c 1802
Shaka takes service with Mthethwa

c 1816
Shaka becomes the Zulu *inkosi* as Mthethwa tributary

c 1817
Dingiswayo, *inkosi* of the Mthethwa, killed by Ndwandwe
Shaka defeats Phakathwayo, *inkosi* of the Qwabe

c 1818
Shaka beats off Ndwandwe attack

c 1819
Shaka drives Ndwandwe across Phongolo River

TIMELINE

1824

APRIL
Shaka's first Mpondo campaign (*amabece impi*)

10 MAY
Julia with Fynn's party lands at Port Natal

20 JUNE
Antelope with Farewell's party lands at Port Natal

AUGUST
Attempted assassination of Shaka at esiKlebheni
Purge of Qwabe
Construction of second kwaBulawayo

8 AUGUST
Shaka's land grant to Farewell

1825

1 OCTOBER
Mary with King's party wrecked at Port Natal

1826

OCTOBER
Shaka and settlers crush Ndwandwe at battle of izinDolowane hills
Campaign opens against Bheje kaMagawuzi of the Khumalo
Campaign against Pedi
Construction of kwaDukuza begins

1827

7 FEBRUARY
Settlers and Zulu defeat Bheje in Ngome forest

FEBRUARY
Fynn establishes station at Mzimkhulu River

24 JULY
Shaka decides to send embassy to the Cape

AUGUST
Death of Nandi
Violent official mourning for Nandi
Shaka suspects Zulu *abantwana* of plotting against him
Shaka quits kwaBulawayo for kwaDukuza

SEPTEMBER
End of official mourning for Nandi

1828

FEBRUARY
Shaka's land grant to King

10 MARCH
Launch of schooner *Elizabeth and Susan*

30 APRIL
First Zulu embassy with King and Sothobe sets sail for the Cape

4 MAY
First Zulu embassy arrives in Algoa Bay

MAY–JUNE
Shaka's second Mpondo campaign (*ihlambo impi*)

JUNE
Aborted plot by *abantwana* to assassinate Shaka at Mkhomazi River

JUNE/JULY
Launch of campaign against Soshangane (*Bhalule impi*)

26 JULY
British attack Ngwane people

7 AUGUST
First Zulu embassy embarks for home from Port Elizabeth

TIMELINE

17 AUGUST
First Zulu embassy arrives back at Port Natal

26 AUGUST
Failed embassy reports to Shaka

27 AUGUST
British defeat and disperse Ngwane people

SEPTEMBER
Abantwana desert the *Bhalule impi*

6/7 SEPTEMBER
Second Zulu embassy under Cane leaves overland for the Cape

17 SEPTEMBER
Shaka's land grant to Isaacs

23 SEPTEMBER
Assassination of Shaka at the kwaNyakamubi *umuzi* at kwaDukuza

OCTOBER
Dingane's and Mhlangana's forces kill Ngwadi at kwaWambaza

NOVEMBER
Assembly decides on Dingane as Shaka's successor
Mhlangana put to death

26 NOVEMBER
British Zulu Mission to Shaka sets out

DECEMBER
Return of *Bhalule impi*
Dingane acclaimed king

1 DECEMBER
Settlers temporarily evacuate Port Natal on *Elizabeth and Susan*

15 DECEMBER
News reaches Port Elizabeth of death of Shaka

26 DECEMBER
Zulu Mission to Shaka countermanded

1829
Dingane purges *abantwana* and Shaka's leading men

FEBRUARY
Revolt of Qwabe under Nqetho
Execution of Mbopha
Dingane rebuilds second kwaDukuza as Shaka's spirit home

1830
Dingane's first campaign against the Bhaca
Dingane's first campaign against the Ndebele

21 NOVEMBER
Dingane's unsuccessful embassy under Cane reaches the Cape

1831
Dingane's second campaign against the Bhaca

APRIL
Settlers temporarily evacuate Port Natal

1832
Dingane's second campaign against the Ndebele

1833

JULY
Settlers temporarily evacuate Port Natal

1836
Dingane's campaign against the Swazi

1837
Dingane's third campaign against the Ndebele

TIMELINE

OCTOBER
Boer invasion of Zululand

1838

4 FEBRUARY
Dingane cedes territory south of Thukela to Boers

6 FEBRUARY
Dingane executes Boer delegation at uMgungundlovu

16–17 FEBRUARY
Boers fight off Zulu attacks at Bloukraans and Weenen

10 APRIL
Zulu defeat Boers at battle of eThaleni

17 APRIL
Zulu defeat Port Natal forces at battle of the Thukela

17–24 APRIL
Zulu sack Port Natal

13–15 AUGUST
Boers defeat Zulu at battle of Veglaer

16 DECEMBER
Boer victory at battle of Ncome (Blood River)

27 DECEMBER
Zulu defeat Boers at battle of White Mfolozi

1839

25 MARCH
Dingane recognizes Boer Republiek Natalia south of Thukela

27 OCTOBER
Mpande allies with Boers against Dingane

1840

29 JANUARY
Mpande defeats Dingane at battle of the Maqongqo hills

FEBRUARY
Dingane killed at eSankoleni by the Swazi and the Nyawo

10 FEBRUARY
Boers recognise Mpande as Zulu king

14 FEBRUARY
Mpande makes further territorial concessions to Boers

1842

5 JULY
Republiek Natalia submits to British authority

1843

12 MAY
Annexation of the District of Natal as a British dependency

5 OCTOBER
British recognise Zulu kingdom north of Thukela River
Mpande rebuilds third kwaDukuza as Shaka's spirit home

1844

31 MAY
District of Port Natal annexed to Cape Colony
Site of Shaka's grave allocated to T Potgieter

1845

30 APRIL
District of Natal separated from Cape

TIMELINE

1856

15 JULY
Natal established as a separate British colony

2 DECEMBER
Cetshwayo defeats rival for succession at battle of Ndondakusuka

1872

SEPTEMBER
Mpande dies at kwaNodwengu and is succeeded by Cetshwayo

1879

11 JANUARY
British invasion of Zulu kingdom

22 JANUARY
Zulu victory at battle of Isandlwana

26 JUNE
British burn third kwaDukuza

4 JULY
Final British victory at battle of Ulundi

1 SEPTEMBER
British dictate peace terms, depose Cetshwayo and break up Zulu kingdom

1882

11 DECEMBER
British restore Cetshwayo to central Zululand and civil war ensues

1884

8 FEBRUARY
Cetshwayo dies and is succeeded by son, Dinuzulu

16 AUGUST
Dinuzulu cedes northwestern Zululand to Boers of New Republic

1887

19 MAY
Britain annexes rest of Zululand as Colony of Zululand

1888

20 JULY
South African Republic incorporates New Republic

1897

30 DECEMBER
Colony of Zululand incorporated into Natal as a province

1932
Shaka memorial at kwaDukuza (Stanger)

1977–1994
Self-governing territory of KwaZulu

Characters

Bheje kaMagawuzi (?) *Inkosi* of the Khumalo, defeated by Shaka in 1827.

Bhibhi (d 1840) Sister of Ndlela kaSompisi. One of Senzangakhona's wives and the mother of Sigujana, his heir. Killed after the battle of the Maqongqo hills.

Major General Richard Bourke (1777–1855) Acting Governor of the Cape, 1826–1828.

John Cane, 'Jana' (c 1800–1838) Trader, settler at Port Natal, 1824–1838. Led Zulu embassies to the Cape in 1828 and 1830. Killed at the battle of the Thukela.

Cetshwayo kaMpande (c 1832–1884) In 1872 succeeded his father, King Mpande, as fourth Zulu king. Deposed by the British in 1879 at the end of the Anglo-Zulu War.

Deputy Quartermaster General Major Abraham Josias Cloete (1794–1886) Cape government representative dealing with Shaka's first embassy in 1828.

Sir Lowry Cole (1772–1842) Governor of the Cape Colony, 1828–1833.

Dingane kaSenzangakhona (c 1788–1840) Zulu *umntwana*. Shaka's half-brother by Mphikase. In 1828 assassinated Shaka, and succeeded him as second Zulu king. Overthrown by Mpande in 1840.

Dingiswayo kaJobe (d 1817) *Inkosi* of Mthethwa. In about 1807 succeeded his father, Jobe, after succession dispute. The young Shaka's patron. Killed by Zwide of the Ndwandwe.

Faku (1780–1867) Mpondo paramount. In 1818 succeeded his father, Ngqungqushe, after succession dispute.

Farewell, Francis George, 'Febana' (1793–1829) Lieutenant, Royal Navy. Trader, settler at Port Natal, 1824–1829. Killed by Qwabe under Nqetho.

Fynn, Henry Francis, 'Mbuyazi' (1803–1861) Trader, settler at Port Natal, 1824–1834.

Hlangabeza kaMabedla (d 1828) *Inkosi* of the Ntshali. Killed by the *Bhalule impi*.

Isaacs, Nathaniel, 'Mis Isisi' (1808–1827) Trader, settler at Port Natal, 1825–1831.

Jacob or Jakot Msimbithi (d 1831) Xhosa interpreter from the eastern Cape in the service of the Port Natal settlers. Executed by Port Natal traders.

Khondlo kaMncinci (?) *Inkosi* of the Qwabe in the late eighteenth century.

King, James Saunders, 'Kamu Kengi' (1795–1828) Discharged midshipman, Royal Navy. Trader, settler at Port Natal, 1825–1828. With Shaka's first embassy to the Cape, 1828.

Maclean, Charles Rawden, 'John Ross' (1815–1887) Trader's assistant at Port Natal, 1825–1828.

Magaye kaDibandlela (d 1829) Trusted tributary *inkosi* of the Cele through whom Shaka administered his lands south of the Thukela. Executed by Dingane.

Maphitha kaSojiyisa (d 1872) *Inkosi* of the Mandlakazi. Shaka's viceroy over the northeastern Zulu kingdom.

Masiphula kaMamba (d 1873) *Inkosi* of the emGazini and King Mpande's chief *induna*. Executed by King Cetshwayo.

Matiwane kaMasumpa (d 1829) *Inkosi* of the Ngwane. Executed by Dingane.

Mbopha kaSitayi (d 1829) Of the eGazini people and Shaka's *inceku*. One of Shaka's assassins. Executed by Dingane.

Mbozamboza (?) *Induna* and official intelligence-gatherer for Shaka. Sothobe's associate in the first Zulu embassy to the Cape, 1828.

CHARACTERS

Mdlaka kaNcidi (d 1829) Shaka's commander-in-chief. Executed by Dingane.

Mhlangana kaSenzangakhona (d 1828) Zulu *umntwana*. Shaka's half-brother by Mzondwase. One of Shaka's assassins. Executed by Dingane.

Mmama (?) Daughter of Jama, the Zulu *inkosi*, twin sister of Mnkabayi, sister of Senzangakhona, and Shaka's aunt.

Mnkabayi (c 1765–1840) Daughter of Jama, the Zulu *inkosi*, twin sister of Mmama, sister of Senzangakhona, and Shaka's aunt. She engineered the accession to the throne of both Shaka and Dingane.

Mpande kaSenzangakhona (c 1798–1872) Zulu *umntwana*. Shaka's half-brother by Songiya. In 1840 overthrew his half-brother, King Dingane, and succeeded him as third Zulu king.

Mxamana kaNtandeka (d 1828) Of the Sibisi people and an *inceku* of Shaka's and his principal *imbongi*. Buried with him.

Mzilikazi kaMashobana (c 1790–1868) Founder of Ndebele kingdom.

Nandi (c 1760–1827) The *iNdlovukazi* or Great She-Elephant. Daughter of Mbhengi kaMhlongo, *inkosi* of the Langeni. Mother of Shaka by Senzangakhona and of Ngwadi and Noncoba, probably by Ngendeyana.

Ndlela kaSompisi (d 1840) Of the Ntuli people and brother of Bhibhi. A general under Shaka and Dingane's chief councillor and commander-in-chief. Executed by Dingane after losing the battle of the Maqongqo hills.

Ngomane kaMqomboli (?) Mthethwa commander-in-chief who became Shaka's chief councillor. Survived Shaka's assassination in retirement.

Ngqengelele kaMvulana (?) *Inkosi* of the Buthelezi people and a favoured protégé of Shaka's.

Ngqojana kaSenzangakhona (d 1835) Zulu *umntwana* and half-brother of Shaka, executed by Dingane.

Ngwadi kaNgendeyana (d 1828) Nandi's son, probably by Ngendeyana. Shaka's half-brother and great favourite. Killed by Dingane and Mhlangana.

Noncoba (c 1786–1856) Shaka's half-sister by his mother Nandi and probably by Ngendeyana.

Nongalaza kaNondela (d 1856) *Inkosi* of the Nyandwini. One of Dingane's leading generals and Mpande's commander-in-chief. Died at the battle of Ndondakusuka.

Nqetho kaKhondlo (d 1830) Shaka's client *inkosi* of the Qwabe. Revolted in 1829 against Dingane.

Ntendeka (d 1828) *Induna* of kwaDlangezwa *ikhanda*. Killed and buried with Shaka.

Nxazonke kaMbhengi (d 1828) Of the Langeni people and uncle of Nandi's. Killed and buried with Shaka.

Nzibe kaSenzangakhona (d 1928) Zulu *umntwana*. Full brother of King Mpande by their mother, Songiya. Died during *Bhalule impi*.

Nzobo kaSobadli (d 1840) A great *induna* of Dingane's. Executed by the Boers.

Ogle, Henry, 'Wohlo' or 'Hohlo' (1800–1860) Trader, settler at Port Natal in 1824, and remained in Natal under Boer and British rule until his death.

Phakathwayo kaKhondlo (died c 1817) *Inkosi* of the Qwabe, killed by Shaka.

Senzangakhona kaJama (c 1762–1816) *Inkosi* of the Zulu, and Shaka's father.

Shaka kaSenzangakhona (c 1781/87–1828) In 1816 overthrew his half-brother, Sigujana, *inkosi* of the Zulu. First Zulu king. Assassinated by Dingane, Mhlangana and Mbopha.

Sigujana kaSenzangakhona (d 1816) Zulu *inkosi*. Bhibhi's son and Senzangakhona's heir. Overthrown and killed by his half-brother Shaka.

Sikhunyana kaZwide (d 1826) *Inkosi* of the Ndwandwe. Succeeded Zwide in 1826 after succession dispute. Killed at the battle of izinDolowane hills.

Silevana (?) Regent of the Nyawo and tributary of Mswati II, the Swazi king.

Soshangane kaZikode (c 1780–1858) Founder of the Gaza kingdom.

Sothobe kaMpangalala (?) *Inkosi* of Sibiya. Leader of Shaka's first embassy to the Cape, 1828. Dingane's viceroy south of the Thukela until 1838.

Zibizendlela kaShaka (?) Putative son of Shaka's by an Mthethwa woman. Supposedly lived in exile with either the Mpondo or the Ndebele.

Zwide kaLanga (c 1758–1825) *Inkosi* of the Ndwandwe.

Kingdoms, Paramountcies and Chiefdoms

Note: a kingdom is a centralising state under a ruling house incorporating various smaller, previously independent polities, or chiefdoms. A paramountcy is a looser association of chiefdoms recognising the overarching authority of a particular ruling house.

Bhaca	Chiefdom situated along the Mngeni River. Under pressure from Shaka, it moved southwards across the Mzimkhulu River.
Bomvana	Chiefdom situated between the Mthatha and Mbashe rivers.
Cele	Paramountcy pushed southwards by the Qwabe across the Thukela River and settled in the coastlands between the Mvoti River to the north and the Mngeni River to the south. Subjugated by Shaka.
Chunu	Chiefdom originally situated in west-central Zululand between the middle reaches of the Mzinyathi River and the headwaters of the Mhlathuze River. Fled south from Shaka across the Thukela River to the middle reaches of the Mkhomazi River.
Drosters	Mixed-race, semi-nomadic hunting communities that had moved north over the Orange River onto the highveld and out of the jurisdiction of the Cape Colony. These Griqua,

	Ooorlams, Bergenaars, Hartenaars and Basters were mounted on horses and armed with muskets.
Gaza	Migratory kingdom that originated as a section of the Ndwandwe that broke away after 1819 in the direction of Delagoa Bay. By 1824 it was halted between Delagoa Bay and the Limpopo River to the north where the Zulu attacked it in 1828.
Hlubi	Paramountcy situated along the upper Mzinyathi River in western Zululand. Dislodged and fragmented in about 1816 by the Ngwane. Some elements remained in the region, but the bulk move west onto the highveld, shattering the Tlokwa before moving southwest towards the Caledon River.
Khumalo	Chiefdom in northwestern Zululand situated at the upper reaches of the Mkhuze River. Defeated and incorporated by Shaka in 1827.
Langeni	Chiefdom in central Zululand on the northern banks of the Mhlathuze River. Conquered and incorporated by Shaka.
Mpondo	Kingdom south of Zululand between the Mzimkhulu River in the north and the Mthatha River in the south, which had its heart along the banks of the Mzimvubu River. Invaded by Shaka in 1824 and 1828.
Mthethwa	Paramountcy in southeastern Zululand between the White Mfolozi and Mhlathuze rivers. Defeated by the Ndwandwe in 1817 and subsequently incorporated by Shaka.
Ndebele	Migratory kingdom that originated as a section of the Khumalo in northwestern Zululand. A former tributary of the Ndwandwe, it broke away after 1819 for the highveld of the interior rather than accept Shaka's rule. By 1828 it had come to rest on the northern slopes of the Magaliesberg to the west of the Pedi paramountcy.
Ndwandwe	Paramountcy in northern Zululand between the Phongolo and Black Mfolozi rivers. Fragmented by Shaka in 1819. Senior section moved north across the Phongolo and by 1825 had established itself as the dominant power between the Lepelle River to the north and the Phongolo River to the south. Defeated and scattered by Shaka in 1826.

Ngwane	Chiefdom originally situated at the headwaters of the White Mfolozi in northwestern Zululand. Dislodged southwards by the Ndwandwe in c. 1815. Subsequently driven further off by Shaka and, after disrupting the Sotho kingdom, finally broken up in 1828 by British-led forces near the Mthatha River.
Ntshali	Chiefdom situated in northern Zululand along the upper reaches of the Black Mfolozi River. In 1828 fled north from Shaka and destroyed near the Assegaai River.
Nyawo	Chiefdom north of Zululand in the foothills of the Lubombo Mountains. Tributary of the Swazi king.
Pedi	Paramountcy under the Maroteng ruling house situated north of Zululand between the Lepelle River and the valley of the Tubatse River. In 1822 it was shattered by the Ndwandwe but recovered by 1828.
Qwabe	Paramountcy in southeastern Zululand between the Mhlathuze and Thukela rivers conquered by Shaka and repeatedly suppressed. King Dingane drove a large section southwards in 1829 over the Mzimkhulu River into the territory of the Bhaca and Mpondo, who broke it up in 1830.
Swazi	Kingdom under the Dlamini ruling house north of Zululand centred in the fortified caves of the Mdimba Mountains in northwest of modern-day Swaziland.
Thembu	Chiefdom originally situated in west-central Zululand on the middle reaches of the Mzinyathi River. Fled south from Shaka across the Thukela River to the headwaters of the Mzimkhulu River.
Thuli	Paramountcy pushed south by the Qwabe across the Thukela River and finally settled in the coastlands and midlands between the Mngeni River in the north and the Mkhomazi River in the south. Subjugated by Shaka.
Tsonga	Small chiefdoms situated on the coastal plains between the Limpopo River in the north and the Mkhuze River in the south. Those south of Delagoa Bay were tributaries of the Zulu king.
Xhosa	Paramountcy between the Mbashe River to the northeast and

Zulu — Cape Colony to the southwest. As a result of defeat in the fifth Frontier War of 1818–1819, the British pushed its western boundary back from the Great Fish to the Keiskamma River. Tributary chiefdom of the Mthethwa paramountcy in the valley of the White Mfolozi River in central Zululand that expanded into a kingdom under King Shaka. His sway extended from the foothills of the Drakensberg Mountains in the west to the Indian Ocean in the east, and from the Phongolo River in the north to the Mzimkhulu River in the south.

Notes

The following abbreviations are used in the notes (for full details, see Reading List):

JSA   C de B Webb and JB Wright (eds), *The James Stuart Archive of Recorded Oral Evidence Relating to the History of the Zulu and Neighbouring Peoples*.
RN   Dr BJT Leverton (ed), *Records of Natal*.
ZKS   C de B Webb and JB Wright (eds), *A Zulu King Speaks: Statements Made by Cetshwayo kaMpande on the History and Customs of His People*.

PREFACE

1 Bird, *Annals I*, p 93.
2 Isaacs, *Travels*, p 151.
3 For a trenchant critique of *Shaka Zulu*, see Hamilton, *Terrific Majesty*, pp 173–5, 17–19, 182–7. In 1987 SABC TV screened a 13-part epic titled *John Ross: An African Adventure*, which told the story of Charles Rawden Maclean ('John Ross'), who, as a boy, lived for three years in Shaka's kingdom. Unlike *Shaka Zulu*, it has not been distributed internationally.
4 Nyembezi, 'Izibongo', Part I, p 114.
5 *Weekly Mail & Guardian*, 30 August–5 September 1991.
6 Wylie, 'White Myths of Shaka', p 82.

INTRODUCTION

1. For two recorded oral accounts of the event, see *JSA 4*, pp 93–5: Mtshapi; and pp 303–304: Ndukwana. See also Bryant, *Olden Times*, pp 671–2.
2. Fynn, *Diary*, pp 293–4.
3. *JSA 3*, p 162: Mkando.
4. *JSA 1*, p 344: Lunguza.
5. *JSA 2*, p 208: Mangati; Fuze, *Black People*, p 94.
6. *ZKS*, pp 96–7: Cetshwayo's evidence to the Cape Government Commission on Native Laws and Customs, 7 July 1881: Additions and Notes IV.
7. Bird, *Annals I*, p 106: evidence of Henry Francis Fynn before the Native Commission, 1852; *JSA 4*, pp 302–3: Ndukwana.
8. *JSA 4*, p 94: Mtshapi.
9. *JSA 2*, p 165: Makuza.
10. *JSA 4*, pp 93–4: Mtshapi.
11. Dingane's chief *ikhanda* was uMgungundlovu, which he established in 1829 in the emaKhosini valley.
12. *JSA 4*, p 94: Mtshapi.

CHAPTER 1

1. *JSA 1*, p 28: Baleni.
2. *ZKS*, p 3.
3. Bryant, *Olden Times*, pp 32–3, 35. See also Wylie, *Myth of Iron*, pp 33–6 for further genealogies.
4. *JSA 4*, p 291: Ndukwana.
5. *JSA 2*, p 253: Mayinga.
6. Maclean, 'John Ross', p 135. Maclean published his memories in 'Loss of the Brig *Mary* at Natal with Early Recollection of that Settlement' in the *Nautical Magazine* in 11 instalments between January 1853 and March 1855.
7. Maclean, 'John Ross', pp 120, 123–4.
8. Maclean, 'John Ross', p 123.
9. Maclean, 'John Ross', p 127.
10. Bryant, *Olden Times*, p 122.
11. Maclean, 'John Ross', p 127.
12. *JSA 2*, p 60: Madikane; p 248: Mayinga.
13. Isaacs, *Travels*, pp 56–7.
14. *JSA 4*, p 271: Ndukwana.
15. *JSA 3*, p 87: Melapi.
16. The assassination attempt and Fynn's attendance on Shaka are described in Fynn, *Diary*, pp 83–6. The editor of Fynn's diary places the attack in August 1824 (p 83, n 1), but the *umkhosi* festival during which it occurred was usually celebrated in late

December when the full moon was about to wane.
17 *JSA 3*, p 80: Melapi.
18 *JSA 1*, p 194: Jantshi.
19 Besides Melapi and Jantshi above, see also *JSA 2*, p 161: Makewu; p 169: Makuza; and *JSA 5*, pp 39, 62: Ngidi.

CHAPTER 2

1 *JSA 2*, p 161: Makewu.
2 See *JSA 5*, pp 39–40: Ngidi.
3 *JSA 1*, p 8: Baleka.
4 Wylie, *Myth of Iron*, pp 101–2.
5 *JSA 5*, p 369: Sivivi.
6 *JSA 3*, p 201: Mkebeni.
7 ZKS, p 4.
8 See *JSA 4*, pp 201–5, 219–30: Ndhlovu.
9 See *JSA 2*, p 51: Madikane.
10 See *JSA 1*, p 5: Baleka; *JSA 3*, p 248: Mmemi; and Bird, *Annals I*, p 164: Theophilus Shepstone, 'The Early History of the Zulu-Kafir Race of South-Eastern Africa' (1875).
11 *JSA 1*, p 189: Jantshi; *JSA 3*, p 105: Mgidhlana; *JSA 4*, pp 199–200: Mbekeni; Fuze, *Black People*, p 59.
12 *JSA 2*, pp 247, 254: Mayinga. However, it was also said that Ngwadi was spoken of as Senzangakhona's son only so as not to anger Shaka. See *JSA 1*, p 191: Jantshi.
13 *JSA 3*, p 200: Mkebeni.
14 Fynn, *Diary*, p 13; *JSA 2*, p 205: Mangati; *JSA 3*, pp 199, 200, 206: Mkebeni; *JSA 5*, pp 59, 76: Ngidi.
15 Cope, *Izibongo*, p 128.
16 *JSA 1*, pp 181–2: Jantshi; *JSA 2*, p 48: Madikane; *JSA 4*, pp 36–7: Mruyi; pp 204–5, 228–9: Ndhlovu; *JSA 5*, p 375: Sivivi; Fuze, *Black People*, p 46.
17 Fynn, *Diary*, p 12.
18 ZKS, p 4.
19 *JSA 1*, p 196: Jantshi; *JSA 2*, p 48: Madikane; p 162: Makewu; *JSA 5*, pp 42, 66: Ngidi.
20 *JSA 3*, p 151: Mkando.
21 *JSA 1*, p 191: Jantshi.
22 Bird, *Annals I*, p 168: N Isaacs, 'History of Chaka'; Fynn, *Diary*, pp 13–14; *JSA 1*, p 182: Jantshi; *JSA 2*, p 80: Magidi; *JSA 4*, p 205: Ndhlovu.
23 ZKS, p 4.
24 *JSA 5*, p 84: Ngidi.
25 *JSA 2*, p 47: Madikane; Rycroft and Ngcobo (eds), *Praises of Dingana*, p 184.
26 *JSA 2*, p 216: Mangati; *JSA 4*, pp 277, 327: Ndukwana.

27 *JSA* 2, pp 47–8, 51: Madikane; *JSA* 4, pp 223–4: Ndhlovu.
28 *JSA* 4, pp 42, 59: Ngidi.
29 *ZKS*, p 4; *JSA* 1, p 199: Jantshi.
30 *JSA* 2, pp 204, 206: Mangati.
31 *JSA* 2, p 247: Mayinga.
32 *JSA* 2, p 91: Magidigidi; *JSA* 3, p 278: Ndukwana; *JSA* 5, p 374: Sivivi.
33 *JSA* 1, pp 40–1: Baleni.
34 *JSA* 5, pp 34, 67, 84: Ngidi; Rycroft and Ngcobo (eds), *Praises of Dingana*, p 184.
35 *JSA* 2, p 92; Magidigidi; *JSA* 5, p 84: Ngidi.
36 *Izibongo* composed by Magolwane kaMkhathini Jiyane and translated in Ndlovu, 'Women's Power in the Zulu Kingdom', p 116.
37 *JSA* 4, p 116: Mtshayankomo; p 360: Ndukwana; *ZKS*, p 4.

CHAPTER 3

1 Fynn, *Diary*, p 85.
2 Kirby (ed), *Andrew Smith*, p 86.
3 Fynn, *Diary*, pp 85–6; Kirby (ed), *Andrew Smith*, p 86.
4 *JSA* 1, pp 177, 183–4: Jantshi; *JSA* 2, pp 170–1: Makuza; pp 185–6: Mandhlakazi; Bryant, *Olden Times*, pp 163–6.
5 *JSA* 4, p 205: Ndhlovu.
6 Theal, *Progress of South Africa*, p 169.
7 *JSA* 3, p 158: Mkando.
8 Fynn, *Diary*, pp 125–7.
9 Fynn, *Diary*, p 89.
10 *JSA* 4, p 264: Ndukwana.
11 *JSA* 2, p 248: Mayinga. The shield was cut from the skin of an *ihwanqa* beast, black with white or grey markings.
12 *JSA* 4, p 263: Ndukwana; Fynn, *Diary*, p 126. See also *JSA* 2, p 247: Mayinga.
13 Fynn, *Diary*, pp 89–90.
14 *JSA* 2, p 187: Mandhlakazi.
15 Cope, *Izibongo*, pp 88, 96.
16 Fuze, *Black People*, p 53.
17 *JSA* 2, p 247: Mayinga.
18 *JSA* 5, p 68: Ngidi.
19 Maclean, 'John Ross', p 68.
20 *JSA* 3, p 87: Melapi.
21 *JSA* 5, p 60: Ngidi.
22 Cope, *Izibongo*, p 92.
23 *RN* I, p 64: Capt CN Moorsom to Commodore Christian, 24 May 1825.
24 *JSA* 3, p 162: Mkando. See pp 162–4 for Mkando's full account, assisted by Dhlozi and Ndukwana.

25 *ZKS*, p 5.
26 *JSA 1*, p 185: Jantshi.
27 *JSA 3*, p 271: Mmemi.
28 Cope, *Izibongo*, p 94.
29 *JSA 4*, p 314: Ndukwana.
30 Cope, *Izibongo*, p 202.

CHAPTER 4

1 *JSA 1*, p 194: Jantshi; p 209: Kambi; *JSA 2*, p 169: Makuza; *JSA 3*, p 80: Melapi; *JSA 4*, p 290: Ndukwana; *JSA 5*, pp 39, 62: Ngidi.
2 Nyembezi, 'Izibongo', Part I, p 113.
3 Wright, 'Reflections on Being "Zulu"', p 36.
4 *JSA 4*, p 326: Ndukwana.
5 Shamase, *Zulu Potentates*, p vi: Ndambi kaSikhakhane kaMlisa.
6 *JSA 2*, p 55: Madikane.
7 *JSA 1*, p 118: Dinya.
8 *JSA 3*, p 158: Mkando.
9 *JSA 5*, p 374: Sivivi.
10 *JSA 1*, p 208: Kambi.
11 *JSA 1*, p 194: Jantshi.
12 *JSA 3*, p 241: Mmemi.
13 *JSA 4*, p 226: Ndhlovu.
14 Fuze, *Black People*, p 54.
15 *JSA 3*, pp 243–5: Mmemi.
16 *JSA 3*, p 31: Mbovu.
17 *JSA 1*, p 211: Kambi.
18 *JSA 5*, p 55: Ngidi.
19 *JSA 2*, p 177: Mandhlakazi.
20 *JSA 1*, pp 182–3: Jantshi.
21 Bird, *Annals I*, pp 149–50: enclosure no 1 in Lt Governor Scott's despatch [sic], no 12, 26 February 1864: 'Inhabitants of the Territory (now the Colony of Natal) … before the Extermination of Native Tribes by Chaka'.
22 Fuze, *Black People*, p 54.
23 *JSA 1*, p 183: Jantshi.
24 *JSA 1*, p 183: Jantshi; *JSA 2*, pp 168–9: Makuza.
25 *JSA 3*, pp 240–1: Mmemi.
26 *JSA 5*, p 55: Ngidi. See also *JSA 2*, pp 177–8: Mandhlakazi.
27 *JSA 2*, p 169: Makuza.
28 *JSA 2*, p 178: Mandhlakazi.
29 Fynn, *Diary*, p 89.
30 *JSA 1*, p 8: Baleka; p 194: Jantshi; p 209: Kambi.
31 *JSA 1*, p 8: Baleka; p 16: Baleni.

32 *JSA 1*, p 194: Jantshi; *JSA 5*, pp 39, 62: Ngidi.
33 *JSA 3*, p 43: Mbovu; p 80: Melapi; p 249: Mmemi.
34 *JSA 5*, pp 39, 62: Ngidi.
35 *JSA 5*, p 374: Sivivi.
36 *JSA 3*, p 242: Mmemi.
37 *JSA 5*, p 79: Ngidi.
38 *JSA 2*, p 253: Mayinga.

CHAPTER 5

1 *JSA 5*, p 75: Ngidi.
2 See *JSA 1*, p 5: Baleka.
3 *JSA 2*, p 230: Maputwana; *JSA 4*, pp 198, 221: Ndhlovu.
4 *JSA 1*, p 179: Jantshi.
5 Fuze, *Black People*, p 88.
6 *JSA 5*, pp 29, 78: Ngidi.
7 *JSA 2*, p 248: Mayinga.
8 Isaacs, *Travels*, p 219.
9 *JSA 3*, p 72: Melapi.
10 Isaacs, *Travels*, pp 152–3.
11 Maclean, 'John Ross', p 135.
12 Gibson, *Story of the Zulus*, p 37.
13 *JSA 2*, p 248: Mayinga.
14 Gibson, *Story of the Zulus*, p 37.
15 Maclean, 'John Ross', pp 112, 136.
16 *JSA 1*, p 7: Baleka.
17 Maclean, 'John Ross', p 129.
18 *JSA 2*, p 248: Mayinga.
19 *JSA 4*, p 219: Ndhlovu.
20 *JSA 1*, p 7: Baleka. See also *JSA 3*, p 85: Melapi.
21 *JSA 3*, p 31: Mbovu; p 85: Melapi.
22 *JSA 4*, p 219: Ndhlovu.
23 *JSA 3*, p 85: Melapi.
24 Kirby (ed), *Andrew Smith*, p 86.
25 *JSA 2*, p 163: Makewu.
26 Isaacs, *Travels*, pp 28–9.
27 Maclean, 'John Ross', p 76. See also Isaacs, *Travels*, p 219; and Kirby (ed), *Andrew Smith*, p 84.
28 *JSA 3*, p 52: Mbulo.
29 *JSA 3*, p 130: Mini.
30 *JSA 2*, p 51: Mayinga. See also *JSA 2*, p 162: Makewu.
31 Maclean, 'John Ross', p 76.

32 *JSA 3*, p 85: Melapi.
33 *JSA 4*, p 232: Ndhlovu.
34 *ZKS*, p 9.
35 Kirby (ed), *Andrew Smith*, p 86.
36 *JSA 5*, pp 53, 90: Ngidi.
37 *JSA 3*, p 31: Mbovu; p 84: Melapi; *JSA 5*, pp 41, 90: Ngidi.
38 *JSA 1*, p 76: Jantshi; *JSA 2*, p 80: Magidi; *JSA 3*, p 205: Mkebeni; *JSA 5*, pp 41, 90: Ngidi.
39 Kirby (ed), *Andrew Smith*, p 84.
40 Maclean, 'John Ross', p 111.
41 Maclean, 'John Ross', p 111.
42 *JSA 5*, p 41: Ngidi.
43 *JSA 2*, p 162: Makewu.
44 *JSA 3*, p 72: Melapi.
45 Maclean, 'John Ross', pp 120–1.
46 Isaacs, *Travels*, p 28.
47 Fuze, *Black People*, p 89.
48 See *JSA 1*, p 189: Jantshi; *JSA 2*, pp 60, 61: Madikane; *JSA 3*, p 31: Mbovu; and *JSA 4*, p 205: Ndhlovu.
49 *JSA 3*, p 72: Melapi.
50 *JSA 2*, p 248: Mayinga.
51 *JSA 2*, p 92: Magidigidi; *JSA 5*, p 40: Ngidi.
52 Bryant, *Olden Times*, p 122.
53 Nyembezi, 'Izibongo', Part II, p 161.
54 *JSA 2*, p 252: Mayinga.
55 *JSA 1*, p 8: Baleka.
56 *JSA 2*, p 247: Mayinga; *JSA 5*, p 40: Ngidi.
57 *JSA 2*, p 248: Mayinga.
58 *JSA 1*, p 57: William Bazley.
59 *JSA 1*, p 8: Baleka.
60 *JSA 5*, p 36: Ngidi.
61 *JSA 1*, p 195: Jantshi.
62 *JSA 5*, p 62: Ngidi.
63 *JSA 3*, p 84: Melapi.
64 *JSA 4*, pp 158–9: Mtshebwe.

CHAPTER 6

1 *JSA 4*, p 285: Ndukwana.
2 For Zulu names for the settlers, see *JSA 1*, p 110: Dinya; and *JSA 2*, p 267: Maziyana.
3 *RN 2*, pp 110–11: S Bannister to Sir Lowry Cole, 3 March 1829; Captain W Hoste, FG Farewell, Certificate of Service, 16 September 1814.

4 Bird, *Annals I*, pp 71–3: Farewell to Somerset, 1 May 1824; PG Brink to Farewell, 5 May 1824.
5 *JSA 2*, p 162: Makewu.
6 Fynn, *Diary*, p 63.
7 *JSA 1*, p 96: Dinya.
8 *JSA 3*, p 73: Melapi.
9 *RN 1*, p 37: Farewell to Somerset, 6 September 1824.
10 For this document, see *RN 1*, pp 38–40: Chaka's grant to FG Farewell, 8 August 1824.
11 Isaacs, *Travels*, p 177.
12 *JSA 1*, p 112: Dinya.
13 Maclean, '*John Ross*', pp 62–3.
14 Maclean, '*John Ross*', pp 149–50.
15 *JSA 1*, p 111: Dinya.
16 ZKS, p 9.
17 Gardiner, *Zooloo Country*, p 407.

CHAPTER 7

1 *JSA 4*, p 7: Mqaikana.
2 Laband, 'Zulu Civilians', p 65.
3 *RN 1*, p 37: Farewell to Lord Charles Somerset, Governor of the Cape, 6 September 1824.
4 For the Zulu account of the *amabece impi*, see *JSA 2*, pp 272–3: Maziyana; *JSA 3*, pp 43–4: Mbovu.
5 Kirby (ed), *Andrew Smith*, p 100.
6 Quoted in Stapleton, 'Faku', p 61.
7 *JSA 2*, p 273: Maziyana.
8 *JSA 2*, p 166: Makuza.
9 Isaacs, *Travels*, pp 52–3.
10 *JSA 2*, p 162: Makewu.
11 Captain Gardiner wrote in 1835 that the Zulu called a firearm an 'issibum'. See Gardiner, *Zooloo Country*, p 68.
12 Maclean, '*John Ross*', p 74.
13 *JSA 1*, p 200: Jantshi.
14 *JSA 2*, p 144: Mahungane.
15 Rycroft and Ngcobo (eds), *Praises of Dingana*, p 75.
16 Bird, *Annals 1*, p 314: Gardiner to Colonel Bell, 18 March 1837.
17 *JSA 5*, p 79: Ngidi.
18 For the izinDolowane campaign, see Fynn, *Diary*, pp 123–8; *JSA 1*, p 186: Jantshi; and *JSA 2*, p 269: Maziyana.
19 Maclean, '*John Ross*', pp 67, 69.
20 Fynn, *Diary*, p 128.
21 Cope, *Izibongo*, p 100.

NOTES

CHAPTER 8

1. Isaacs, *Travels*, p 77.
2. *JSA 2*, p 161: Makewu.
3. *JSA 5*, p 39: Ngidi.
4. Maclean, 'John Ross', pp 118–20.
5. Isaacs, *Travels*, p 77.
6. *JSA 5*, p 62: Ngidi.
7. *JSA 3*, p 73: Melapi.
8. *RN 2*, p 18: notes attached to D Campbell, Civil Commissioner of Albany, to Col Bell, 10 October 1828.
9. *RN 1*, p 269: Maj Gen R Bourke to William Huskisson, 26 August 1828. It says something for the slowness of communications at that time between London and the Cape that Huskisson, whom Bourke clearly imagined to be in office as Secretary of State for War and Colonies, had resigned from the cabinet in May 1828.
10. *JSA 4*, p 219: Ndhlovu.
11. Bryant, *Olden Times*, pp 596–8.
12. Bryant, *Olden Times*, pp 60–5.
13. *ZKS*, p 10.
14. Isaacs, *Travels*, p 88.
15. Fynn, *Diary*, p 130; Isaacs, *Travels*, p 89.
16. Isaacs, *Travels*, pp 90–5, 100.
17. *JSA 2*, p 267: Maziyana.
18. Fynn, *Diary*, pp 130–1.
19. Isaacs, *Travels*, pp 86, 105.
20. Isaacs, *Travels*, p 77.
21. *RN 1*, p 37: Farewell to Lord Charles Somerset, 6 September 1824.
22. Wright, 'Dynamics of Power', pp 356–7.
23. Isaacs, *Travels*, p 106.

CHAPTER 9

1. *JSA 1*, p 13: Baleka; Fynn, *Diary*, p 136, quoting her praises.
2. *JSA 4*, p 87: Mtshapi.
3. Cope, *Izibongo*, p 174.
4. Isaacs, *Travels*, p 108.
5. Bryant, *Olden Times*, p 608; Lugg, *Historic Natal and Zululand*, p 126.
6. Fynn, *Diary*, p 132.
7. *JSA 5*, p 35: Ngidi.
8. *JSA 1*, pp 19–25: Jantshi; *JSA 2*, p 45: Madhlebe; *JSA 3*, p 218: Mkehlengana; *JSA 5*, p 72: Ngidi.
9. *JSA 3*, p 86: Melapi; p 109: Mgidhlana; *JSA 5*, p 35: Ngidi.

10 *ZKS*, p 97: Cetshwayo's evidence to the Cape Government Commission on Native Laws and Customs, 7 July 1881: Additions and Notes VI.
11 *JSA 1*, p 57: Bazley.
12 Fuze, *Black People*, p 60.
13 *JSA 1*, p 57: Bazley.
14 Fuze, *Black People*, p 14.
15 *JSA 1*, p 311: Lunguza.
16 *JSA 5*, p 35: Ngidi.
17 *JSA 1*, p 57: Bazley.
18 *JSA 1*, p 8: Baleka; *JSA 3*, p 31: Mbovu; p 86: Melapi; *JSA 5*, p 35: Ngidi.
19 *JSA 1*, p 311: Lunguza.
20 *JSA 4*, p 330: Ndukwana.
21 *JSA 3*, p 109: Mgidhlana.
22 *JSA 3*, p 218: Mkehlengana.

CHAPTER 10

1 *JSA 1*, p 57: Bazley.
2 Fuze, *Black People*, pp 63–4.
3 *JSA 1*, p 42: Baleni.
4 Gibson, *Story of the Zulus*, p 34.
5 *JSA 1*, pp 19, 30: Baleni; *JSA 4*, p 292: Ndukwana; Fuze, *Black People*, p 64.
6 Fynn, *Diary*, p 135.
7 Isaacs, *Travels*, p 109.
8 *ZKS*, p 97: Cetshwayo's evidence to the Cape Government Commission on Native Laws and Customs, 7 July 1881: Additions and Notes VI.
9 *JSA 3*, p 109: Mgidhlana.
10 Bryant, *Olden Times*, photograph opposite p 608. The site of Nandi's grave was refurbished in 2011 and a suitable monument erected.
11 *ZKS*, p 97: Cetshwayo's evidence to the Cape Government Commission on Native Laws and Customs, 7 July 1881: Additions and Notes VI.
12 Laband, *Rope of Sand*, pp 164–5.
13 Fynn, *Diary*, pp 135–6.
14 *JSA 4*, p 293: Ndukwana. See also *JSA 5*, p 72: Ngidi; and Fuze, *Black People*, p 64.
15 *JSA 5*, p 72: Ngidi; Fynn, *Diary*, p 136.
16 Gibson, *Story of the Zulus*, p 35.
17 *JSA 5*, p 36: Ngidi.
18 *JSA 3*, p 128: Mini.
19 *JSA 1*, p 307: Lunguza.
20 Fynn, *Diary*, p 136; Fuze, *Black People*, p 64.
21 *ZKS*, p 97: Cetshwayo's evidence to the Cape Government Commission on Native Laws and Customs, 7 July 1881: Additions and Notes VI.
22 Fynn, *Diary*, p 139.

23 Bryant, *Olden Times*, pp 614–15.
24 *JSA 1*, p 100: Dinya; *JSA 3*, p 85: Melapi.
25 Isaacs, *Travels*, p 113.
26 *JSA 4*, p 342: Ndukwana; *JSA 5*, pp 40–1: Ngidi.
27 *JSA 5*, pp 35, 90: Ngidi.
28 Fynn, *Diary*, pp 137–8.
29 *JSA 3*, p 88: Melapi; p 270: Mmemi; *JSA 5*, p 72: Ngidi.

CHAPTER 11

1 Isaacs, *Travels*, p 113.
2 Isaacs, *Travels*, p 115.
3 *RN 1*, pp 247–8: notarial deed signed by JA Chaboud on 29 July 1828 verifying the 'Scrawling fishbone signature' of Shaka, Jacob's mark, and Isaacs' signature as witness on the document of February 1828.
4 Isaacs, *Travels*, p 117.
5 Isaacs, *Travels*, p 119.
6 Isaacs, *Travels*, pp 117–18; *RN 1*; p 154: DP Francis, Port Captain to Lt Col John Bell, Acting Secretary to the Government, 9 May 1828.
7 *JSA 2*, pp 247, 252, 254, 257, 258: Mayinga; *JSA 3*, pp 81, 86: Melapi.
8 *JSA 2*, pp 166–7: Makuza.
9 Isaacs, *Travels*, p 120.
10 Cope, *Izibongo*, p 180.
11 *RN 1*, pp 156–7: King to JW van der Riet, Civil Commissioner, Uitenhage, 10 May 1928.
12 *JSA 2*, p 267: Maziyana.
13 *RN 1*, p 238: Maj AJ Cloete to Bell, 25 July 1828.
14 See Isaacs, *Travels*, pp 119–24.
15 Isaacs, *Travels*, p 123.
16 *RN 1*, pp 172–3: Bell to Cloete, 14 June 1828; p 207: Bell to Cloete, 11 July 1828.
17 *RN 1*, p 244: Maj Gen R Bourke to Commodore Skipsey, 27 July 1828.
18 *RN 1*, p 255: Bell to Cloete, 8 August 1828.
19 Maclean, *'John Ross'*, pp 135–6.
20 *JSA 5*, p 5: Nduna.
21 *RN 1*, pp 249–50: King to Cloete, 30 July 1828.
22 *RN 1*; pp 191–3: Cloete to Bell, 4 July 1828; p 193: King to Cloete, 4 July 1828; pp 209–10: Cloete to Bell, 11 July 1828; p 211: Cloete to King, 5 July 1828.

CHAPTER 12

1. *RN 1*, p 157: King to Van der Riet, 10 May 1828; p 163: King to Van der Riet, 24 May 1828; pp 219–20: King to Van der Riet, 13 July 1828.
2. *RN 2*, p 133: Farewell to J Barrow, 15 March 1829.
3. *RN 2*, pp 113–14: Bell to Farewell, 6 March 1829.
4. *RN 1*, p 269: Bourke to Huskisson, 26 August 1828.
5. Isaacs, *Travels*, p 113; Fynn, *Diary*, p 139; Bryant, *Olden Times*, pp 613–14.
6. Fynn, *Diary*, p 139.
7. *JSA 1*, p 77: Christian Cane; *JSA 3*, p 145: Mkando.
8. Isaacs, *Travels*, p 113; *RN 1*, p 186: Cloete to Van der Riet, 27 June 1828; *JSA 2*, p 273: Maziyana.
9. *JSA 2*, p 61: Madikane; p 273: Maziyana; *JSA 3*, p 55: Mcotoyi.
10. *RN 1*, p 174: WJ Shrewsbury to Lt Col Somerset, 12 June 1828.
11. Cope, *Izibongo*, p 94.
12. *RN 2*, p 12: Farewell to Maj Dundas, 10 September 1828.
13. *JSA 2*, p 274: Maziyana; *JSA 5*, pp 41, 55–6: Ngidi. Mnkabi died there, and was carried back to Zululand to be buried.
14. Fynn, *Diary*, pp 143–9; Isaacs, *Travels*, p 126.
15. *RN 1*, pp 233–4: Bourke to Commodore Skipsey, 17 July 1828.
16. *RN 1*, pp 273–4: Maj Dundas's report, 15 August 1828; p 269: Bourke to Huskisson, 26 August 1828.
17. Fynn, *Diary*, p 144.
18. Fynn, *Diary*, pp 144–51; Isaacs, *Travels*, pp 126–7; *RN 1*, p 197: Brownlee to Capt Duncan Campbell, Civil Commissioner of Albany, 2 July 1828; p 204: Shrewsbury to Lt Col Somerset, 2 July 1828; pp 204–5: Shaw to Lt Col Somerset, 8 July 1828.
19. Stapleton, 'Faku', p 65; *JSA 2*, p 274: Maziyana.
20. *JSA 2*, p 249: Mayinga; *JSA 3*, p 44: Mbovu; *JSA 4*, p 27: Mqaikana; p 82: Mtshapi.
21. *JSA 3*, p 217: Mkehlengana.
22. *RN 1*, pp 236–7: Maj Dundas to Lt Col Somerset, 14 July 1828; Isaacs, *Travels*, p 127.
23. *RN 1*, p 196: Lt Col Somerset to Bell, 4 July 1828.
24. *RN 1*, pp 180–1: Bell to Dundas, 21 June 1828; p 205: Lt Col Somerset to Campbell, 10 July 1828.
25. *RN 1*, pp 258–60: Maj Dundas to Lt Col Somerset, 1 August 1828.
26. *RN 1*, pp 261–2: Cmdt JS van Wyk to Lt Col Somerset, 21 August 1828.
27. A strong force of Cape troops and local African allies under Lt Col Henry Somerset attacked the Ngwane again on 27 August 1828 and entirely broke them up. The attack was a demonstration of British military power in a region that the Cape now claimed was in its sphere of interest.
28. *JSA 1*, p 186: Jantshi; *JSA 2*, p 61: Madikane; p 274: Maziyana; *JSA 3*, p 66: Mcotoyi.
29. *JSA 2*, p 249: Mayinga; *JSA 3*, p 83: Melaphi; Fynn, *Diary*, pp 151, 158.

NOTES

CHAPTER 13

1 *RN 1*, p 255: Cloete to Bell, 7 August 1828.
2 *RN 2*, p 57: Isaacs to Sir GL Cole, Governor of the Cape, 19 December 1828.
3 Fynn, *Diary*, p 154.
4 *RN 1*, p 230: King to Cloete, 1 August 1828.
5 *RN 2*, p 60: Farewell's statement to Capt R Aitchison: 19 December 1828. Farewell declared that King died on 3 September; Isaacs wrote that he expired on 7 September (*RN 2*, p 75: Fynn to Lt Col Somerset, 9 September 1828).
6 Isaacs, *Travels*, pp 135–6.
7 *RN 1*, p 228: Cloete to Bell, 18 July 1828; p 255: Cloete to Bell, 7 August 1828; p 269: Bourke to Huskisson, 26 August 1828; Isaacs, *Travels*, p 132.
8 *RN 2*, p 57: Isaacs to Cole, 19 December 1828.
9 *RN 2*, p 11: Farewell to Maj Dundas, 10 September 1828. For the decidedly mingy presents selected by the authorities, see *RN 1*, p 222: Bourke to Commodore Skipsey, 15 July 1828; and p 223: Bell to Cloete, 15 July 1828.
10 *RN 2*, pp, 16–17: Campbell to Bell, 10 October 1828; p 29: statement of John Cane, 10 November 1828.
11 *RN 2*, p 30: statement of John Cane, 10 November 1828; p 57: Isaacs to Cole, 19 December 1828.
12 Isaacs, *Travels*, pp 128–35; Fynn, *Diary*, p 155; *RN 2*, p 75: Fynn to Lt Col Somerset, 9 September 1828.
13 Gibson, *Story of the Zulus*, p 36.
14 Isaacs, *Travels*, pp 128–35.
15 *RN 2*, p 36: JA Chabaud, Notary Public to Cole, 14 November 1828.
16 *RN 2*, p 17: Campbell to Bell, 10 October 1828; p 29: statement of John Cane, 10 October 1828.
17 *RN 2*, p 20: message from Shaka.
18 *RN 2*, p 19: statement of John Cane, 7 October 1828; pp 28–31: statement of John Cane, 10 November 1828.
19 See *RN 2*, p 19: statement of Monagali, 8 October 1828; and pp 27–8: statement of Managarda, 10 November 1828.
20 *RN 2*, p 20: statement of Monagali, 8 October 1828.
21 Isaacs, *Travels*, pp 141–2.
22 *RN 2*, pp 22–3: Bell to Aitchison, 11 October 1828.
23 *RN 2*, p 87: Cole to Sir George Murray, 31 January 1828.
24 *RN 2*, pp 43–4: Memorandum for John Cane by Bell, 26 November 1828.
25 *RN 2*, pp 93–5: Bell to Aitchison, 24 November 1828.
26 *RN 2*, p 68: Bell to Aitchison, 26 December 1828.
27 *RN 2*, p 109: Aitchison to Campbell, 2 March 1829.
28 *RN 2*, p 49: Farewell to Lt Col Somerset, 15 December 1828. See also *RN 2*, p 52: Campbell to Aitchison, 19 December 1828. However, in *RN 2*, p 133: Farewell to J Barrow, 15 March 1829, Farewell stated that Shaka was killed on 21 September.

CHAPTER 14

1 Fynn, *Diary*, p 153.
2 *RN 2*, p 17: notes attached to Sir Lowry Cole to Sir George Murray, 31 January 1829.
3 Isaacs, *Travels*, p 127.
4 *JSA 4*, p 80: Mtshapi.
5 *JSA 3*, p 31: Mbovu.
6 *JSA 3*, p 83: Melapi.
7 *JSA 3*, p 217: Mkehlengana.
8 Fynn, *Diary*, p 153; *JSA 4*, p 81: Mtshapi.
9 *JSA 3*, p 56: Mcotoyi.
10 *JSA 2*, p 251: Mayinga.
11 *ZKS*, p 7; *JSA 1*, p 95: Dinya; *JSA 3*, p 56: Mcotoyi.
12 *JSA 1*, p 95: Dinya.
13 *JSA 2*, p 61: Madikane; *JSA 4*, p 264: Ndukwana.
14 *JSA 1*, p 95: Dinya.
15 *RN 2*, p 60: Farewell's statement to Capt Aitchison, 19 December 1828; Fynn, *Diary*, p 161; Bryant, *Olden Times*, p 627.
16 Fynn, *Diary*, p 153.
17 *ZKS*, p 7; *JSA 3*, p 88: Melapi.
18 *JSA 1*, p 6: Baleka; Bryant, *Olden Times*, p 627.
19 *JSA 4*, p 81: Mtshapi.
20 *RN 2*, p 60: Farewell's statement to Capt Aitchison, 19 December 1828; Fynn, *Diary*, p 161; Isaacs, *Travels*, p 172; Bryant, *Olden Times*, p 628.
21 *JSA 1*, p 187: Jantshi; *JSA 4*, p 80: Mtshapi.
22 *JSA 2*, p 163: Makewu.
23 *ZKS*, pp 7–8.
24 *JSA 2*, p 250: Mayinga; *JSA 5*, p 57: Ngidi.
25 *JSA 4*, p 80: Mtshapi.
26 Fynn, *Diary*, p 153; *JSA 5*, p 57: Ngidi.
27 Isaacs, *Travels*, p 143.
28 Fynn, *Diary*, p 156.
29 *JSA 1*, p 95: Dinya.
30 *JSA 2*, p 110: Mahaya.
31 *JSA 3*, p 55: Mcotoyi.
32 *RN 2*, p 18: notes attached to Sir Lowry Cole to Sir George Murray, 31 January 1829.
33 Isaacs, *Travels*, pp 173, 252; *ZKS*, p 10; *JSA 2*, p 71: Mageza; *JSA 5*, p 57: Ngidi.
34 Fynn, *Diary*, p 153.
35 *RN 2*, p 60: Farewell's statement to Capt Aitchison, 19 December 1828.
36 *JSA 2*, p 297: Maziyana.
37 *JSA 4*, p 264: Ndukwana.

NOTES

CHAPTER 15

1. Rycroft and Ngcobo (eds), *Praises of Dingana*, p 71. See also Nyembezi, 'Izibongo', Part I, p 122: 'The deserter of the army'.
2. *JSA* 5, p 57: Ngidi.
3. *JSA* 1, p 95: Dinya; Bryant, *Olden Times*, p 660.
4. Fynn, *Diary*, p 174.
5. *JSA* 1, p 96: Dinya.
6. *RN* 2, p 60: Farewell's statement to Capt Aitchison, 19 December 1828; p 74: Fynn to Lt Col Somerset, 28 November 1828; *JSA* 1, p 187: Jantshi.
7. Isaacs, *Travels*, p 143; *RN* 2, p 60: Farewell's statement to Capt Aitchison, 19 December 1828.
8. Fynn, *Diary*, pp 155–6. Cane has 1000 women put to death (*RN* 2, p 52: Campbell to Bell, 19 December 1828) and Farewell 2 000 at the rate of 300 a day (*RN* 2, p 60: Farewell's statement to Capt Aitchison, 19 December 1828).
9. *RN* 2, p 52: Campbell to Bell, 19 December 1828.
10. Isaacs, *Travels*, p 219.
11. Isaacs, *Travels*, p 177: 29 April 1829.
12. Rycroft and Ngcobo (eds), *Praises of Dingana*, p 91.
13. Nyembezi, 'Izibongo', Part II, p 160.
14. Quoted by Ndlovu, 'King Dingane', p 106.
15. Nyembezi, 'Izibongo', Part II, p 160.
16. Isaacs, *Travels*, p 289.
17. Nyembezi, 'Izibongo', Part II, p 161.
18. Rycroft and Ngcobo (eds), *Praises of Dingana*, p 89.
19. Isaacs, *Travels*, pp 179, 289.
20. *JSA* 1, p 321: Lunguza; *JSA* 5, p 369: Sivivi.
21. *JSA* 2, p 92: Magidigidi; Shamase, *Zulu Potentates*, p 29.
22. Rycroft and Ngcobo (eds), *Praises of Dingana*, p 81; see also p 83; and Nyembezi, 'Izibongo', Part II, p 161.
23. *JSA* 1, p 318: Lunguza.
24. Rycroft and Ngcobo (eds), *Praises of Dingana*, p 93.
25. *JSA* 1, p 321: Lunguza; *JSA* 5, p 369: Sivivi.
26. Isaacs, *Travels*, pp 179, 289.
27. *JSA* 3, p 56: Mcotoyi.
28. *JSA* 1, pp 195–6: Jantshi; Maclean, 'John Ross', p 111.
29. Fuze, *Black People*, p 89.
30. *JSA* 1, p 196: Jantshi; *JSA* 4, p 239: Ndongeni.
31. Bryant, *Olden Times*, p 52.
32. Fynn, *Diary*, p 156.
33. Bryant, *Olden Times*, p 52.
34. *JSA* 4, p 346: Ndukwana.
35. *JSA* 1, pp 191, 194: Jantshi; *JSA* 2, p 250: Mayinga; Bryant, *Olden Times*, p 660. Hamu

grew up to be highly dissatisfied with his status as Nzibe's son. He resented that he was not Mpande's heir and harboured regal aspirations.
36 *JSA 4*, p 117: Mtshayankomo.
37 *JSA 4*, pp 291, 346: Ndukwana. Mbopha was also known as Tumelisa or Tubelisa.
38 Bryant, *Olden Times*, pp 659–60.
39 Maclean, 'John Ross', p 111.
40 Nyembezi, 'Izibongo', Part I, p 110.
41 Fuze, *Black People*, p 71; Bryant, *Olden Times*, pp 659–60.
42 Fynn, *Diary*, p 156.
43 *JSA 2*, p 93: Magidigidi.
44 Maclean, 'John Ross', p 111.
45 *JSA 1*, p 6: Baleka.
46 Fuze, *Black People*, p 71.
47 *JSA 2*, p 161: Makewu.
48 *JSA 1*, p 187: Jantshi.
49 Fynn, *Diary*, p 156; Bird, *Annals I*, p 96: Fynn's account; Bryant, *Olden Times*, p 660.

CHAPTER 16

1 Bryant, *Olden Times*, p 662: note.
2 Fynn, *Diary*, p 156.
3 Isaacs, *Travels*, pp 142–3.
4 *RN 2*, p 49: Farewell to Lt Col Somerset, 15 December 1828; p 60: Farewell's statement to Capt Aitchison, 19 December 1828.
5 *RN 2*, p 133: Farewell to JM Barrow, 15 March 1829.
6 *JSA 3*, p 217: Mkehlengana.
7 *JSA 1*, p 95: Dinya.
8 *JSA 2*, p 295: Maziyana.
9 Isaacs, *Travels*, p 143; Fuze, *Black People*, p 70.
10 Fynn, *Diary*, p 157; Bird, *Annals I*, p 97: Fynn's account; Isaacs, *Travels*, p 143; ZKS, p 8; Fuze, *Black People*, pp 70–2.
11 ZKS, p 8; *JSA 1*, p 95: Dinya; *JSA 2*, p 295: Maziyana; *JSA 3*, p 66: Mcotoyi; *JSA 5*, p 64: Ngidi.
12 Fynn, *Diary*, p 156; Bird, *Annals I*, p 96: Fynn's account; *JSA 4*, p 291: Ndukwana; Fuze, *Black People*, p 70.
13 ZKS, p 8; testimony of Matingwana kaNdinizana as recounted to Socwatsha kaPapu, interviewed by Stuart in 1913 (quoted in Eldredge, *Creation of the Zulu Kingdom*, p 271).
14 Isaacs, *Travels*, p 143.
15 *JSA 1*, p 96: Dinya; Bird, *Annals I*, pp 96–7: Fynn's account. One account had Mbopha driving cattle about as a diversion, rather than people. See *JSA 2*, p 163: Makewu.

16 Kirby (ed), *Andrew Smith*, p 41; Bird, *Annals I*, p 97: Fynn's account; Bryant, *Olden Times*, p 662; Fuze, *Black People*, p 70.
17 Matingwana's testimony, quoted in Eldredge, *Creation of the Zulu Kingdom*, p 272.
18 *JSA 2*, pp 294–5: Maziyana.
19 Maclean, 'John Ross', p 111.
20 Isaacs, *Travels*, p 143.
21 *JSA 2*, p 163: Makewu.
22 *JSA 4*, p 291: Ndukwana.
23 *JSA 1*, p 187: Jantshi.
24 *JSA 1*, p 194: Jantshi. See note 23.
25 Bird, *Annals I*, p 97: Fynn's account; Bryant, *Olden Times*, p 662; Fuze, *Black People*, p 71.
26 Kirby (ed), *Andrew Smith*, p 41.
27 Bird, *Annals I*, p 97: Fynn's account; Isaacs, *Travels*, p 143.
28 *JSA 2*, p 163: Makewu.
29 Kirby (ed), *Andrew Smith*, p 41.
30 Isaacs, *Travels*, p 143.
31 *JSA 1*, p 194: Jantshi; *JSA 4*, pp 291–2: Ndukwana.
32 *JSA 1*, p 194: Jantshi; *JSA 4*, p 291: Ndukwana.
33 *JSA 2*, p 295: Maziyana. See also Kirby (ed), *Andrew Smith*, p 51; and Isaacs, *Travels*, p 143.
34 *JSA 5*, p 167: Nsuze.
35 *JSA 2*, p 295: Maziyana.
36 *JSA 5*, p 167: Nsuze.
37 *RN 2*, p 74: Fynn to Lt Col Somerset, 28 November 1828. See also Bird, *Annals I*, p 97: Fynn's account; Fynn, *Diary*, p 157; and Kirby (ed), *Andrew Smith*, p 41. The English translation of the Zulu wording varies from one version to the next, but the meaning is the same. Essentially the same formulation can be found as an element in longer versions of Shaka's last words preserved in oral memory: 'Is it the sons of my father who are killing me?' (*JSA 1*, p 96: Dinya); 'Children of my father, are you killing me, I who am of your house and king of the Zulu?' (*JSA 1*, p 307: Lunguza); and, most dramatically of all, 'You stab me like this my father's sons, what have I done? You would strike and stab thus the wild beast of Mtetwa who shatters and destroys the nations he invades?' (Socwatsha's testimony, quoted in Eldredge, *Creation of the Zulu Kingdom*, p 272).
38 *JSA 3*, p 206: Mkebeni.
39 See *JSA 1*, p 96: Dinya; p 307: Lunguza; *JSA 3*, p 155: Mkando; and *JSA 4*, p 200: Ndhlovu.
40 *JSA 1*, p 307: Lunguza; Lugg, *Historic Natal and Zululand*, p 83.
41 *JSA 3*, p 155: Mkando.

CHAPTER 17

1. Kirby (ed), *Andrew Smith*, p 41.
2. ZKS, p 8; Bird, *Annals I*, p 97: Fynn's account; Fynn, *Diary*, p 157; Isaacs, *Travels*, p 143; Fuze, *Black People*, p 72.
3. Isaacs, *Travels*, p 143.
4. *JSA 3*, p 270: Mmemi; Bird, *Annals I*, p 97: Fynn's account; Fynn, *Diary*, p 157; Isaacs, *Travels*, p 143.
5. Fynn, *Diary*, p 157; RN 2, p 60: Farewell's statement to Capt Aitchison, 19 December 1828; p 61: Farewell to Bell, 19 December 1828.
6. *JSA 3*, p 270: Mmemi.
7. Bryant, *Olden Times*, p 666.
8. Socwatsha's testimony, quoted in Eldredge, *Creation of the Zulu Kingdom*, p 274.
9. Bird, *Annals I*, p 97: Fynn's account; Fynn, *Diary*, p 157; Gibson, *Story of the Zulus*, p 41; Fuze, *Black People*, p 71.
10. *JSA 4*, p 20: Mqaikana; Socwatsha's testimony, quoted in Eldredge, *Creation of the Zulu Kingdom*, pp 274–5.
11. *JSA 4*, p 125: Mtshayankomo.
12. Bryant, *Olden Times*, p 666.
13. Fynn, *Diary*, p 157.
14. *JSA 5*, pp 43, 64: Ngidi; Socwatsha's testimony, quoted in Eldredge, *Creation of the Zulu Kingdom*, p 274.
15. Fynn, *Diary*, p 158; *JSA 3*, pp 108–9: Mgidhlana; Gibson, *Story of the Zulus*, p 42; Bryant, *Olden Times*, p 666; Fuze, *Black People*, p 27; Lugg, *Historic Natal and Zululand*, pp 84, 111.
16. *JSA 3*, p 109: Mgidhlana.
17. RN 2, p 184: JC Chase, Notice respecting the late expedition overland to the Portuguese settlement at Delagoa Bay, October 1829.
18. On 5 October 1843 King Mpande recognised the boundaries of what would finally become the British Colony of Natal in 1856, but was then known as the District of Port Natal.
19. Bryant, *Olden Times*, pp 240, 671. In 2006, the official name of Stanger was changed to KwaDukuza.
20. *JSA 2*, p 161: Makewu.

CHAPTER 18

1. Isaacs, *Travels*, p 144.
2. RN 2, p 49: Farewell to Lt Col Somerset, 15 December 1828; Isaacs, *Travels*, p 144.
3. Isaacs, *Travels*, p 162; RN 2, p 51: JW van der Riet, Civil Commissioner, to H Hudson, Resident Magistrate, 17 December 1828.
4. RN 2, p 49: Farewell to Lt Col Somerset, 15 December 1828.

NOTES

5   Fynn, *Diary*, p 158; *JSA 3*, p 82: Melapi; *JSA 5*, p 57: Ngidi; Bryant, *Olden Times*, pp 667–8.
6   Bryant, *Olden Times*, p 668.
7   Isaacs, *Travels*, p 161.
8   *RN 2*, p 58: Isaacs to Cole, 19 December 1828; p 61: Farewell to Bell, 19 December 1828; p 74: Fynn to Lt Col Somerset, 28 November 1828.
9   *JSA 4*, p 307: Ndukwana.
10 Isaacs, *Travels*, pp 161–2.
11 *RN 2*, p 58: Isaacs to Cole, 19 December 1828; p 74: Fynn to Lt Col Somerset, 28 November 1828; Fynn, *Diary*, pp 159–60; *JSA 3*, p 248: Mmemi; *JSA 5*, pp 57, 83: Ngidi; Bryant, *Olden Times*, pp 668–9.
12 *RN 2*, p 74: Fynn to Lt Col Somerset, 28 November 1828.
13 *JSA 3*, p 74: Melapi.
14 *RN 2*, p 50: Farewell to Lt Col Somerset, 15 December 1828; p 61: Farewell to Bell, 19 December 1828.
15 *RN 2*, p 60: Farewell's statement to Capt Aitchison, 19 December 1828.
16 Isaacs, *Travels*, p 144.
17 *JSA 1*, p 312: Lunguza.
18 *RN 2*, p 58: Isaacs to Cole, 19 December 1828; p 74: Fynn to Lt Col Somerset, 28 November 1828.
19 *JSA 1*, p 196: Jantshi.
20 *JSA 3*, p 217: Mkehlengana. See also *JSA 2*, p 162: Makuza.
21 *JSA 4*, p 346: Ndukwana.
22 *JSA 4*, pp 291–2, 346: Ndukwana.
23 *JSA 3*, p 217: Mkehlengana.
24 *JSA 1*, p 196: Jantshi; *JSA 2*, p 163: Makewu; *JSA 4*, p 292: Ndukwana.
25 *JSA 1*, p 6: Baleka; Nyembezi, 'Izibongo', Part I, pp 122–3.
26 Rycroft and Ncobo (eds), *Praises of Dingana*, p 71.

CHAPTER 19

1   *JSA 1*, p 187: Jantshi; Fynn, *Diary*, p 161; Bryant, *Olden Times*, p 665.
2   *ZKS*, p 7; Bryant, *Olden Times*, p 628.
3   *JSA 3*, p 83: Melapi.
4   Isaacs, *Travels*, p 173.
5   *RN 2*, p 60: Farewell's statement to Capt Aitchison, 19 December 1828.
6   *RN 2*, pp 49–50: Farewell to Lt Col Somerset, 15 December 1828; p 60: Farewell's statement to Capt Aitchison, 19 December 1828.
7   Isaacs, *Travels*, p 173.
8   *JSA 1*, p 6: Baleka.
9   Isaacs, *Travels*, p 161; *JSA 1*, p 196: Jantshi; *JSA 2*, p 49: Madikane.
10 *ZKS*, pp 97–8: Cetshwayo's evidence to the Cape Government Commission on Native

Laws and Customs, 7 July 1881: Additions and Notes VII.
11 Isaacs, *Travels*, p 177.
12 *JSA 1*, pp 329–30: Lunguza.
13 *JSA 1*, p 196: Jantshi.
14 *JSA 1*, p 29: Baleni.
15 *ZKS*, p 10.
16 Rycroft and Ngcobo (eds), *Praises of Dingana*, p 95.
17 *JSA 1*, p 19: Baleni.
18 *JSA 3*, p 74: Melapi; *JSA 4*, p 318: Ndukwana.
19 Rycroft and Ngcobo (eds), *Praises of Dingana*, pp 87, 175.
20 Bird, *Annals I*, p 289: Capt Gardiner, February 1835.
21 Ironically, Gqugqu was executed in 1843 by King Mpande, who feared that the only surviving son of Senzangakhona besides himself constituted a threat to his reign.
22 Nyembezi, 'Izibongo', Part II, p 162.
23 *JSA 4*, p 214: Ndhlovu.
24 *JSA 1*, p 6: Baleka; p 19: Baleni; *JSA 3*, p 266: Mmemi; *JSA 4*, p 317: Ndukwana.
25 Fynn, *Diary*, pp 162–3.
26 *ZKS*, p 8.
27 Bryant, *Olden Times*, pp 632, 670.
28 *ZKS*, p 10; Bryant, *Olden Times*, p 671.
29 For a list of henchmen executed, see *JSA 2*, p 272: Maziyana; and also those named in Dingane's praises, Rycroft and Ngcobo (eds), *Praises of Dingana*, pp 87, 89.
30 Fynn, *Diary*, p 167; *JSA 1*, pp 104–6: Dinya; p 210: Kambi; *JSA 3*, pp 82, 88: Melapi.
31 *ZKS*, p 10; Bryant, *Olden Times*, p 671.
32 *JSA 1*, p 194: Jantshi; *JSA 4*, p 291: Ndukwana; Bryant, *Olden Times*, pp 670–1.

CHAPTER 20

1 *JSA 1*, p 196: Jantshi.
2 Bird, *Annals I*, pp 196–7: Campbell to Bell, 26 November 1830.
3 *JSA 4*, p 94: Mtshapi.
4 *JSA 4*, p 107: Mtshayankomo.
5 *JSA 3*, p 123: Mgundeni.
6 Rycroft and Ngcobo (eds), *Praises of Dingana*, p 87.
7 For details of Dingane's death, see *JSA 3*, pp 260–1: Mmemi; *JSA 4*, p 68: Mtshapi; Gibson, *Story of the Zulus*, p 90; Bryant, *Olden Times*, pp 325–6; Fuze, *Black People*, pp 82–4; and Lugg, *Historic Natal and Zululand*, pp 162–8. In 1947, HC Lugg succeeded in locating the grave and photographing it. The stones were still there but the site was thickly covered in trees and bush.

Reading List

Angus, George French. *The Kaffirs Illustrated in a Series of Drawings* (London: G Barclay for J Hogarth, 1849).

Ballard, Charles. 'Trade, Tribute and Migrant Labour: Zulu and Colonial Exploitation of the Delagoa Bay Hinterland 1818–1879' in *Before and After Shaka: Papers in Nguni History*, edited by JB Peires (Grahamstown: Rhodes University, Institute of Social and Economic Research, 1981).

Ballard, CC. 'Natal 1824–44: The Frontier Interregnum', *Journal of Natal and Zulu History*, IV (1982): 49–64.

Ballard, Charles. 'Drought and Economic Distress: South Africa in the 1800s', *Journal of Interdisciplinary History*, 17, 2 (Autumn 1986): 359–78.

Ballard, Charles. *The House of Shaka: The Zulu Monarchy Illustrated* (Durban: Emoyeni Books, 1988).

Ballard, Charles. 'Traders, Trekkers and Colonists' in *Natal and Zululand from Earliest Times to 1910: A New History*, edited by Andrew Duminy and Bill Guest (Pietermaritzburg: University of Natal Press and Shuter & Shooter, 1989).

Becker, Peter. *Rule of Fear: The Life and Times of Dingane, King of the Zulu* (London: Longmans, 1964).

Berning, Gillian. '*Indaba Yamakhos' Ayibanjelwa Mlando* / The Matter of Kings is Not Kept' in *Zulu Treasures: Of Kings and Commoners. A Celebration of the Material Culture of the Zulu People*, coordinated by Marilee Wood (Ulundi: KwaZulu Cultural Museum; Durban: The Local History Museums, 1996).

Bird, John. *The Annals of Natal 1495 to 1845*. 2 vols, facsimile reprint (Cape Town: C Struik, 1965).

Bonner, Philip. 'The Dynamics of Late Eighteenth Century, Early Nineteenth Century Northern Nguni Society – Some Hypotheses' in *Before and After Shaka: Papers in*

Nguni History, edited by JB Peires (Grahamstown: Rhodes University, Institute of Social and Economic Research, 1981).

Bonner, Philip. *Kings, Commoners and Concessionaires: The Evolution and Dissolution of the Nineteenth-Century Swazi State* (Johannesburg: Ravan, 1983).

Brookes, Edgar H and Colin de B Webb. *A History of Natal* (Pietermaritzburg: University of Natal Press, 1965).

Bryant, the Rev AT. *Olden Times in Zululand and Natal Containing Earlier Political History of the Eastern-Nguni Clans* (London: Longmans, Green, 1929).

Bryant, AT. *The Zulu People as They Were before the White Man Came* (Pietermaritzburg: Shuter & Shooter, 1949).

Bulpin, TV. *Shaka's Country: A Book of Zululand*, 3rd edition (Cape Town: Howard Timmins, 1956).

Buthelezi, Mbongiseni. 'The Empire Talks Back: Re-examining the Legacies of Shaka and Zulu Power in Post-apartheid South Africa' in *Zulu Identities: Being Zulu, Past and Present*, edited by Benedict Carton, John Laband and Jabulani Sithole (Pietermaritzburg: University of KwaZulu-Natal Press, 2008).

Cameron, Trewhella and SB Spies (eds). *An Illustrated History of South Africa* (Johannesburg: Jonathan Ball Publishers, 1986).

Carton, Benedict and Malcolm Draper. 'Bulls in the Boardroom: The Zulu Warrior Ethic and the Spirit of South African Capitalism' in *Zulu Identities: Being Zulu, Past and Present*, edited by Benedict Carton, John Laband and Jabulani Sithole (Pietermaritzburg: University of KwaZulu-Natal Press, 2008).

Chase, John Centlivres. *The Natal Papers: A Reprint of All Notices and Public Documents Connected with That Territory Including a Description of the Country and a History of Events from 1498 to 1843 in Two Parts*, facsimile reprint (Cape Town: C Struik, 1968).

Christopher, Joseph. *Natal, Cape of Good Hope* (London: Effingham Wilson, 1850).

Cobbing, Julian. 'The Ndebele State' in *Before and After Shaka: Papers in Nguni History*, edited by JB Peires (Grahamstown: Rhodes University, Institute of Social and Economic Research, 1981).

Colenbrander, Peter. 'The Zulu Kingdom, 1828–1879' in *Natal and Zululand from Earliest Times to 1910: A New History*, edited by Andrew Duminy and Bill Guest (Pietermaritzburg: University of Natal Press and Shuter & Shooter, 1989).

Cooper, Barbara M. 'Oral Sources and the Challenge of African History' in *Writing African History*, edited by John Edward Philips (Rochester, NY: University of Rochester Press, 2006).

Cope, Nicholas. *To Bind the Nation: Solomon kaDinuzulu and Zulu Nationalism 1913–1933* (Pietermaritzburg: University of Natal Press, 1993).

Cope, Trevor. *Izibongo: Zulu Praise Poems* (Oxford: Oxford University Press, 1968).

Cubbin, Anthony Edward. 'Origins of the British Settlement at Port Natal, May 1824–June 1842' (unpublished PhD thesis, University of the Orange Free State, 1983).

Dlamini, Nsizwa. 'Monuments of Division: Apartheid and Post-apartheid Struggles over Zulu Nationalist Heritage Sites' in *Zulu Identities: Being Zulu, Past and Present*, edited by Benedict Carton, John Laband and Jabulani Sithole (Pietermaritzburg:

University of KwaZulu-Natal Press, 2008).

Eldredge, Elizabeth A. 'Delagoa Bay and the Hinterland in the Early Nineteenth Century: Politics, Trade, Slaves, and Slave Riding' in *Slavery in South Africa: Captive Labor on the Dutch Frontier*, edited by Elizabeth A Eldredge and Fred Morton (Boulder: Westview Press; Pietermaritzburg: University of Natal Press, 1994).

Eldredge, Elizabeth A. 'Sources of Conflict in Southern Africa c 1800–1830' in *The Mfecane Aftermath: Reconstructive Debates in Southern African History*, edited by Carolyn Hamilton (Johannesburg: Wits University Press; Pietermaritzburg: University of Natal Press, 1995).

Eldredge, Elizabeth A. *The Creation of the Zulu Kingdom, 1815–1828: War, Shaka and the Consolidation of Power* (Cambridge: Cambridge University Press, 2014).

Eldredge, Elizabeth A. *Kingdoms and Chiefdoms in Southeastern Africa* (Rochester, NY: University of Rochester Press, 2015).

Etherington, Norman. *The Great Treks: The Transformation of Southern Africa, 1815–1854* (Harlow, Essex: Longman, 2001).

Falola, Toyin. 'Mission and Colonial Documents' in *Writing African History*, edited by John Edward Philips (Rochester, NY: University of Rochester Press, 2006).

Fuze, Magema M. *The Black People and Whence They Came: A Zulu View*, translated by HC Lugg and edited by AT Cope (Pietermaritzburg: University of Natal Press; Durban: Killie Campbell Africana Library, 1979).

Gardiner, Capt Allen Francis. *Narrative of a Journey to the Zooloo Country in South Africa, Undertaken in 1835*, facsimile reprint (Cape Town: C Struik, 1966).

Gibson, James Young. *The Story of the Zulus*, new edition (London: Longmans, Green, 1911).

Giliomee, Hermann and Bernard Mbenga. *New History of South Africa* (Cape Town: Tafelberg, 2007).

Gluckman, M. 'The Kingdom of the Zulus in South Africa' in *African Political Systems*, edited by M Fortes and EE Evans-Pritchard (Oxford: Oxford University Press, 1940): 25–55.

Gluckman, M. 'The Individual in a Social Framework: The Rise of King Shaka of Zululand', *Journal of African Studies*, 1, 2 (Summer 1974): 113–44.

Grout, L. *Zulu-Land; or, Life among the Zulu-Kafirs of Natal and Zulu-land* (London: Trubner, 1862).

Guy, Jeff. *The Destruction of the Zulu Kingdom: The Civil War in Zululand, 1879–1884* (London: Longman, 1979).

Guy, Jeff. 'Ecological Factors in the Rise of Shaka and the Zulu Kingdom' in *Economy and Society in Pre-Industrial South Africa*, edited by Shula Marks and Anthony Atmore (London: Longman, 1980): 102–19.

Hamilton, Carolyn. '"The Character and Objects of Shaka": A Reconsideration of the Making of Shaka as Mfecane Motor' in *The Mfecane Aftermath: Reconstructive Debates in Southern African History*, edited by Carolyn Hamilton (Johannesburg: Wits University Press; Pietermaritzburg: University of Natal Press, 1995).

Hamilton, Carolyn. *Terrific Majesty: The Powers of Shaka Zulu and the Limits of Historical Invention* (Cape Town and Johannesburg: David Philip, 1998).

Hamilton, Carolyn and John Wright. 'The Making of the *Amalala*: Ethnicity, Ideology and Relations of Subordination in a Precolonial Context', *South African Historical Journal*, 22 (1990): 3–23.

Hammond-Tooke, WD. 'Descent Groups, Chiefdoms and South African Historiography', *Journal of Southern African Studies*, 11, 2 (April 1985): 307–19.

Hammond-Tooke, David. *The Roots of Black South Africa* (Johannesburg: Jonathan Ball Publishers, 1993).

Hammond-Tooke, WD. 'Cattle Symbolism in Zulu Culture' in *Zulu Identities: Being Zulu, Past and Present*, edited by Benedict Carton, John Laband and Jabulani Sithole (Pietermaritzburg: University of KwaZulu-Natal Press, 2008).

Hanretta, Shaun. 'Women, Marginality and the Zulu State: Women's Institutions and Power in the Early Nineteenth Century', *Journal of African History*, 39 (1998): 389–415.

Harries, Patrick. 'Slavery amongst the Gaza Nguni: Its Changing Shape and Function and its Relationship to Other Forms of Exploitation' in *Before and After Shaka: Papers in Nguni History*, edited by JB Peires (Grahamstown: Rhodes University, Institute of Social and Economic Research, 1981).

Harries, Patrick. 'Ethnicity and the Ingwavuma Land Deal: The Zulu Northern Frontier in the Nineteenth Century', *Journal of Natal and Zulu History*, VI (1983): 1–27.

Henige, David. 'Oral Tradition as a Means of Reconstructing the Past' in *Writing African History*, edited by John Edward Philips (Rochester, NY: University of Rochester Press, 2006).

Holden, Rev William C. *History of the Colony of Natal, South Africa* (London: Alexander Heylin, 1855).

Isaacs, Nathaniel. *Travels and Adventures in Eastern Africa – Descriptive of the Zoolus, Their Manners, Customs with a Sketch of Natal*, edited by Louis Herman and Percival R Kirby (Cape Town: C Struik, 1970).

Jenkinson, Thomas B. *Amazulu: The Zulus, Their Past History, Manners, Customs, and Language* (London: WH Allen, 1882).

Kennedy, Philip A. 'Mpande and the Zulu Kingship', *Journal of Natal and Zulu History*, IV (1981): 21–38.

Kirby, Percival R (ed). *Andrew Smith and Natal: Documents Relating to the Early History of That Province* (Cape Town: Van Riebeeck Society, 1955).

Knight, Ian. *The Anatomy of the Zulu Army from Shaka to Cetshwayo 1818–1879* (London: Greenhill Books, 1995).

Knight, Ian. *Zulu Rising: The Epic Story of Isandlwana and Rorke's Drift* (London: Macmillan, 2010).

Koopman, A. 'Dingiswayo Rides Again', *Journal of Natal and Zulu History*, II (1979): 1–12.

Krige, Eileen Jensen. *The Social System of the Zulus*, 2nd edition (Pietermaritzburg: Shuter & Shooter, 1974).

Kunene, Mazisi. *Emperor Shaka the Great: A Zulu Epic* (London: Heinemann, 1979).

Laband, John. *Rope of Sand: The Rise and Fall of the Zulu Kingdom* (Johannesburg: Jonathan Ball Publishers, 1995).

Laband, John. 'Zulu Civilians during the Rise and Fall of the Zulu Kingdom, c 1817–1879' in *Daily Lives of Civilians in Wartime Africa: From Slavery Days to Rwandan Genocide*, edited by John Laband (Westport, CT, and London: Greenwood Press, 2007).

Laband, John. '"Bloodstained Grandeur": Colonial and Imperial Stereotypes of Zulu Warriors and Zulu Warfare' in *Zulu Identities: Being Zulu, Past and Present*, edited by Benedict Carton, John Laband and Jabulani Sithole (Pietermaritzburg: University of KwaZulu-Natal Press, 2008).

Laband, John. 'The Rise and Fall of the Zulu Kingdom' in *Zulu Identities: Being Zulu, Past and Present*, edited by Benedict Carton, John Laband and Jabulani Sithole (Pietermaritzburg: University of KwaZulu-Natal Press, 2008).

Laband, John. *Historical Dictionary of the Zulu Wars* (Lanham, MD: The Scarecrow Press, 2009).

Laband, John. '"Fighting Stick of Thunder": Firearms and the Zulu Kingdom: The Cultural Ambiguities of Transferring Weapons Technology', *War & Society*, 33, 4 (October 2014): 229–43.

Laband, John. *Zulu Warriors: The Battle for the South African Frontier* (New Haven and London: Yale University Press, 2014).

Laband, John. 'Zulu Wars' in *Oxford Bibliographies Online: Military History*, edited by Dennis Showalter (New York: Oxford University Press, 2015).

Lambert, Michael. 'Ancient Greek and Zulu Sacrificial Ritual: A Comparative Analysis', *Numen*, 40 (1993): 293–318.

Leverton, Dr BJT (ed). *Records of Natal, Volume One 1823–August 1828* (Pretoria: Government Printer, 1984).

Leverton, Dr BJT (ed). *Records of Natal, Volume Two September 1828–July 1835* (Pretoria: Government Printer, 1989).

Liesegang, Gerhard. 'Nguni Migrations between Delagoa Bay and the Zambezi, 1821–1839', *African Historical Studies*, 3, 2 (1970): 317–37.

Liesegang, Gerhard. 'Notes on the Internal Structure of the Gaza Kingdom of Southern Mozambique, 1840–1895' in *Before and After Shaka: Papers in Nguni History*, edited by JB Peires (Grahamstown: Rhodes University, Institute of Social and Economic Research, 1981).

Lugg, HC. *Historic Natal and Zululand* (Pietermaritzburg: Shuter & Shooter, 1949).

Mackeurtan, Graham. *The Cradle Days of Natal (1497–1845)* (London: Longmans, Green, 1930).

Maclean, Charles Rawden. *The Natal Papers of 'John Ross'*, edited by Stephen Gray (Pietermaritzburg: University of Natal Press; Durban: Killie Campbell Africana Library, 1992).

Maggs, Tim. 'The Iron Age Farming Communities' in *Natal and Zululand from Earliest Times to 1910: A New History*, edited by Andrew Duminy and Bill Guest (Pietermaritzburg: University of Natal Press and Shuter & Shooter, 1989).

Mahoney, Michael R. *The Other Zulus: The Spread of Zulu Ethnicity in Colonial South Africa* (Durham and London: Duke University Press, 2012).

Martens, Jeremy. 'Enlightenment Theories of Civilisation and Savagery in British Natal:

The Colonial Origins of the (Zulu) African Barbarism Myth' in *Zulu Identities: Being Zulu, Past and Present*, edited by Benedict Carton, John Laband and Jabulani Sithole (Pietermaritzburg: University of KwaZulu-Natal Press, 2008).

Maylam, Paul. *A History of the African People of South Africa: From the Early Iron Age to the 1970s* (London: Croom Helm, 1989).

Ndlovu, Sifiso. 'A Reassessment of Women's Power in the Zulu Kingdom' in *Zulu Identities: Being Zulu, Past and Present*, edited by Benedict Carton, John Laband and Jabulani Sithole (Pietermaritzburg: University of KwaZulu-Natal Press, 2008).

Ndlovu, Sifiso. 'Zulu Nationalist Representations of King Dingane' in *Zulu Identities: Being Zulu, Past and Present*, edited by Benedict Carton, John Laband and Jabulani Sithole (Pietermaritzburg: University of KwaZulu-Natal Press, 2008).

Ngubane, Harriet. *Body and Mind in Zulu Medicine: An Ethnography of Health and Disease in Nyuswa-Zulu Thought and Practice* (London: Academic Press, 1977).

Ntuli, Deuteronomy Bhekinkosi. '"Praises Will Remain"' in *Zulu Treasures: Of Kings and Commoners. A Celebration of the Material Culture of the Zulu People*, coordinated by Marilee Wood (Ulundi: KwaZulu Cultural Museum; Durban: The Local History Museums, 1996).

Nyembezi, CLS. 'The Historical Background to the Izibongo of the Zulu Military Age, Part I', *African Studies* 7, 2–3 (June 1948): 110–25.

Nyembezi, CLS. 'The Historical Background to the Izibongo of the Zulu Military Age, Part II', *African Studies* 7, 4 (June 1948): 157–74.

Okoye, Felix NC. 'Dingane: a Reappraisal', *Journal of African History*, X, 2 (1969): 221–35.

Omer-Cooper, JD. *The Zulu Aftermath: A Nineteenth-Century Revolution in Bantu Africa* (London: Longman, 1966).

Omer-Cooper, John. 'The Mfecane Survives its Critics' in *The Mfecane Aftermath: Reconstructive Debates in Southern African History*, edited by Carolyn Hamilton (Johannesburg: Wits University Press; Pietermaritzburg: University of Natal Press, 1995).

Papini, Robert. 'Some Zulu Uses for the Animal Domains: Livestock (*imfuyo*) and Game (*izilwane*) in *Zulu Treasures: Of Kings and Commoners. A Celebration of the Material Culture of the Zulu People*, coordinated by Marilee Wood (Ulundi: KwaZulu Cultural Museum; Durban: The Local History Museums, 1996).

Peires, Jeff. 'Matiwane's Road to Mbholompo: A Reprieve for the Mfecane?' in *The Mfecane Aftermath: Reconstructive Debates in Southern African History*, edited by Carolyn Hamilton (Johannesburg: Wits University Press; Pietermaritzburg: University of Natal Press, 1995).

Poland, Marguerite. 'Zulu Cattle: Colour Patterns and Imagery in the Names of Zulu Cattle' in *Zulu Treasures: Of Kings and Commoners. A Celebration of the Material Culture of the Zulu People*, coordinated by Marilee Wood (Ulundi: KwaZulu Cultural Museum; Durban: The Local History Museums, 1996).

Poland, Marguerite, David Hammond-Tooke and Leigh Voigt. *The Abundant Herds: A Celebration of the Nguni Cattle of the Zulu People* (Vlaeberg, South Africa: Fernwood Press, 2003).

Ritter, EA. *Shaka Zulu* (Harmondsworth: Penguin Books, 1985).

Roberts, B. *The Zulu Kings* (London: Sphere Books, 1974).
Roodt, Frans. 'Zulu Metalworking' in *Zulu Treasures: Of Kings and Commoners. A Celebration of the Material Culture of the Zulu People*, coordinated by Marilee Wood (Ulundi: KwaZulu Cultural Museum; Durban: The Local History Museums, 1996).
Rycroft, DK and AB Ngcobo (eds). *The Praises of Dingana (Izibongo zikaDingana)* (Pietermaritzburg: University of Natal Press; Durban: Killie Campbell Africana Library, 1988).
Saunders, Christopher (ed). *Reader's Digest Illustrated History of South Africa: The Real Story*, 3rd edition (Cape Town: The Reader's Digest Association South Africa, 1994).
Shamase, MZ. *Zulu Potentates from Earliest to Zwelithini KaBhekuzulu* (Durban: SM Publications, 1996).
Smail, JL. *From the Land of the Zulu Kings* (Durban: AJ Pope, 1979).
Stapleton, Timothy J. '"Him Who Destroys All": Reassessing the Early Career of Faku, King of the Mpondo, c 1818–1829', *South African Historical Journal*, 38 (May 1998): 55–78.
Stapleton, Timothy J. *Faku: Rulership and Colonisation in the Mpondo Kingdom (c. 1780–1867)* (Waterloo, Canada: Wilfrid Laurier University Press, 2001).
Stuart, James and D McK Malcolm (eds). *The Diary of Henry Francis Fynn* (Pietermaritzburg: Shuter & Shooter, 1969).
Tabler, Edward C. *Pioneers of Natal and South-Eastern Africa 1552–1878* (Cape Town and Rotterdam: AA Balkema, 1977).
Taylor, Stephen. *Shaka's Children: A History of the Zulu People* (London: HarperCollins, 1994).
Temkin, Ben. *Buthelezi: A Biography* (London and Portland, OR: Frank Cass, 2003).
Theal, DG McC, *Progress of South Africa in the Century* (London: Linscott, 1900).
Thornton, John. 'European Documents and African History' in *Writing African History*, edited by John Edward Philips (Rochester, NY: University of Rochester Press, 2006).
Van Schalkwyk, Len. 'Origins' in *Zulu Treasures: Of Kings and Commoners. A Celebration of the Material Culture of the Zulu People*, coordinated by Marilee Wood (Ulundi: KwaZulu Cultural Museum; Durban: The Local History Museums, 1996).
Von Sicard, H. 'Shaka and the North', *African Studies*, 14, 4 (January 1955): 145–53.
Waetjen, Thembisa and Gerhard Maré. 'Shaka's Aeroplane: The Take-off and Landing of Inkatha, Modern Zulu Nationalism and Royal Politics' in *Zulu Identities: Being Zulu, Past and Present*, edited by Benedict Carton, John Laband and Jabulani Sithole (Pietermaritzburg: University of KwaZulu-Natal Press, 2008).
War Office: Intelligence Division. *Précis of Information Concerning Zululand with a Map. Corrected to December, 1894* (London: Her Majesty's Stationery Office, 1894).
Webb, C de B and JB Wright (eds and translators). *The James Stuart Archive of Recorded Oral Evidence Relating to the History of the Zulu and Neighbouring Peoples*, 5 vols (Pietermaritzburg: University of Natal Press; Durban: Killie Campbell Africana Library, 1976, 1979, 1982, 1986, 2001).
Webb, C de B and JB Wright (eds). *A Zulu King Speaks: Statements Made by Cetshwayo*

kaMpande on the History and Customs of His People (Pietermaritzburg: University of Natal Press; Durban: Killie Campbell Africana Library, 1978).

Whitelaw, Gavin. 'A Brief Archaeology of Precolonial Farming in KwaZulu-Natal' in *Zulu Identities: Being Zulu, Past and Present*, edited by Benedict Carton, John Laband and Jabulani Sithole (Pietermaritzburg: University of KwaZulu-Natal Press, 2008).

Wood, Marilee. 'Zulu Beadwork' in *Zulu Treasures: Of Kings and Commoners. A Celebration of the Material Culture of the Zulu People*, coordinated by Marilee Wood (Ulundi: KwaZulu Cultural Museum; Durban: The Local History Museums, 1996).

Wright, John. 'Pre-Shakan Age-Group Formations among the Northern Nguni', *Natalia*, 8 (1978): 22–30.

Wright, John. 'Control of Women's Labour in the Zulu Kingdom' in *Before and After Shaka: Papers in Nguni History*, edited by JB Peires (Grahamstown: Rhodes University, Institute of Social and Economic Research, 1981).

Wright, John. 'The Dynamics of Power and Conflict in Late 18th and Early 19th Centuries: A Critical Reconstruction' (unpublished PhD thesis, University of the Witwatersrand, 1989).

Wright, John. 'AT Bryant and the "Wars of Shaka"', *History in Africa*, 18 (1991): 409–25.

Wright, John. 'Beyond the Concept of the "Zulu Explosion": Comments on the Current Debate' in *The Mfecane Aftermath: Reconstructive Debates in Southern African History*, edited by Carolyn Hamilton (Johannesburg: Wits University Press; Pietermaritzburg: University of Natal Press, 1995).

Wright, John. 'Political Transformations in the Thukela–Mzimkhulu Region in the Late Eighteenth and Early Nineteenth Centuries' in *The Mfecane Aftermath: Reconstructive Debates in Southern African History*, edited by Carolyn Hamilton (Johannesburg: Wits University Press; Pietermaritzburg: University of Natal Press, 1995).

Wright, John. 'Reflections on the Politics of Being "Zulu"' in *Zulu Identities: Being Zulu, Past and Present*, edited by Benedict Carton, John Laband and Jabulani Sithole (Pietermaritzburg: University of KwaZulu-Natal Press, 2008).

Wright, John. 'Revisiting the Stereotype of Shaka's "Devastations"' in *Zulu Identities: Being Zulu, Past and Present*, edited by Benedict Carton, John Laband and Jabulani Sithole (Pietermaritzburg: University of KwaZulu-Natal Press, 2008).

Wright, John. 'Turbulent Times: Political Transformations in the North and East, 1760s–1830s' in *The Cambridge History of South Africa, Volume I: From Early Times to 1885*, edited by Carolyn Hamilton, Bernard K Mbenga and Robert Ross (Cambridge: Cambridge University Press, 2012).

Wright, John and Carolyn Hamilton. 'Traditions and Transformations: The Phongolo-Mzimkhulu Region the Late Eighteenth and Early Nineteenth Centuries' in *Natal and Zululand from Earliest Times to 1910: A New History*, edited by Andrew Duminy and Bill Guest (Pietermaritzburg: University of Natal Press and Shuter & Shooter, 1989).

Wright, John and Carolyn Hamilton. 'Ethnicity and Political Change before 1840' in *Political Economy and Identities in KwaZulu-Natal: Historical and Social Perspectives*, edited by Robert Morrell (Durban: Indicator Press, 1996).

Wylie, Dan. 'Textual Incest: Nathaniel Isaacs and the Development of the Shaka Myth', *History in Africa*, 19 (1992): 411–33.
Wylie, Dan. 'Language and Assassination: Cultural Negations in White Writers' Portrayal of Shaka and the Zulu' in *The Mfecane Aftermath: Reconstructive Debates in Southern African History*, edited by Carolyn Hamilton (Johannesburg: Wits University Press; Pietermaritzburg: University of Natal Press, 1995).
Wylie, Dan. *Savage Delight: White Myths of Shaka* (Pietermaritzburg: University of Natal Press, 2000).
Wylie, Dan. *Myth of Iron: Shaka in History* (Pietermaritzburg: University of KwaZulu-Natal Press, 2006).
Wylie, Dan. 'White Myths of Shaka' in *Zulu Identities: Being Zulu, Past and Present*, edited by Benedict Carton, John Laband and Jabulani Sithole (Pietermaritzburg: University of KwaZulu-Natal Press, 2008).
Wylie, Dan. *Shaka: A Pocket Biography* (Johannesburg: Jacana, 2011).

Acknowledgements

The composition of any book is a protracted and gruelling procedure, but it is not as lonely as it is often made out to be. Ever since I first embarked on writing one some forty years ago, Fenella has steadfastly continued to hearten and reassure me during the recurring process, and shrewdly to critique the initial drafts.

Jonathan Ball made this particular book possible through his engaged and enthusiastic support at every stage, and I am particularly indebted to him. Alfred LeMaitre, the freelance editor and project manager, has exhibited great patience and tact as well as admirable proficiency in shepherding the book to completion, and I am fortunate to have worked with him. My thanks are also due to Ester Levinrad, Ceri Prenter and Farieda Classen, the in-house team at Jonathan Ball Publishers, as well as to Kevin Shenton, who was responsible for design and typesetting, and to Tessa Botha, who compiled the index. The proofreader, Lesley Hay-Whitton, expertly and meticulously put my manuscript through a fine sieve. She saved me from many a slip, but any remaining mistakes are mine alone. Sinothi Thabethe, the Director of the Local History Museums, Durban, and Rebecca Naidoo, the Museum Officer, both generously assisted with the illustrations.

In the course of decades of engagement with the history of the Zulu kingdom, I have benefited immeasurably from the learning and companionship of many experts in the same field. Their indispensable works – without which I could not have attempted this study of Shaka's assassination – spill out of my overloaded bookcases. Regrettably, not all of these fine scholars are still living, and I dedicate this book to the memory of Paul Thompson (1940–2017), colleague, companion on many a field trip, co-author and friend of forty-five years.

Index

Page numbers in *italics* indicate illustrations; the letter 'n' after a page number indicates a note. Note that Zulu words are entered under the stem, not under the prefix.

adornments 3, 4, 6–7, *8*, 16–17, 35,
African National Congress 167
Aitchison, Captain RS 115, 116
amnesty 37
ancestors' shades 7–9
Anglo-Zulu War (1879) 13, 28, 144, 165
animal skins 6, 16, 138
Anne (schooner) 84
Antelope (brig) 67
appearance *see* physical appearance
assassinations
  under Dingane 151, 154–155, 156–157, 159
  and fight between snakes 7–9
  Mawewe 23
  Ngwadi 149
  Shaka, first attempt on 13–14, 18–19, 26, 30–31, 42, 49–50
  Shaka, second attempt on 124–125, 127, 133
  Shaka, killing of 136–140
  Shaka's last words 140, 207n
  Sigujana 25–26, 27
  in traditional societies ix
  see also executions
assegais 16

baggage-carriers 73, 123
Baleka (informant) 20–21, 49, 57, 58, 63
Baleni (informant) 96
Barends, Barend 83
battle at Ndondakusuka 61
battle, description of 33–35, 37

battle of izinDolowane hills 78–79, 84
battle of Ncome (Blood River) 163
battle of the Maqongqo hills 9, 27, 163
battle of the Thukela 162
battle of the White Mfolozi 163
battle of Veglaer 162
Bazley, William 63, 91, 92
beer 4, *4*, 73
Bees (iziNyosi) regiment 123, 148, 149
beetles, intestinal 55–56
Bhaca people *32*, 75, 160–161, 187
Bhalule impi
  accept succession of Dingane 153
  accompanied by Shaka's brothers 121
  attack on Gaza people 121–123
  Shaka's purpose in launching 120, 121, 123–124, 126
  sheds large numbers of conscripts 128
  size of 122–123
  suffers catastrophic losses 152–153
  see also warriors
Bheje kaMagawuzi 83, 84
Bhibhi (wife of Senzangakhona) 22, 27–28, 132
blankets 6, 59, 65, 114
Blood River, battle of 163
blood sacrifices 7
Boers 161–163, 164–165
boundaries
  British Natal 165, 208n
  Zulu kingdom 66, 73, 190
Bourke, Major General Richard 82, 105, 108
brass adornments 4, 6–7
British authorities 165
  see also Cape Colony government
Bryant, Rev AT 13, 97, 136
buffalo thorn 97, *97*

burial customs 96–98, 142–143, 165, 167
burial sites
  Dingane 164, 167
  Mnkabayi 29
  Mpande 167
  Nandi 97, *97*, 98
  Shaka 143, 144, 165, *166*
  Valley of the Kings 13–14
Buthelezi people 150

Cane, John
  description of Dingane 129
  embassy to Cape for Dingane 160
  embassy to Cape for Shaka 114–116, 119, 125, 126
  final years of 158
  joins Shaka's battles 83
  settles in Port Natal 70
Cape Colony government
  Dingane's desire to contact 160
  nervous of Zulu incursions 111
  refuses to annex Port Natal 67–68, 112, 115
  and Shaka's attack on Mpondo 108, 148
  Shaka's desire to contact 65–66, 85–86
  Shaka's fear of revolt 82
  Shaka's first embassy to 103–106, 112–113
  Shaka's second embassy to 113–115, 119
Cape Mounted Riflemen 115
Cape Town 13, 70, 84, 114
captives 5, 38–39, 61
cattle
  appropriation of Farewell's cattle 157
  daily inspection by king 5
  and death of Nandi 96, 98
  illustration of *4*
  indicator of wealth 2, 149
  ilobolo system 21
  as payment of tribute 39, 84, 111, 137
  raids on 23, 74, 75, 83, 85, 110–111, 122, 160–161
  red cattle 119
  rights of their carers 6
  rounded up after Shaka's death 148
  sacrifices of 9, 14, 19, 108, 141–142
  seized in combat 33, 37, 79, 161
  sent to starving *Bhalule impi* 149–150
  Shaka gift to King 84
  Sothobe's accurate estimate of 104
cattle byres 1–2, *2*, 138
cattle guards 148
Cele, Henry xi, 64
Cele people 45, 56, 92, 156, 187
ceremonial dress 6, 15–16, *15*, *36*
Cetshwayo kaMpande
  appointing of next king 153
  assassination of Shaka 138
  coronation in 1873 *36*
  death of Senzangakhona 25
  defeated in Anglo-Zulu War 13, 165, 167
  Dingane's killing of his brothers 154
  dream 21

exclamation when angry 133
legitimacy of Shaka 21, 22, 56
Mdlaka's challenge to Dingane 155, 156
Nandi's death/burial 91, 97–98, 99
oNdini homestead *3*
Shaka's lack of progeny 60
snakes as ancestors' shades 7
Ceza mountain 128
charms, medicinal 33–34, 47–48, 108
Chase, JC 144
chiefdoms
  defeated chiefdoms 38, 46
  fluid membership of 40
  insider vs outsider 44–45
  loyalty to Shaka 39, 43, 65
  and Shaka's defeat of Qwabe 48–49
  Shaka's threat to eastern Cape 104, 105, 107
  warfare between 23–24
children 5, 38, 60–61, 73, 78–79, 92–93, 96, 123, 155
Chunu people 32, 48–49, 187
circumcision 63
civilians in warfare 37–38
cleansing rituals 30, 79
Cloete, Major AJ 104, 105
clothing
  ceremonial dress 6, 15–16, *15*, *36*
  praise singers 17
  royal children 5
  women 3–4
coil, sacred 28
Cole, Sir Lowry 115, 116
Commission on Native Laws and Customs 91, 97
council, royal 2
cowardice 35, 110
cruelty
  of Dingane 153–154
  of Shaka 57, 58, 129
crying tree 93, 122

dancing 17, 18, 47, 59, 131
deadman's tree 93, 122
Delagoa Bay 12, 32, 38, 41, 65, 67, 68
dialects 44, 45, 64
Dingane kaSenzangakhona
  acclaimed as king 153
  appreciates value of firearms 77, 157
  assassinations under 149, 151, 154–155, 156–157
  battles against the Boers 161–163, 167
  campaigns against other peoples 160–161
  ceremony for Shaka's spirit 144
  chosen as king 150–151
  conspiracy to kill Shaka 124–125, 128–129, 131–134
  death of 164
  defeated by Mpande 163
  denounced by Mpande 9
  desires contact with British 160
  fewer adornments than Shaka 16
  illustration of *131*

INDEX

invades Swazi kingdom 163
lack of progeny 60
motive for killing Shaka 128, 131
paternity of Ngwadi 22
physical appearance 130–131
portrayed as villain by IFP 166–167
reassurance after Shaka's assassination 147, 148
rehabilitated by ANC 167
relationship with Mhlangana 132, 142, 148–149
relations with traders 147, 157, 160
reputation for treachery 129
Shaka delegates authority to 20
and Shaka's assassination 138–139
'smelled out' by diviners 100
support from Mnkabayi 133, 134
Dingiswayo kaJobe
death of 31, 39
plot against Senzangakhona 24–25
praise-name for Shaka 56
reliance on Zulu chiefdom 24
Shaka's patron 23, 24
supports Shaka's seizure of power 26
usurps the throne 23
Dinya (informant) 68, 70, 124, 137
diviners 10, 30, 100
Dlamini (Swazi) people 38
Drakensberg 66, 110, 190
dreams 21, 112, 134–135
drosters (gangs) 32, 66, 187–188
Dundas, Major WB 111
Durban 67, 158
dysentery 91–92, 93, 122

ear plugs 3
elephant ivory 77, 85, 90
Elizabeth and Susan (schooner) 86, 103, 112, 116, 147, 148
emaKhosini valley 13, 20, 159, 163
executions
for cowardice 110
under Dingane 154–155, 156–157, 159, 162
of diviners 100
instrument of policy 57
modes of 58, 93
under Mpande 208n
place of execution 159
under Shaka 26, 49, 99, 100, 110
see also assassinations

Faku (Mpondo paramount)
attacks on Mpondo 75–76, 110
moves away from Shaka 76
peace envoys to Shaka 111
succeeds his father 74
Farewell, Elizabeth 103
Farewell, Francis George
arrives in Port Elizabeth 116
choosing of Dingane as king 150
conspiracy to kill Shaka 129
date of Shaka's assassination 136–137
death of 157–158
fort on Port Natal 71
founder of Port Natal 67
joins Shaka's battles 110
leaves Port Natal after assassination 148
loses Shaka's favour 85, 102
possible emissary for Shaka 85
reasons for Gaza campaign 126
returns to Port Natal 112
rivalry with King 84, 85, 112–113
sails with King to Cape 103
Shaka 'careless with people's lives' 110
Shaka's atrocities against women 129
size of Zulu army 74–75
trade negotiations with Shaka 68
views on Shaka x
feathers 16, 104
Febana (Farewell's Zulu name) 67
firearms *see* muskets
first-fruits ceremonies 14–18, 155
food 4, 5, 73–74, 98, 99, 122, 152
Frontier Wars 77, 85
Fuze, Magema 35, 56, 62, 92, 95–96
Fynn, Henry Francis
account of a battle 33–34
admires Shaka's headdress 16
arrives in Port Natal 66–67
assassination attempt on Shaka 18, 19, 30, 69
assassination of Shaka 136, 139
burial of Shaka 143
conspiracy to kill Shaka 124
and death of King 112
death of Nandi 90–91, 91–92, 95, 99
establishes own station 84–85
final years of 158
fondness between Dingane and Mhlangana 132
illustration of 70
joins Shaka's battles 79, 110
Nandi's grave site 97
reports on deaths of women 129
Shaka's desire to contact British 86
Shaka's dream of being killed 134
Shaka's vanity 59
trade negotiations with Shaka 68
views on Shaka x
Zulu still believed Shaka alive 155

Gardiner, Captain Allen 72, 77, 154
Gaza people 32, 41, 119, 120, 121–123, 152, 188
Gibixhegu 51
Gibson, James Young 57, 96, 113
gifts 103, 113, 114–115, 160
Gqugqu (son of Senzangakhona) 154, 208n
Grahamstown 106, 114, 116, 160
grass coil (sacred) 28
graves *see* burial sites
Griqua people 66, 83
Gwembeshe (Bazley's Zulu name) 91

Halstead, Thomas 70

221

Hamu (son of Mpande) 133
headdresses 8, *15*, 16, *36*
healers *see* traditional healers
herdsmen 6, 39, 44
Heritage Day 136
Hintsa (Xhosa paramount) 85
hippopotamus ivory 71, 90, 103
historical sources xiii–xiv
Hlangabeza kaMabedla 120, 121
uHlomendlini regiment 125, 148, 149, 156, 160
Hlubi people *12*, *32*, 188
HMS *Helicon* (sloop-of-war) 112
Home Guards *see* uHlomendlini regiment
homesteads, family 1, *12*, 13, 25, 28, *32*, 48, 90, 95, 101, 137, 139–140, 141, 142, 144, 149, 156, 157, 163–164
homesteads, royal 1–3, 7–8, *12*, 13, 14, 17, 18, 20, 28, *32*, 40, 46, 47, 51, *81*, 82, 144, 159–160, 162, 163, 165, 192n
  see also kwaBulawayo; kwaDukuza
horses 68, 83, 162
hunter-traders *see* trader-hunters
hunting 71, 77, 85, 90, 103

Inkatha Freedom Party xii–xiii, 165–167
Isaacs, Nathaniel
  arrival in Port Natal 71
  assassination of Shaka 136, 139
  British reception of Shaka's embassy 105
  choosing of Dingane as king 150
  conspiracy to kill Shaka 124, 129
  and death of King 112
  descriptions of Dingane 129, 130, 131
  final years of 157–158
  joins Shaka's battles 83, 84
  killings after Nandi's death 96
  losses suffered by *Bhalule impi* 152–153
  meaning of 'kwaDukuza' 81
  returns to Port Natal 112
  sails with King to Cape 103
  Shaka angry with 113
  Shaka's attitude to trade 69
  Shaka endows with lands 115
  Shaka's anger towards British 113
  Shaka's character 57
  Shaka's desire to contact British 86
  Shaka's fear of conspiracies 99
  Shaka's physical activity 59
  Shaka's physical appearance 62
  spelling of Shaka's name 55
  traders' panic after assassination 147
  views on Shaka x, 56
  warriors' dance with Shaka 17
ivory 65, 69, 71, 76, 85, 90, 103, 113, 114
izinDolowane hills, battle of 78–79, 84

Jantshi (informant) 18, 46–47, 49, 55–56, 76, 91, 131, 139, 150
Jele people 41

jewellery *see* adornments
Jobe kaKhayi 21, 23
JR Thompson & Co. 67
Julia (sloop) 67

Kambi (informant) 46
uKhandempemvu regiment 5, 6
Khathide (Phakathwayo's heir) 48
Khoekhoen 71, 72, 83
Khondlo kaMncinci 45, 46
Khumalo people *32*, 41, 83, 84, 188
King George IV 86, 102, 115
King, James Saunders
  abandons Port Natal 85
  admires Shaka's headdress 16
  arrival in Port Natal 70–71
  death of 112–113, 115
  illustration of Shaka *xii*
  joins Shaka's battles 84, 85
  returns to Port Natal 112
  rivalry with Farewell 84, 85, 112–113
  sets sail for Cape 103
  Shaka angry with 113, 115, 126
  Shaka's attack on Mpondo 107, 108
  Shaka's embassy to British 85–86, 104, 105, 106
  signs treaty with Shaka 102
King Mswati II 164
King Sobhuza I 122
Kunene, Mazisi xi
Kutshwayo kaNswakele 58
kwaBulawayo homestead
  first and second homesteads *12*, *32*, 50–51, 55
  killing of Qwabe 49
  killings after death of Nandi 96
  remains administrative centre 81
  Shaka meets with traders 68
  Shaka moves away from 100–101
kwaDukuza homestead
  burned in Anglo-Zulu War 144
  Dingane moves away from 159
  establishment of kwaNyakamubi 101
  James King appointed as 'chief' 102
  layout 80
  place of Shaka's assassination 137
  presumed site of Shaka's grave 165, *166*
  rebuilt by Dingane/Mpande 144
  return of Dingane and Mhlangana 134
  Shaka's purported cutting open of pregnant woman 58
  Shaka's purpose in building 82
  Shaka watches the sea 59
  site of village of Stanger 144
kwaNkatha (place of execution) 159
KwaZulu Monuments Council 167

Langazana (wife of Senzangakhona) 28
legitimacy of Shaka 21–22
leopard skins 16
Lepelle River *32*, 83, 119

INDEX

ilobolo system 21, 71
Lourenço Marques *12, 32*, 41, 65, 68
Lucunge (councillor) 68, 125
Lunguza (informant) 5, 92, 93, 131

Macassar hair oil 60, 113, 115
Maclean, Charles Rawden
    amnesty to survivors 37
    arrival in Port Natal 71
    assassination of Shaka 138
    attends first-fruits ceremony 14–16
    conspiracy to kill Shaka 133
    description of kwaDukuza 80
    description of Mbopha 134
    description of Port Natal settlers 71
    returns to Port Natal 112
    sails with King to Cape 103
    Shaka's character 57
    Shaka's compact with Dingane 61, 131
    Shaka's concern over white hairs 60
    Shaka's relations with traders 59
    Sothobe's impression of 'white' cities 106
    spends three years with Shaka 14
    subjects in awe of Shaka 62
    TV series *John Ross* 191n
    warriors' reactions to muskets 77
    Zulu form of execution 58
Madhlebe (informant) 91
Madikane (informant) 44
Madzikane (Bhaca chief) 75
Mafokose (wife of Sothobe) 103
Magaye kaDibandlela 56, 64, 68, 82, 125, 156
magic potions 25, 28, 31
Magidigidi (informant) 134
Magolwana kaMkhathini 161
Mahlabathini plain 1, 13, 29, 144
maids-of-honour 3–5, 17, 19, 61, 89, 141
Makewu (informant) 20, 134, 139, 144
Makuza (informant) 75, 103
Malandela (father of Qwabe and Zulu) 45
malaria 122, 132
Maphitha kaSojiyisa 41–42, 110
Maqongqo hills, battle of 9, 27, 163
marriage 21, 38–39, 71
    see also ilobolo system
Mary (brig) 70
Masawuzana (son of Mteli) 99
Masiphula kaMamba 6–7, 8
Matabele people 41
Matingwana (informant) 138
Matiwane kaMasumpa 111
matricide, rumours of 91–94, 133
mats, royal 21, 62
Mawewe (Dingiswayo's brother) 23
Mayinga (informant) 22, 56, 57, 63, 104
Maziyana (informant) 74, 137, 138
Mbelebeleni homestead *12, 32*, 46
Mbo chiefdom 23
Mbopha kaSitayi
    acts as interim regent 142, 148, 150

    assassination of Ngwadi 149
    assassination of Shaka 138–139
    executed by Dingane 157
    influence of Mnkabayi 133–134, 157
    plot to kill Mhlangana 151
    second attempt on Shaka's life 125
    Shaka confides dream to his sister 135
    Shaka's trusted advisor 133
Mbozamboza (chief) 103, 104, 106, 109, 114
Mbulo (informant) 59
Mbuyazi (Fynn's Zulu name) 66
Mbuyazi (Shaka's possible son) 61
Mcotoyi (Thuli chief) 124, 125, 131
Mdlaka kaNcidi 74, 75, 109, 121, 122, 155, 156
medicinal charms 33–34, 47–48, 108
Melapi (informant) 56, 58, 60, 62–63, 104
Melapi (son of Magaye) 82
mercenaries 161
mfecane (crushing) 33
Mfihlo (Shaka's half-brother) 100, 154
Mfokozana *see* Sigujana kaSenzangakhona
Mfunda (Shaka's grandmother) 45
Mgidhlana (son of Mpande) 93
uMgungundlovu homestead *81*, 144, 159–160, 162, 163, 192n
Mhlangana kaSenzangakhona
    assassination of Ngwadi 149
    conspiracy to kill Shaka 124–125, 131–132, 133, 134
    death of 151
    insists on right to be king 150
    reassurance after Shaka's assassination 147, 148
    relationship with Dingane 142, 148–149
    as rightful heir 132
    role in Shaka's assassination 138, 139
    Shaka delegates authority to 20
    'smelled out' by diviners 100
    support from Mnkabayi 133
migrations *32*, 33, 37, 40–41
milk, sour 4, 73, 98
Mini (informant) 98
missionaries x, 31, 114, 129, 160
Mkando (informant) 38, 140
Mkebeni kaDabulamanzi 140
Mkehlengana (informant) 91, 137
Mkhonto (son of Magaye) 156
Mkomoyi (father of Makuza) 103
Mlahla (father of Mbulo) 59
Mmama (sister of Mnkabayi) 27, 28, 133
Mmemi (informant) 40, 47
Mnkabayi kaJama (sister of Senzangakhona)
    becomes Shaka's enemy 133–134
    burial site 29
    chooses Dingane as king 150
    plot to kill Mhlangana 151
    praises 28–29, 133
    rules over Shaka's homesteads 28
    support for Shaka 27
    taste for power 26
Mnkabi (wife of Senzangakhona) 110

Mnongose (Qwabe chief) 99
Monase (wife of Mpande) 61
mourning
    assassination attempt on Shaka 19
    death of Nandi 95–96, 98–99, 102, 108, 120
    no mourning for Shaka 142
Mpande kaSenzangakhona
    and Boers 161, 162, 164
    building of kwaNodwengu 144
    burial of 98
    death of 165
    defeat of Dingane 27, 163
    escapes assassination 154–155
    favoured by Mdlaka 155
    and fight between snakes 9–10, 161
    forced to share power with Cetshwayo 60
    illustration of *8*
    liked to hear Dingane's praises 161
    not involved in conspiracy against Shaka 132
    raises seed for Nzibe 132–133
    recognised as king by British 165
    views on royal succession 9
Mphikase (wife of Senzangakhona) 132, 163
Mpondo kingdom *12*, *32*, 66, 74, 75–76, 108, 109–111, 121, 124, 188
Mqayana (healer) 47–48
Msimbithi, Jacob (interpreter) 68, 76, 102, 103, 113, 115
Mteli kaLufuta 99
Mthethwa people 21, 23, 24, 31, 38, 188
Mtshapi (informant) 7, 119, 122
Mtshebwe (son of Magaye) 64
Mudli kaNkwelo kaNdaba 26
muskets 66, 69, 71, 75–76, 78, 82–83, 84, 110, 157
Mxamana kaNtandeka 137, 141, 143
Mzilikazi kaMashobana 41, 66, 79, 161
Mzondwase (wife of Senzangakhona) 132

Nandi (wife of Senzangakhona)
    burial of 96–98, *97*
    death of 28, 89, 90–94, 133
    marries Ngendeyana 22
    mourning period for 95–96, 98–99, 102, 108, 120
    physical appearance/character 89–90
    pregnant with Shaka 55
    Senzangakhona's favourite wife 21–22
    Shaka as 'illegitimate child' 27
    Shaka's reaction to her death 95–96
    Shaka's retribution on Qwabe 49–50
    and story of Shaka's son 92–93
Natal, annexation of 144, 208n
Natal Native Commission 91
Ncome, battle of 163
Ndamase (son of Faku) 75
Ndangane (councillor) 126
Ndebele people *32*, 41, 66, 161, 188
Ndhlovu (informant) 22, 31, 58, 83
Ndlela kaSompisi 155
Ndondakusuka, battle at 61

Ndongeni (son of Xoki) 132
Ndukwana (informant) 7, 17, 34, 98, 139
Ndwandwe people 23, 24, 30–31, 38, 39–40, 41, 42, 50, 76–79, 111, 188–189
Ngendeyana 22, 25
Ngidi (informant) 26, 48, 51, 55, 56, 63–64, 81, 91, 92, 100
Ngomane kaMqomboli 24, 26, 98, 108, 156
Ngqengelele kaMvulana 150, 151
Ngqojana kaSenzangakhona
    assassination of Shaka 138
    death of 154
    'smelled out' by diviners 100
Ngqungqushe (Mpondo paramount) 74
Nguni cattle 2, *2*
    see also cattle
Ngunuza kaNsiyana 143
Ngwadi (son of Nandi) 22, 25–26, 149, 151, 193n
Ngwane people 111, 189, 202n
Nobiya (son of Sothobe) 103
Nomkwayimba *see* Sigujana kaSenzangakhona
Noncoba (daughter of Nandi) 22, 28, 90, 150
Nongalaza kaNondela 148
Nongila (Shaka's spy) 18
Nono (brother of Phakathwayo) 46
nose, Shaka's 63
Nqetho kaKhondlo 46, 156, 157, 161
Ntendeka (councillor) 143
Ntombaze (mother of Zwide) 31
Ntshali people *12*, *32*, 120, 121, 189
Nxazonke kaMbhengi 137, 141, 143
Nyawo people *12*, 164, 189
iziNyosi (Bees) regiment 123, 148, 149
Nzibe (royal prince) 132
Nzobo kaSobadli 153–154, 159, 160

occult forces
    bewitching of Dingiswayo 31
    and distinctive necklace 35
    plot against Senzangakhona 24–25
    Shaka's defeat of Qwabe 47–48
    use of poison 93
Ogle, Henry 70, 110
oNdini homestead *3*

Pedi Maroteng paramountcy 41
Pedi people *32*, 83, 189
penis sheaths 5, 6
penis, slurs about Shaka's 45, 46–47
Phakathwayo kaKhondlo 43, 45, 46–47, 48, 150
physical appearance
    Dingane 130–132
    Mbopha 134
    Mnkabayi 28
    Nandi 89
    Port Natal settlers 71
    Shaka 62–63, 64
    Sothobe 104
poisoning of Nandi 93

INDEX

population of Zulu kingdom 74
porridge 4, 98
Port Elizabeth 103, 106, 107
Port Natal 12, 32, 66–68, 69–71, 112, 115
  see also trader-hunters
Port St Johns 74
Portugal 38, 41, 65, 68, 122
Potgieter, T 144
potions, magic 25, 28, 31
Powell, Joseph 70
praises
  Dingane 77, 128, 129–130, 130–131, 151, 154, 161
  fate of civilians in war 38
  Maphitha 42
  Mnkabayi 28–29, 133
  Mpande 154
  Nandi 90
  Shaka xi, 35, 40, 43, 63, 79, 109
  Sothobe 104
  sung by warriors 5
  Zwide 24
  see also songs
praise singers 17, 137, 161
princes, royal
  complex succession procedures 20
  possibility of violent usurpation 26
  'smelled out' by diviners 100
progeny, lack of 60

Qwabe people 12, 43–44, 45, 46, 47–48, 49–50, 82, 99, 130, 156, 157, 189

regiments
  uHlomendlini 125, 148, 149, 156, 160
  uKhandempemvu 5, 6
  iziNyosi (the Bees) 123, 148, 149
  Shaka's influence on 23
  iziToyatoyi 164
  see also warriors
religious beliefs 7
Republiek Natalia 163, 165
Retief, Piet 162
rituals
  ahead of battles 30, 33–34
  cleansing after battles 79
  religious 2
  Shaka purified after Nandi's death 108
  slitting open of belly 140
  for spirits of the dead 143–144
  stabbing of corpses 140
  transition from childhood to adulthood 3
Ross, John see Maclean, Charles Rawden
royal children 5, 155
royal council 2
royal enclosures 2–5, 61, 80, 159–160
royal mats 21, 62
royal women 3, 26–27, 27, 28, 96

sacrifices 7, 9, 14, 19, 108, 141–142
Senzangakhona kaJama
  decides to kill Shaka 21
  establishment of esiKlebheni 13
  line of descent 14
  occult plot against 24–25
  various wives 21, 22, 28, 131–132
sexual intercourse 60
shades of ancestors 7–9
Shaka kaSenzangakhona
  character traits 56–60, 61
  fathering of possible children 60–61, 92
  illustration of xii
  physical appearance 62–63, 64
  portrayed as hero by IFP 166
  pronunciation/origin of name 55–56
  slurs about his penis 45, 46–47
  speech defect 63–64
Shaka Zulu (film) xi, 191n
shields xiii, 17
  see also war-shields
Sibisi people 137
Sibiya people 103
Sigujana kaSenzangakhona
  assassination of 25–26, 128, 131–132, 151
  death of his mother 27
  recognised by Senzangakhona 22–23
Sikwayo (would-be assassin) 43, 48
Silevana (Nyawo regent) 164
Sivivi (informant) 50
slave trade 38, 71, 157
Smith, Andrew
  assassination attempt on Shaka 30
  assassination of Shaka 138, 139
  Shaka's character 58–59
  Shaka's possible children 61
  Shaka's sexual relations 60
snakes 7–9, 161
snuff 63, 96, 131
Soga, John 75
Somerset, Lord Charles 68
Songiya (wife of Senzangakhona) 28, 132
songs 56, 82, 123, 126
  see also praises
Sonyezane Dlamini 164
Sophane (Shaka's half-brother) 100, 138, 154
Soshangane kaZikode 41, 119, 120, 122, 124
Sothobe kaMpangalala
  assassination of Shaka 141
  conspiracy to kill Shaka 125–126
  Dingane entrusts power to 156–157, 160
  Shaka's embassy to British 103, 104–105, 113
spears xii, 6, 24, 34, 43, 44, 139, 143, 162
speech defect, Shaka's 63–64
stabbing-spears 6, 24, 34, 162
Stanger 80, 144
Stanger, William 144
statues of Shaka xiii
Stuart, James 5
succession, royal 9, 20, 26–27, 46, 77–78
Swazi people 12, 32, 38, 121, 122, 161, 163, 189

Theal, George McCall 33
Thembu people 12, 32, 48–49, 189
throwing-spears 24, 34
Thukela, battle of 162
Thuli people 45, 124, 189
iziToyatoyi regiment 164
trade
   Dingane's restrictions on 160
   in ivory 65, 69, 71, 77, 85, 90, 103
   with Portuguese 65
   Shaka's desire to trade with British 65–66, 85
trader-hunters
   assist Shaka in battles 77, 78, 82–83, 83–84, 110
   defeated by Dingane 162
   desire for British protection 67–68, 103, 107, 114
   discontent with Shaka 69
   first meeting with Shaka 68–69
   friendly relations with Boers 162
   hunting activities 71
   introduction of blankets 6
   leave Port Natal after assassination 147–148
   relations with Dingane 157, 160
   rivalry between 84–85, 112
   settlement at Port Natal 69–71
   Shaka appoints as chiefs 71
   Shaka as bloodthirsty 31, 33
   and Shaka's attack on Mpondo 107–108
   Shaka's relations with 59, 112–113
   source of information on Shaka xiii
traditional healers 18–19, 33–34, 93, 108
treaties 69, 102, 113
trees
   buffalo thorn 97, 97
   deadman's (or crying) tree 93, 122
Tsonga people 12, 32, 122, 152, 190

Utimuni (Shaka's nephew) 15

Valley of the Kings 13–14
Veglaer, battle of 162
Voortrekkers 129, 156, 158

warfare
   battles between chiefdoms 23–24
   description of battle 33–37
   fate of civilians 37–38
   limited nature of 33
   Shaka's passion for 56
   Shaka's style of fighting 37
warriors
   ceremonial dress 6, 15–16, 15, 36
   daily routine 6
   Dingane moves to win approval of 153
   and first-fruits ceremony 14, 15–16, 17
   heroes in battle 34–35, 37
   illustrations of 15, 36
   life on campaigns 73–74
   living quarters 5
   no time to recuperate 83, 119–120, 121
   praise-singing/dancing 5, 17
   reaction to white traders 68
   ritual cleansing of 30, 33–34, 79
   treatment of cowards 35, 110
   see also *Bhalule impi*
war-shields
   distinctive colours/patterns 8, 15, 16, 34
   illustrations of xii, 8, 15, 36
   of older warriors 123
   protection of 6
   and Shaka's statue xiii
war songs 123
White Mfolozi, battle of 163
witches 25, 93, 100
wizards 154
women
   brewing beer 4
   as captives 5, 38–39, 61
   executions of 58
   maids-of-honour 3–5, 17, 19, 61, 89, 141
   massacres of 40, 78–79, 96
   reports of Shaka's atrocities against 58, 129
   royal women 3, 26–27, 27, 28, 96
wooden sticks 34
Wylie, Dan x, xi, xiii, 21

Xhosa people 32, 77, 85, 190
Xoki (father of Ndongeni) 132

Zibizendlela (Shaka's possible son) 60–61
Zulu army 73–74, 109, 110, 122–123
Zulu kingdom
   boundaries 66, 73, 190
   ethnic distinctions 44
   at outset of Shaka's reign 12
   population 74
   shattered in Anglo-Zulu War 165
Zulu language 2
Zulu nationalism xi–xii, 165–167
Zwangendaba kaZiguda 41
Zwide kaLanga
   bewitching of Dingiswayo 31
   death of 77
   defeated by Shaka 39–40
   praises 24
   regroups after defeat 41
   suspect in assassination attempt on Shaka 30, 42

CPSIA information can be obtained
at www.ICGtesting.com
Printed in the USA
BVHW050954270223
659303BV00011B/238